Erich Maria Remarque

ALL QUIET ON THE WESTERN FRONT

Joseph Roth

JOB

The German Library: Volume 68

Volkmar Sander, General Editor

Erich Maria Remarque

ALL QUIET ON THE WESTERN FRONT

Joseph Roth

JOB
(abridged)

Edited by Helmuth Kiesel

CONTINUUM · NEW YORK

2004

The Continuum International Publishing Group Inc
15 East 26 Street, New York, NY 10010

The Continuum International Publishing Group Ltd
The Tower Building, 11 York Road, London SE1 7NX

The German Library is published in cooperation with Deutsches Haus,
New York University.

This volume has been supported by Inter Nationes and the Erich Maria Remarque
Chair at New York University

Printed in the United States of America

Library of Congress Cataloging-in-Publication Data

Remarque, Erich Maria, 1898–1970.
  [Im Westen Nichts Neues. English]
  All quiet on the western front ; and Job / Erich Maria Remarque and Joseph
Roth ; edited by Helmuth Kiesel.
    p. cm. — (German library ; v. 68)
  "For the purposes of this volume, the text of Roth's novel was shortened
by twenty percent."—Intro.
  Includes bibliographical references.
  ISBN 0-8264-1652-7 (hardcover : alk. paper) — ISBN 0-8264-1653-5
(pbk. : alk. paper)
  I. Roth, Joseph, 1894–1939. Hiob, Roman eines einfachen Mannes. English.
Selections   II. Kiesel, Helmuth, 1947–   III. Wheen, A. W. (Arthur Wesley),
1897–   IV. Thompson, Dorothy, 1893–1961.   V. Title.   VI. Series.
PT2635.E681713   2004
833'.912—dc22   2004020897

Contents

Introduction

This volume 68 of The German Library in 100 Volumes presents two novels: Erich Maria Remarque's *Im Westen Nichts Neues (All Quiet on the Western Front*, 1929) and a generous selection from Joseph Roth's *Hiob (Job*, 1930).

Written during the last years of the Weimar Republic, they reflect widely discussed issues and urgent problems of that age. In particular, the significance of the First World War to the front line troops, who were to play an important part in the Weimar Republic; and further, the problem of Jewish identity in a newly mobilized society with dreams of a modern nationalism. Both novels were extremely successful and were widely distributed in Germany and elsewhere. Both novels are examples of a more traditional narrative style than that of the avant-garde approach used so effectively by Alfred Döblin in *Berlin Alexanderplatz* (1929), and take a prominent and important place in modern German literature.

Erich Maria Remarque—whose name was in fact Erich Paul Remark—was born June 22, 1898, the son of a bookbinder. On completing basic schooling, he attended the Catholic Teacher Training Institution in Osnabrück. Two years after the beginning of World War I, in November 1916, he was called up and began his military service with hard training in a camp in the Luneburg Heath. In the beginning of June 1917, his Unit was commanded to undertake trench duties on the Western Front, at Flanders. Although frequently under fire, the Unit was not involved in dangerous battles. The trench warfare and assaults described in *All Quiet on the Western Front* were not, therefore, part of the author's immediate experience. Remarque's unit was mobilized against the attacking English forces toward the end of July 1917, but Remarque was seriously wounded early in the advance. He spent a long period in the

Field Hospital, and was finally released to clerical duties in the Hospital offices. After the War, Remarque worked for two years as an advertising copywriter for a rubber factory in Hannover. He then worked as a Sports Editor in Berlin.

Remarque had begun to gather material for a book during the war, but it was not until the period 1927–1928 that he could begin to work on it. It may be that Remarque needed this ten-year gestation to develop the necessary writing skills. It may also be that the approaching ten-year anniversary of the War was stirring public memories. In 1928 and 1929, a number of books appeared that dealt with the Great War, as it was then known, and which considered the War in the light of the political developments that had followed it.

This distance is equally fundamental to Remarque's novel. On the one hand, *All Quiet on the Western Front* is a report of experiences, speaking of immediacies, and recounted throughout in the present tense. However, this novel is also unmistakeably the speech of a man who had become aware of how much he, and those of his generation who had survived, had been affected by the trauma of the Great War. In suffering from and practicing brutal violence, they had been separated from the normal processes of individual development, and had become estranged from civilian life. *All Quiet on the Western Front* is, not least, a novel of those age groups which, during the '20s, became what the American writer Gertrude Stein referred to as the "Lost Generation."

The hero and storyteller of this novel does not have to continue the tale, having fallen in the last weeks of the War—as is made clear in the use of the preterit tense in the last paragraph. For him, though, the awareness of having been spoiled by war for "normal" life had already crystallized during the War itself.

All Quiet on the Western Front describes the War from the viewpoint of the so-called simple soldier, the *Muschkoten*, as the Infantry was then known. It is described by its hero, Paul Böhmer, a man of good education with literary aspirations. He is absorbed by the colorful mix of comrades in his Unit, and brings their collective experiences to life. Not for nothing does the novel begin with the pronoun "we." This "we" is a group of eight Infantrymen who develop a particularly close relationship born of the time shared on the Front, of which this story reports. The group consists of four high school students, a fitter and turner, a turf-cutter, a farmer, and a forty-year-old soldier of wide experience and considerable insight. Of course, we are best informed about Paul Böhmer, the storyteller. We also hear from him, though, of the experiences and sufferings of his comrades, of the dangers, difficulties, losses, hardships, and the astonishing events they underwent, and of their reactions, based on character and on social and occupational backgrounds. It was apparently Remarque's wish to display as broad as possible a spectrum of typical situations and behavior patterns.

According to a *New York Times* Book Review from January 27, 1946, he described his novel, with a certain understatement, as being "simply a collection of the best stories I told, and that my friends told, as we sat over drinks and relived the War." Remarque, then, derived the novel from a series of stories and episodes. These he recounts with masterly control of facet, to produce a scintillating, precise account of the War.

We become acquainted with the group when, after weeks at the Front, they have withdrawn to the rear and are attempting to recuperate. We are observers as they dig trenches, come under artillery fire, are wreathed in gas vapors, and are plagued by lice and rats. We live through offensive and counter-offensive with them. Hear, as they become death-seeking animals. We endure with the storyteller, who can only survive by stabbing a French soldier seeking shelter in the same bomb-crater to death. We see those who, frenzied by war, begin to rebel, perhaps even run away, probably to later be shot as deserters. We read also of how easy life in the rear can be—especially when one can come by piglets, or a goose. Particularly, too, when a couple of hungry Frenchwomen, for the sake of a little bread and sausage from the debilitated soldiers' rations, give them a good time. We even join the protagonist on home leave—but, of course, merely to see how mothers fear and grieve. We are with him at the end, in the military hospital, to see in detail what weapons and military medicine do to people.

The first half of the novel (up to the beginning of the home leave) is marked by the fatalistic, sarcastic heroism the soldiers adopt as a shield against the horrors to which they are exposed. The second half is filled with descriptions of suffering and grievance. More and more, the War loses the initial adventurous overtones. But such moments still occur in the military hospital—above all, happiness is found in comradeship. So from beginning to end in this description of the war, its horrors of destruction and complexities of suffering are set against such moments of trial and proven friendship, of good luck and survival. This juxtaposition is in part responsible for the extraordinary force of Remarque's novel. The effect is not only forbidding; it also shows war as something which can be endured, and which offers a unique experience in life. This accords with the hero's acceptance, without regret, of a return to the Front, from home leave or from the military hospital. He is prepared to share his comrades' fate, and is an admirer to the end of those "Magnificent Officers of the Front Line" who "in every difficult situation are in the vanguard" and who sweep the troops along with them.

In brief, the novel allows for an identification with the heroism that ignores pain and death—as does the novel's hero, who naturally expects to survive. That he dies in the end—apparently painlessly, undramatically—carries the sense of the pacifist message Remarque wished to express. It seems forced, however, and not readily believable.

On completing the manuscript, which is said to have taken only six weeks, Remarque offered it to Germany's then most reputable publisher, Samuel Fischer. For unknown reasons, the script was rejected, it was then accepted by Ullstein, initially for publication in the widely read "Vossischen Zeitung." The series began on November 10, 1928, ten years to the day of the Kaiser's abdication, which had made possible the end of the Great War, to which the book now called attention.

Prophyläen Publishers, a branch of Ullstein, released the book at the end of January 1929. An extraordinary number were sold in a short time: 600,000 copies in the first three months, and over a million within half a year. This became an enduring success: *All Quiet on the Western Front* was reprinted constantly, and in an increasing number of languages, until the rise to power of National Socialism. Today the novel appears in some fifty languages, and between fifteen and twenty million copies have been sold. It qualifies as the most successful German-language book of the twentieth century.

This success is no doubt also due in part to Lewis Milestone's melodramatic film version. Produced in Hollywood in 1930, it drew crowds all around the world, provoked debate, and was banned in some places. Fierce argument accompanied the film, particularly in Germany. The German premiere, in a renowned cinema in Berlin, was bombed by a group of Nazis, led by Goebbels, later the Minister of Propaganda. This occurred during other attempts to show the film, until December 12, when, by order of the Reichstag, the film was banned.

Early in 1933, the National Socialists ordered a large-scale "cleansing" of Germany's libraries. *All Quiet on the Western Front* belonged to the list of banned books, which, on the tenth of May, were ritually burned in all German Universities. As reasons were given that the book exercised "literary betrayal of the soldiers of the World War" and the danger the book posed to "the education of the people in the spirit of military valor." By this time, Remarque was already out of the country—he had left Germany a few days before Hitler took power. Until 1939, he lived mainly close to Ascona, in Italy, and in Paris. In 1939 he moved to the United States. He died on September 25, 1970, in Locarno, Switzerland.

Like Erich Maria Remarque, so can Joseph Roth be characterized as a member of the so-called Lost Generation. Often, and with justice, Roth said that World War I had cost him his homeland and turned him into a nomad. He tried to turn this loss to advantage, in that he lead a European existence and adopted cosmopolitan manners; but the constant pain of his loss is clearly reflected in his most famous and important novels, in *Hiob* and *Radetskymarsch*.

(Moses) Joseph Roth was born on September 2, 1894, in Brody. Then a middle-sized merchant township marked by a strong Jewish influence, it lies about a hundred kilometers east of Lemberg, and today belongs to the Ukraine. At the time of Roth's birth, Brody was part of the Kingdom of Galizia and Lodomeria. This was the most easterly province of the multicultural State of Austria, which was a result of the first division of Poland in 1772.

Roth's father Nachum was a Jewish grain handler, who, before his son was born, fell mentally ill during a business trip and spent the rest of his life in care. Thus, Roth grew up without a father. After initial study at an enlightened Jewish school, he was able, thanks to his mother's wealthy family, to attend the public Gymnasium in Brody. He subsequently studied Germanistics, in the Winter Semester of 1913–14 in Lemberg, and beginning in the Summer Semester of 1914 in Vienna. In September 1916, Roth was called up.

After basic training, he was commanded to serve in Lemberg—not in a fighting Unit, however, but as part of the Press Service.

After the war he returned to Vienna and began to work as a freelance journalist. In 1920 he moved to Berlin, where he worked on a succession of respected newspapers. These included the liberal *Berliner Tageblatt*, and the equally liberal *Prager Tagblatt*. Also, the social democratic newspapers *Vorwärts* (Berlin) and *Arbeiterzeitung* (Vienna) in 1923, and then the most respected of German newspapers, *Frankfurter Zeitung*. Roth wrote not only feature articles, but also modern novels. The topical contents and short chapters made these ideal for serialization in daily newspapers, and as such paid good fees.

In his early years as a journalist he presented a Socialist viewpoint, and made his stand clear by calling himself "Joseph the Red." It is to be noted that Roth's socialism was purely a matter of emotion, derived from the observation of daily life and not bound by theory or Party dogma. Subsequent to the mid–'20s, this socialist tendency was overlaid by a development of socially critical and conservative ideas, which were fed by memories of the Austrian Monarchy, and by an inclination to Catholicism as the tie between the conservative and the cosmopolitan. In Chapter 13 of *Radetzky-marsch*, the famous description of a Viennese Corpus Christi procession gives this new attitude a concentrated aesthetic expression.

Roth never forgot his Jewish origins; nor did he overlook the problems of Jewish existence in a nationalistic Europe. Indeed, he dedicated a series of essays reflecting the situation of Jews in the European capitals of Vienna, Berlin, and Paris, in America, and in the Soviet Union. These were published in book form as *The Wandering Jew*. The title was not merely descriptive, but also a statement of policy. Roth saw Jewish existence as being a matter of constant migration.

Whilst understanding the Zionist longing for a Jewish Homeland in Palestina, nonetheless to him it seemed to be mistaken, given historic persecution and current Pogroms, as being founded on the same concept of a nation-state as had already brought much suffering to Europe and indeed to the world. As he put it in *The Wandering Jew*, "The Epoch of Jewish Nationalism has passed for the Jews. Do they really seek this again? Do they really envy the European States?"

From 1925 on, Roth traveled extensively throughout France (1925), the Soviet Union (1926), Albania (1927), Poland, and Italy (1928), and sent detailed reports to the *Frankfurter Zeitung*. Roth had married in 1922. In 1928, his wife was diagnosed as schizophrenic, and had to be consigned to a clinic for nervous diseases. In the following years, Roth was particularly productive as a novelist, and with *Hiob* (1930) and *Radetzkymarsch* (1932) he reached the apex of his abilities. At the same time, his life became much more complicated. Roth lived with a sequence of different women, and had to take care of their financial needs. His work did not always provide him with the means to do so.

In 1933, immediately after Hitler took power, he left Germany, and lived by choice in a small Parisian hotel. He had been an enthusiastic drinker in the '20s, and now developed into a serious alcoholic, apparently wishing to drink himself to death.

He was in the Parisian café Tournon on May 23, 1929, when he learned of the suicide of the German-Jewish revolutionary and poet, Ernst Toller. In despair over the political situation, Toller had hanged himself in New York the day before. At this, Roth broke down, and was taken to the Hospital Neckar, where he died four days later, on May 27, 1939. On May 30, Joseph Roth was buried in the "Thiais" Cemetary. It is said that an altercation occurred at the graveside between Austrian Monarchists and communist writers, as well as between Jews and Catholics, as each of these groups claimed Roth to have been exclusively one of their own.

Roth's novel, *Hiob* is the story of the sufferings of an average but good Jewish citizen at the time of World War I. There are probably two motivating factors which led to the novel. In the first instance, after 1928, the negative affect on Roth's life of his wife's sickness. In the second, the knowledge, reflected in *The Wandering Jew*, of the lack of any really secure place, in the modern world of that time, for a traditional Jewish lifestyle.

The "simple man" of whom the story tells is a pious and God-fearing Jew living with his family in a Wolhynish village, on the border of Czarist Russia and Galizia–Austria. Mendel Singer—for such is his name—is a teacher, and has a family: his wife Deborah, two strong sons, called Joseph and Schemarjah, and a very pretty daughter called Mirjam. The youngest child, another son called

Menuchim, has been marked from birth by a disease that prevents both physical and mental development.

Mendel rejects treatment in a Russian hospital suggested by the district doctor, as he does not want his son associating with Russian children, and eating non–kosher food. So it is that Menuchim remains an apathetic gnome, with a huge head, a skinny body, and bent limbs, unable to control himself, or to talk. It is impossible for Mendel to protect his other children from the influence of their Russian environment. It is not necessary at this point to give a detailed account of how this influence is manifested; suffice it to say that one of the sons has cause to escape across the border and emigrate to America. Mendel fears that his family's Jewish identity will be completely lost under the influence of Russian society. Several years later, leaving the sickly Menuchim behind, he and the rest of the family follow his son.

Of course, America isn't the Promised Land either. Hardly has Mendel settled in New York that he realizes he has not found Canaan, but simply exchanged one form of Egypt for another, and is living still in a Diaspora that threatens his identity. This situation is made more acute by the First World War, which causes the deaths, one after the other, of Mendel's immigrant family, and brings him, parallel to the biblical Job, into dispute with his God. Indeed, Mendel goes one step further than Job. He turns away from God, and begins, in demonstration of his stance, to eat pork. Mendel's life now takes a turn for the better. Unexpectedly, Menuchim, left behind in Russia, appears in New York, giving his father the feeling that God does still work miracles and that Jewish life will endure.

This wondrous end to Roth's *Hiob* was the cause of several extremes in critical reviews. Some saw the happy ending as being completely unrealistic, and therefore kitsch and illegitimate. As an allegory of traditional Jewry in a modern mobile society, it was held to gloss over the inherent pressure for the surrender of Jewish lifestyle, and to ignore the exercise of persecution.

Others understood the conclusion to be Utopian, the sense and justice of it lying precisely in the way in which the difference between the wish for an undisturbed Jewish existence and the reality of the Diaspora is shown. This version is held to be verified by the use Roth makes of the legendary Utopian and the ironically distanced tones with which he tells the story of his Hiob.

Still others saw in *Hiob* a song of praise for the dangerous obstinacy of those Jews who let nothing, neither the threats of Nationalism nor the temptations of modern life, distract them from the observance of the rites of their fathers and who did so in the one place where only the Jews, grown wise politically, could, according to Roth, inhabit: the Diaspora. The novel makes it clear that to achieve this can be self-destructive. Whether this achievement is possible and purposeful is not clearly stated. Then, looked at closely, Mendel Singer has failed at almost all points. He loses not only his homeland, but also his profession as a teacher, his family, and his faith, to which last he returns only at the very end.

Furthermore, this happy end should not distract from the point that his son Menuchim is an exponent of a different way of Jewish life. He is not only the product of traditional Jewry, but also of just that modern medical treatment from which his father, in Czarist Russia, had tried to protect him. In addition, he had received an education in music in the Czarist Army. The international musician, as he arrives in New York and meets his father, leads a very different life from that of the small Wolhynish village schoolmaster, Mendel Singer.

An American edition of *Hiob* appeared in 1931, an English edition in 1933, and other translations followed. A stage version was produced in Paris in 1939, and, also in the thirties, a film was produced in Hollywood. In this version, the story was set in Catholic South Tyrol and of the Jewish teacher was made a Catholic sacristan.

For the purposes of this volume, the text of Roth's novel was shortened by twenty percent. The excisions are marked with ellipses. The number then given can be found in a brief overview of the edited passages at the end of the text.

Remarque and Roth, and especially the novels printed here, are the subjects of a number of studies, which have been used for this preface but to which only inadequate justice could be done here. For additional detail of the authors and their works, reference should be made to three extensive biographies:

Wilhelm von Sternburg: *"Als wäre alles das letzte Mal": Erich Maria Remarque: eine Biographie.* Köln: Kiepenheuer & Witsch, 1998 (und 2000 als KiWi-Pocket-book).

David Bronsen: *Joseph Roth: eine Biographie.* Köln: Kiepenheuer & Witsch, 1974 (und 1993 als KiWi-Pocket-book mit gekürztem Text).

Helmuth Nürnberger: *Joseph Roth in Selbstzeugnissen und Bilddokumenten.* Reinbek bei Hamburg: Rowohlt, 1981 (9. Auflage 1999).

Finally, there is a new edition of *All Quiet on the Western Front* planned for 2004, with different text versions and a detailed history of its conception and its controversial early reception: Thomas F. Schneider: *Erich Maria Remarques Roman "Im Westen nichts Neues": Text, Edition, Entstehung, Distribution und Rezeption (1928–1930).* Tübingen: Niemeyer, 2004.

H. K.
Translated by Virginia Wurdak

In the United States Erich Maria Remarque married Paulette Goddard, the film actress and former wife of Charles Chaplin. On her death, she donated Remarque's papers to New York University, together with a sizable bequest. This volume has also been partially sponsored by these funds.

Erich Maria Remarque

All Quiet on the Western Front

This book is to be neither an accusation nor a confession, and least of all an adventure, for death is not an adventure to those who stand face to face with it. It will try simply to tell of a generation of men who, even though they may have escaped shells, were destroyed by the war.

1

We are at rest five miles behind the front. Yesterday we were relieved, and now our bellies are full of beef and haricot beans. We are satisfied and at peace. Each man has another mess-tin full for the evening; and, what is more, there is a double ration of sausage and bread. That puts a man in fine trim. We have not had such luck as this for a long time. The cook with his carroty head is begging us to eat; he beckons with his ladle to every one that passes, and spoons him out a great dollop. He does not see how he can empty his stewpot in time for coffee. Tjaden and Müller have produced two washbasins and had them filled up to the brim as a reserve. In Tjaden this is voracity, in Müller it is foresight. Where Tjaden puts it all is a mystery, for he is and always will be as thin as a rake.

What's more important still is the issue of a double ration of smokes. Ten cigars, twenty cigarettes, and two quids of chew per man; now that is decent. I have exchanged my chewing tobacco with Katczinsky for his cigarettes, which means I have forty altogether. That's enough for a day.

It is true we have no right to this windfall. The Prussian is not so generous. We have only a miscalculation to thank for it.

Fourteen days ago we had to go up and relieve the front line. It was fairly quiet on our sector, so the quartermaster who remained in the rear had requisitioned the usual quantity of rations and provided for the full company of one hundred and fifty men. But on the last day an astonishing number of English heavies opened up on us with high-explosive, drumming ceaselessly on our position, so that we suffered severely and came back only eighty strong.

Last night we moved back and settled down to get a good sleep for once: Katczinsky is right when he says it would not be such a bad war if only one could get a little more sleep. In the line we have had next to none, and fourteen days is a long time at one stretch.

It was noon before the first of us crawled out of our quarters. Half an hour later every man had his mess-tin and we gathered at the cookhouse, which smelt greasy and nourishing. At the head of the queue of course were the hungriest—little Albert Kropp, the clearest thinker among us and therefore only a lance-corporal; Müller, who still carries his school textbooks with him, dreams of examinations, and during a bombardment mutters propositions in physics; Leer, who wears a full beard and has a preference for the girls from officers' brothels. He swears that they are obliged by an army order to wear silk chemises and to bathe before entertaining guests of the rank of captain and upwards. And as the fourth, myself, Paul Bäumer. All four are nineteen years of age, and all four joined up from the same class as volunteers for the war.

Close behind us were our friends: Tjaden, a skinny locksmith of our own age, the biggest eater of the company. He sits down to eat as thin as a grasshopper and gets up as big as a bug in the family way; Haie Westhus, of the same age, a peat-digger, who can easily hold a ration-loaf in his hand and say: Guess what I've got in my fist; then Detering, a peasant, who thinks of nothing but his farmyard and his wife; and finally Stanislaus Katczinsky, the leader of our group, shrewd, cunning, and hard-bitten, forty years of age, with a face of the soil, blue eyes, bent shoulders, and a remarkable nose for dirty weather, good food, and soft jobs.

Our gang formed the head of the queue before the cookhouse. We were growing impatient, for the cook paid no attention to us.

Finally Katczinsky called to him: "Say, Heinrich, open up the soup-kitchen. Anyone can see the beans are done."

He shook his head sleepily: "You must all be there first." Tjaden grinned: "We are all here."

The sergeant-cook still took no notice. "That may do for you," he said. "But where are the others?"

"They won't be fed by you today. They're either in the dressing-station or pushing up daisies."

The cook was quite disconcerted as the facts dawned on him. He was staggered. "And I have cooked for one hundred and fifty men—"

Kropp poked him in the ribs. "Then for once we'll have enough. Come on, begin!"

Suddenly a vision came over Tjaden. His sharp, mousy features began to shine, his eyes grew small with cunning, his jaws twitched, and he whispered hoarsely: "Man! then you've got bread for one hundred and fifty men too, eh?"

The sergeant-cook nodded absent-minded, and bewildered.

Tjaden seized him by the tunic. "And sausage?"

Ginger nodded again.

Tjaden's chaps quivered. "Tobacco too?"

"Yes, everything."

Tjaden beamed: "What a bean-feast! That's all for us! Each man gets—wait a bit—yes, practically two issues."

Then Ginger stirred himself and said: "That won't do."

We got excited and began to crowd around.

"Why won't that do, you old carrot?" demanded Katczinsky.

"Eighty men can't have what is meant for a hundred and fifty."

"We'll soon show you," growled Müller.

"I don't care about the stew, but I can only issue rations for eighty men," persisted Ginger.

Katczinsky got angry. "You might be generous for once. You haven't drawn food for eighty men. You've drawn it for the Second Company. Good. Let's have it then. We are the Second Company."

We began to jostle the fellow. No one felt kindly toward him, for it was his fault that the food often came up to us in the line too late and cold. Under shellfire he wouldn't bring his kitchen up near enough, so that our soup-carriers had to go much farther than those of the other companies. Now Bulcke of the First Company is a much better fellow. He is as fat as a hamster in winter, but he trundles his pots when it comes to that right up to the very front line.

We were in just the right mood, and there would certainly have been a dust-up if our company commander had not appeared. He informed himself of the dispute, and only remarked: "Yes, we did have heavy losses yesterday."

He glanced into the dixie. "The beans look good."

Ginger nodded. "Cooked with meat and fat."

The lieutenant looked at us. He knew what we were thinking. And he knew many other things too, because he came to the company as a non-com. and was promoted from the ranks. He lifted the lid from the dixie again and sniffed. Then passing on he said: "Bring me a plate full. Serve out all the rations. We can do with them."

Ginger looked sheepish as Tjaden danced round him.

"It doesn't cost you anything! Anyone would think the quartermaster's store belonged to him! And now get on with it, you old blubber-sticker, and don't you miscount either."

"You be hanged!" spat out Ginger. When things get beyond him he throws up the sponge altogether; he just goes to pieces. And as if to show that all things were equal to him, of his own free will he issued in addition half a pound of synthetic honey to each man.

Today is wonderfully good. The mail has come, and almost every man has a few letters and papers. We stroll over to the meadow behind the billets. Kropp has the round lid of a margarine tub under his arm.

On the right side of the meadow a large common latrine has been built, a roofed and durable construction. But that is for recruits who as yet have not learned how to make the most of whatever comes their way. We want something better. Scattered about everywhere there are separate, individual boxes for the same purpose. They are square, neat boxes with wooden sides all round, and have unimpeachably satisfactory seats. On the sides are hand grips enabling one to shift them about.

We move three together in a ring and sit down comfortably. And it will be two hours before we get up again.

I well remember how embarrassed we were as recruits in barracks when we had to use the general latrine. There were no doors and twenty men sat side by side as in a railway carriage, so that they could be reviewed all at one glance, for soldiers must always be under supervision.

Since then we have learned better than to be shy about such trifling immodesties. In time things far worse than that came easy to us.

Here in the open air though, the business is entirely a pleasure. I no longer understand why we should always have shied at these things before. They are, in fact, just as natural as eating and drinking. We might perhaps have paid no particular attention to them had they not figured so large in our experience, nor been such novelties to our minds—to the old hands they had long been a mere matter of course.

The soldier is on friendlier terms than other men with his stomach and intestines. Three-quarters of his vocabulary is derived from these regions, and they give an intimate flavor to expressions of his greatest joy as well as of his deepest indignation. It is impossible to express oneself in any other way so clearly and pithily. Our families and our teachers will be shocked when we go home, but here it is the universal language.

Enforced publicity has in our eyes restored the character of complete innocence to all these things. More than that, they are so much a matter of course that their comfortable performance is fully as much enjoyed as the playing of a safe top running flush. Not for nothing was the word "latrine-rumor" invented; these places are the regimental gossip-shop and common-rooms.

We feel ourselves for the time being better off than in any palatial white-tiled "convenience." *There* it can only be hygienic; *here* it is beautiful.

These are wonderfully care-free hours. Over us is the blue sky. On the horizon float the bright yellow, sunlit observation-balloons, and the many little white clouds of the anti-aircraft shells. Often they rise in a sheaf as they follow after an airman. We hear the muffled rumble of the front only as very distant thunder, bumble-bees droning by quite drown it. Around us stretches the flowery meadow. The grasses sway their tall spears; the white butterflies flutter around and float on the soft warm wind of the late summer. We read letters and newspapers and smoke. We take off our caps and lay them down beside us. The wind plays with our hair; it plays with our words and thoughts. The three boxes stand in the midst of the glowing, red field-poppies.

We set the lid of the margarine tub on our knees and so have a good table for a game of skat. Kropp has the cards with him. After every *misère ouverte* we have a round of nap. One could sit like this for ever.

The notes of an accordion float across from the billets. Often we lay aside the cards and look about us. One of us will say: "Well, boys. . . ." Or "It was a near thing that time. . . ." And for a moment we fall silent. There is in each of us a feeling of constraint. We are all sensible of it; it needs no words to communicate it. It might easily have happened that we should not be sitting here on our boxes today; it came damn near to that. And so everything is new and brave, red poppies and good food, cigarettes and summer breeze.

Kropp asks: "Anyone seen Kemmerich lately?"

"He's up at St. Joseph's," I tell him.

Müller explains that he has a flesh wound in his thigh; a good blighty.

We decide to go and see him this afternoon.

Kropp pulls out a letter. "Kantorek sends you all his best wishes."

We laugh. Müller throws his cigarette away and says: "I wish he was here."

Kantorek had been our schoolmaster, a stern little man in a gray tail-coat, with a face like a shrew mouse. He was about the same size as Corporal Himmelstoss, the "terror of Klosterberg." It is very queer that the unhappiness of the world is so often brought on by small men. They are so much more energetic and uncompromising than the big fellows. I have always taken good care to keep out of sections with small company commanders. They are mostly confounded little martinets.

During drill-time Kantorek gave us long lectures until the whole of our class went, under his shepherding, to the District Commandant and volunteered. I can see him now, as he used to glare at us through his spectacles and say in a moving voice: "Won't you join up, Comrades?"

These teachers always carry their feelings ready in their waistcoat pockets, and trot them out by the hour. But we didn't think of that then.

There was, indeed, one of us who hesitated and did not want to fall into line. That was Joseph Behm, a plump, homely fellow. But he did allow himself to be persuaded, otherwise he would have been ostracized. And perhaps more of us thought as he did, but no one could very well stand out, because at that time even one's parents were ready with the word "coward"; no one had the vaguest idea what we were in for. The wisest were just the poor and simple people. They knew the war to be a misfortune, whereas those who were better off, and should have been able to see more clearly what the consequences would be, were beside themselves with joy.

Katczinsky said that was a result of their upbringing. It made them stupid. And what Kat said, he had thought about.

Strange to say, Behm was one of the first to fall. He got hit in the eye during an attack, and we left him lying for dead. We couldn't bring him with us, because we had to come back helter-skelter. In the afternoon suddenly we heard him call, and saw him crawling about in No Man's Land. He had only been knocked unconscious. Because he could not see, and was mad with pain, he failed to keep under cover, and so was shot down before anyone could go and fetch him in.

Naturally we couldn't blame Kantorek for this. Where would the world be if one brought every man to book? There were thousands of Kantoreks, all of whom were convinced that they were acting for the best—in a way that cost them nothing.

And that is why they let us down so badly.

For us lads of eighteen they ought to have been mediators and guides to the world of maturity, the world of work, of duty, of culture, of progress—to the future. We often made fun of them and played jokes on them, but in our hearts we trusted them. The idea of authority, which they represented, was associated in our minds with a greater insight and a more humane wisdom. But the first death we saw shattered this belief. We had to recognize that our generation was more to be trusted than theirs. They surpassed us only in phrases and cleverness. The first bombardment showed us our mistake, and under it the world as they had taught it to us broke in pieces.

While they continued to write and talk, we saw the wounded and dying. While they taught that duty to one's country is the greatest thing, we already knew that death-throes are stronger. But for all that we were no mutineers, no deserters, no cowards—they were very free with all these expressions. We loved our country as much as they; we went courageously into every action; but also we distinguished the false from true, we had suddenly learned to see. And we saw that there was nothing of their world left. We were all at once terribly alone; and alone we must see it through.

Before going over to see Kemmerich we pack up his things: he will need them on the way back.

In the dressing station there is great activity: it reeks as ever of carbolic, pus, and sweat. We are accustomed to a good deal in the billets, but this makes us feel faint. We ask for Kemmerich. He lies in a large room and receives us with feeble expressions of joy and helpless agitation. While he was unconscious someone had stolen his watch.

Müller shakes his head: "I always told you that nobody should carry as good a watch as that."

Müller is rather crude and tactless, otherwise he would hold his tongue, for anybody can see that Kemmerich will never come out of this place again. Whether he finds his watch or not will make no difference, at the most one will only be able to send it to his people.

"How goes it, Franz?" asks Kropp.

Kemmerich's head sinks.

"Not so bad . . . but I have such a damned pain in my foot."

We look at his bed covering. His leg lies under a wire basket. The bed covering arches over it. I kick Müller on the shin, for he is just about to tell Kemmerich what the orderlies told us outside: that Kemmerich has lost his foot. The leg is amputated. He looks ghastly, yellow and wan. In his face there are already the strained lines that we know so well, we have seen them now hundreds of times. They are not so much lines as marks. Under the skin the life no longer pulses, it has already pressed out the boundaries of the body. Death is working through from within. It already has command in the eyes. Here lies our comrade, Kemmerich, who a little while ago was roasting horse flesh with us and squatting in the shell-holes. He it is still and yet it is not he any longer. His features have become uncertain and faint, like a photographic plate from which two pictures have been taken. Even his voice sounds like ashes.

I think of the time when we went away. His mother, a good plump matron, brought him to the station. She wept continually, her face was bloated and swollen. Kemmerich felt embarrassed, for she was the least composed of all; she simply dissolved into fat and water. Then she caught sight of me and took hold of my arm again and again, and implored me to look after Franz out there. Indeed he did have a face like a child, and such frail bones that after four weeks' pack-carrying he already had flat feet. But how can a man look after anyone in the field!

"Now you will soon be going home," says Kropp. "You would have had to wait at least three or four months for your leave."

Kemmerich nods. I cannot bear to look at his hands, they are like wax. Under the nails is the dirt of the trenches, it shows through blue-black like poison. It strikes me that these nails will continue to grow like lean fantastic cellar-plants long after Kemmerich breathes no more. I see the picture before me. They twist themselves into corkscrews and grow and grow, and with them the hair on the decaying skull, just like grass in a good soil, just like grass, how can it be possible——

Müller leans over. "We have brought your things, Franz."

Kemmerich signs with his hands. "Put them under the bed."

Müller does so. Kemmerich starts on again about the watch. How can one calm him without making him suspicious?

Müller reappears with a pair of airman's boots. They are fine English boots of soft, yellow leather which reach to the knees and lace up all the way—they are things to be coveted.

Müller is delighted at the sight of them. He matches their soles against his own clumsy boots and says: "Will you be taking them with you then, Franz?"

We all three have the same thought; even if he should get better, he would be able to use only one—they are no use to him. But as things are now it is a pity that they should stay here; the orderlies will of course grab them as soon as he is dead.

"Won't you leave them with us?" Müller repeats.

Kemmerich doesn't want to. They are his most prized possessions.

"Well, we could exchange," suggests Müller again. "Out here one can make some use of them." Still Kemmerich is not to be moved.

I tread on Müller's foot; reluctantly he puts the fine boots back again under the bed.

We talk a little more and then take our leave.

"Cheerio, Franz."

I promise him to come back in the morning. Müller talks of doing so, too. He is thinking of the lace-up boots and means to be on the spot.

Kemmerich groans. He is feverish. We get hold of an orderly outside and ask him to give Kemmerich a dose of morphia.

He refuses. "If we were to give morphia to everyone we would have to have tubs full——"

"You only attend to officers properly," says Kropp viciously.

I hastily intervene and give him a cigarette. He takes it.

"Are you usually allowed to give it, then?" I ask him.

He is annoyed. "If you don't think so, then why do you ask?"

I press a few more cigarettes into his hand. "Do us the favor——"

"Well, all right," he says.

Kropp goes in with him. He doesn't trust him and wants to see. We wait outside.

Müller returns to the subject of the boots. "They would fit me perfectly. In these boots I get blister after blister. Do you think he will last till tomorrow after drill? If he passes out in the night, we know where the boots——"

Kropp returns. "Do you think——?" he asks.

"Done for," said Müller emphatically.

We go back to the huts. I think of the letter that I must write tomorrow to Kemmerich's mother. I am freezing. I could do with a tot of rum. Müller pulls up some grass and chews it. Suddenly little Kropp throws his cigarette away, stamps on it savagely, and looking around him with a broken and distracted face, stammers "Damned shit, the damned shit!"

We walk on for a long time. Kropp has calmed himself; we understand, he saw red; out there every man gets like that sometime.

"What has Kantorek written to you?" Müller asks him.

He laughs. "We are the Iron Youth."

We all three smile bitterly, Kropp rails: he is glad that he can speak.

Yes, that's the way they think, these hundred thousand Kantoreks! Iron Youth! Youth! We are none of us more than twenty years old. But young? Youth? That is long ago. We are old folk.

2

It is strange to think that at home in the drawer of my writing table there lies the beginning of a play called "Saul" and a bundle of poems. Many an evening I have worked over them—we all did something of the kind—but that has become so unreal to me I cannot comprehend it any more. Our early life is cut off from the moment we came here, and that without our lifting a hand. We often try to look back on it and to find an explanation, but never quite succeed. For us young men of twenty everything is extraordinarily vague, for Kropp, Müller, Leer, and for me, for all of us whom Kantorek calls the "Iron Youth." All the older men are linked up with their previous life. They have wives, children, occupations, and interests, they have a background which is so strong that the war cannot obliterate it. We young men of twenty, however, have only our parents, and some, perhaps, a girl—that is not much, for at our age the influence of parents is at its weakest and girls have not yet got a hold over us. Besides this there was little else—some enthusiasm, a few hobbies, and our school. Beyond this our life did not extend. And of this nothing remains.

Kantorek would say that we stood on the threshold of life. And so it would seem. We had as yet taken no root. The war swept us away. For the others, the older men, it is but an interruption. They are able to think beyond it. We, however, have been gripped by it and do not know what the end may be. We know only that in some strange and melancholy way to have become a waste land. All the same, we are not often sad.

Though Müller would be delighted to have Kemmerich's boots, he is really quite as sympathetic as another who could not bear to think of such a thing for grief. He merely sees things clearly. Were Kemmerich able to make any use of the boots, then Müller would rather go bare-foot over barbed wire than scheme how to get hold of them. But as it is the boots are quite inappropriate to Kemmerich's circumstances, whereas Müller can make good use of them. Kemmerich will die; it is immaterial who gets them. Why, then, should Müller not succeed to them? He has more right than a hospital orderly. When Kemmerich is dead it will be too late. Therefore Müller is already on the watch.

We have lost all sense of other considerations, because they are artificial. Only the facts are real and important for us. And good boots are scarce.

Once it was different. When we went to the district commandant to enlist, we were a class of twenty young men, many of whom proudly shaved for the first time before going to the barracks. We had no definite plans for our future. Our thoughts of a career and occupation were as yet of too unpractical a character to furnish any scheme of life. We were still crammed full of vague ideas which gave to life, and to the war also an ideal and almost romantic character. We were trained in the army for ten weeks and in this time more profoundly influenced than by ten years at school. We learned that a bright button is weightier than four volumes of Schopenhauer. At first astonished, then embittered, and finally indifferent, we recognized that what matters is not the mind but the boot brush, not intelligence but the system, not freedom but drill. We became soldiers with eagerness and enthusiasm, but they have done everything to knock that out of us. After three weeks it was no longer incomprehensible to us that a braided postman should have more authority over us than had formerly our parents, our teachers, and the whole gamut of culture from Plato to Goethe. With our young, awakened eyes we saw that the classical conception of the Fatherland held by our teachers resolved itself here into a renunciation of personality such as one would not ask of the meanest servants— salutes, springing to attention, parade-marches, presenting arms, right wheel, left wheel, clicking the heels, insults, and a thousand pettifogging details. We had fancied our task would be different, only to find we were to be trained for heroism as though we were circus-ponies. But we soon accustomed ourselves to it. We learned in fact that some of these things were necessary, but the rest merely show. Soldiers have a fine nose for such distinctions.

By threes and fours our class was scattered over the platoons amongst Frisian fishermen, peasants, and laborers with whom we soon made friends. Kropp, Müller, Kemmerich, and I went to No. 9 platoon under Corporal Himmelstoss.

He had the reputation of being the strictest disciplinarian in the camp, and was proud of it. He was a small undersized fellow with a foxy, waxed mustache, who had seen twelve years' service and was in civil life a postman. He had a special dislike of Kropp, Tjaden, Westhus, and me, because he sensed a quiet defiance.

I have remade his bed fourteen times in one morning. Each time he had some fault to find and pulled it to pieces. I have kneaded a pair of prehistoric boots that were as hard as iron for twenty hours—with intervals of course—until they became as soft as butter and not even Himmelstoss could find anything more to do to them; under his orders I have scrubbed out the Corporals' Mess with a tooth-brush. Kropp and I were given the job of clearing the barrack-square of snow with a hand-broom and a dust-pan, and we would have gone on till we were frozen had not a lieutenant accidentally appeared who sent us off, and hauled Himmelstoss over the coals. But the only result of this was to make Himmelstoss hate us more. For six weeks consecutively I did guard every Sunday and was hut-orderly for the same length of time. With a full pack and rifle I have had to practice on a wet, soft, newly-ploughed field the "Prepare to advance, advance!" and the "Lie down!" until I was one lump of mud and finally collapsed. Four hours later I had to report to Himmelstoss with my clothes scrubbed clean, my hands chafed and bleeding. Together with Kropp, Westhus, and Tjaden I have stood at attention in a hard frost without gloves for a quarter of an hour at a stretch, while Himmelstoss watched for the slightest movement of our bare fingers on the steel barrel of the rifle. I have run eight times from the top floor of the barracks down to the courtyard in my shirt at two o'clock in the morning because my drawers projected three inches beyond the edge of the stool on which one had to stack all one's things. Alongside me ran the corporal, Himmelstoss, and trod on my bare toes. At bayonet-practice I had constantly to fight with Himmelstoss, I with a heavy iron weapon, whilst he had a handy wooden one with which he easily struck my arms till they were black and blue. Once, indeed, I became so infuriated that I ran at him blindly and gave him a mighty jab in the stomach and knocked him down. When he reported me the company commander laughed at him and told him he ought to keep his eyes open; he understood Himmelstoss, and apparently was not displeased at his discomfiture. I became a past master on the parallel bars and excelled at physical jerks;—we have trembled at the mere sound of his voice, but his runaway post-horse never got the better of us.

One Sunday as Kropp and I were lugging a latrine-bucket on a pole across the barrack-yard, Himmelstoss came by, all polished up and spry for going out. He planted himself in front of us and asked how we liked the job. In spite of ourselves we tripped and emptied the bucket over his legs. He raved, but the limit had been reached.

"That means clink," he yelled.

But Kropp had had enough. "There'll be an inquiry first," he said, "and then we'll unload."

"Mind how you speak to a non-commissioned officer!" bawled Himmelstoss. "Have you lost your senses? You wait till you're spoken to. What will you do, anyway?"

"Show you up, Corporal," said Kropp, his thumbs in line with the seams of his trousers.

Himmelstoss saw that we meant it and went off without saying a word. But before he disappeared he growled: "You'll drink this!"—but that was the end of his authority. He tried it on once more in the ploughed field with his "Prepare to advance, advance" and "Lie down." We obeyed each order, since an order's an order and has to be obeyed. But we did it so slowly that Himmelstoss became desperate. Carefully we went down on our knees, then on our hands, and so on; in the meantime, quite infuriated, he had given another command. But before we had even begun to sweat he was hoarse. After that he left us in peace. He did indeed always refer to us as swine, but there was, nevertheless, a certain respect in his tone.

There were many other staff corporals, the majority of whom were more decent. But above all each of them wanted to keep his good job there as long as possible, and this he could do only by being strict with the recruits.

So we were put through every conceivable refinement of parade-ground soldiering till we often howled with rage. Many of us became ill through it; Wolf actually died of inflammation of the lung. But we would have felt ridiculous had we hauled down our colors. We became hard, suspicious, pitiless, vicious, tough—and that was good; for these attributes were just what we lacked. Had we gone into the trenches without this period of training most of us would certainly have gone mad. Only thus were we prepared for what awaited us. We did not break down, but adapted ourselves; our twenty years, which made many another thing so grievous, helped us in this. But by far the most important result was that it awakened in us a strong, practical sense of *esprit de corps*, which in the field developed into the finest thing that arose out of the war—comradeship.

I sit by Kemmerich's bed. He is sinking steadily. Around us is great commotion. A hospital train has arrived and the wounded fit to be moved are being selected. The doctor passes by Kemmerich's bed without once looking at him.

"Next time, Franz," I say.

He raises himself on the pillow with his elbows. "They have amputated my leg."

He knows it too then. I nod and answer: "You must be thankful you've come off with that."

He is silent.

I resume: "It might have been both legs, Franz. Wegeler has lost his right arm. That's much worse. Besides, you will be going home." He looks at me. "Do you think so?"

"Of course."

"Do you think so?" he repeats.

"Sure, Franz. Once you've got over the operation."

He beckons me to bend down. I stoop over him and he whispers: "I don't think so."

"Don't talk rubbish, Franz, in a couple of days you'll see for yourself. What is it anyway—an amputated leg? Here they patch up far worse things than that."

He lifts one hand. "Look here though, these fingers."

"That's the result of the operation. Just eat decently and you'll soon be well again. Do they look after you properly?"

He points to a dish that is still half full. I get excited. "Franz, you must eat. Eating is the main thing. That looks good too."

He turns away. After a pause he says slowly: "I wanted to become a head-forester once."

"So you may still," I assure him. "There are splendid artificial limbs now, you'd hardly know there was anything missing. They are fixed on to the muscles. You can move the fingers and work and even write with an artificial hand. And besides, they will always be making new improvements."

For a while he lies still. Then he says: "You can take my lace-up boots with you for Müller."

I nod and wonder what to say to encourage him. His lips have fallen away, his mouth has become larger, his teeth stick out and look as though they were made of chalk. The flesh melts, the forehead bulges more prominently, the cheekbones protrude. The skeleton is working itself through. The eyes are already sunken in. In a couple of hours it will be over.

He is not the first that I have seen thus; but we grew up together and that always makes it a bit different. I have copied his essays. At school he used to wear a brown coat with a belt and shiny sleeves. He was the only one of us, too, who could do the giant's turn on the horizontal bar. His hair flew in his face like silk when he did it. Kantorek was proud of him. But he couldn't stand cigarettes. His skin was very white; he had something of the girl about him.

I glance at my boots. They are big and clumsy, the breeches are tucked into them, and standing up one looks well-built and powerful in these great drainpipes. But when we go bathing and strip, suddenly we have slender legs again and slight shoulders. We are no longer soldiers but little more than boys; no one would believe that we could carry packs. It is a strange moment when we stand naked; then we become civilians, and almost feel ourselves to be so. When bathing Franz Kemmerich looked as slight and frail as a child. There he lies now—but why? The whole world ought to pass by this bed and say: "This is Franz Kemmerich, nineteen and a half years old, he doesn't want to die. Let him not die!"

My thoughts become confused. This atmosphere of carbolic and gangrene clogs the lungs, it is a thick gruel, it suffocates.

It grows dark. Kemmerich's face changes color, it lifts from the pillow and is so pale that it gleams. The mouth moves slightly. I draw near to him. He whispers: "If you find my watch, send it home——"

I do not reply. It is no use any more. No one can console him. I am wretched with helplessness. This forehead with its hollow temples, this mouth that now seems all teeth, this sharp nose! And the fat, weeping woman at home to whom I must write. If only the letter were sent off already!

Hospital orderlies go to and fro with bottles and pails. One of them comes up, casts a glance at Kemmerich and goes away again. You can see he is waiting, apparently he wants the bed.

I bend over Franz and talk to him as though that could save him: "Perhaps you will go to the convalescent home at Klosterberg, among the villas, Franz. Then you can look out from the window across the fields to the two trees on the horizon. It is the loveliest time of the year now, when the corn ripens; at evening the fields in the sunlight look like mother-of-pearl. And the lane of poplars by the Klosterbach, where we used to catch stickle-backs! You can build an aquarium again and keep fish in it, and you can go without asking anyone, you can even play the piano if you want to."

I lean down over his face which lies in the shadow. He still breathes, lightly. His face is wet, he is crying. What a fine mess I have made of it with my foolish talk!

"But Franz"—I put my arm around his shoulder and put my face against his. "Will you sleep now?"

He does not answer. The tears run down his cheeks. I would like to wipe them away but my handkerchief is too dirty.

An hour passes. I sit tensely and watch his every movement in case he may perhaps say something. What if he were to open his mouth and cry out! But he only weeps, his head turned aside. He does not speak of his mother or his brothers and sisters. He says nothing; all that lies behind him; he is entirely alone now with his little life of nineteen years, and cries because it leaves him. This is the most disturbing and hardest parting that I ever have seen, although it was pretty bad too with Tiedjen, who called for his mother—a big bear of a fellow who, with wild eyes full of terror, held off the doctor from his bed with a dagger until he collapsed.

Suddenly Kemmerich groans and begins to gurgle.

I jump up, stumble outside and demand: "Where is the doctor? Where is the doctor?"

As I catch sight of the white apron I seize hold of it: "Come quick, Franz Kemmerich is dying."

He frees himself and asks an orderly standing by: "Which will that be?"

He says: "Bed 26, amputated thigh."

He sniffs: "How should I know anything about it, I've amputated five legs today"; he shoves me away, says to the hospital orderly "You see to it," and hurries off to the operating room.

I tremble with rage as I go along with the orderly. The man looks at me and says: "One operation after another since five o'clock this morning. You know, today alone there have been sixteen deaths—yours is the seventeenth. There will probably be twenty altogether——"

I become faint, all at once I cannot do any more. I won't revile any more, it is senseless, I could drop down and never rise up again.

We are by Kemmerich's bed. He is dead. The face is still wet from the tears. The eyes are half open and yellow like old horn buttons. The orderly pokes me in the ribs, "Are you taking his things with you?" I nod.

He goes on: "We must take him away at once, we want the bed. Outside they are lying on the floor."

I collect Kemmerich's things, and untie his identification disc. The orderly asks about the paybook. I say that it is probably in the orderly room, and go. Behind me they are already hauling Franz on to a waterproof sheet.

Outside the door I am aware of the darkness and the wind as a deliverance. I breathe as deep as I can, and feel the breeze in my face, warm and soft as never before. Thoughts of girls, of flowery meadows, of white clouds suddenly come into my head. My feet begin to move forward in my boots, I go quicker, I run. Soldiers pass by me, I hear their voices without understanding. The earth is streaming with forces which pour into me through the soles of my feet. The night crackles electrically, the front thunders like a concert of drums. My limbs move supplely, I feel my joints strong, I breathe the air deeply. The night lives, I live. I feel a hunger, greater than comes from the belly alone.

Müller stands in front of the hut waiting for me. I give him the boots. We go in and he tries them on. They fit well.

He roots among his supplies and offers me a fine piece of saveloy. With it goes hot tea and rum.

3

Reinforcements have arrived. The vacancies have been filled and the sacks of straw in the huts are already booked. Some of them are old hands, but there are twenty-five men of a later draft from the base. They are about two years younger than us. Kropp nudges me: "Seen the infants?"

I nod. We stick out our chests, shave in the open, shove our hands in our pockets, inspect the recruits and feel ourselves stone-age veterans.

Katczinsky joins us. We stroll past the horseboxes and go over to the reinforcements, who are already being issued with gas masks and coffee.

"Long time since you've had anything decent to eat, eh?" Kat asks one of the youngsters.

He grimaces. "For breakfast, turnip bread—lunch, turnip stew—supper, turnip cutlets and turnip salad." Kat gives a knowing whistle.

"Bread made of turnips? You've been in luck, it's nothing new for it to be made of sawdust. But what do you say to haricot beans? Have some?"

The youngster turns red: "You can't kid me."

Katczinsky merely says: "Fetch your mess tin."

We follow curiously. He takes us to a tub beside his straw sack. Sure enough it is half full of beef and beans. Katczinsky plants himself in front of it like a general and says:

"Sharp eyes and light fingers! That's what the Prussians say."

We are surprised. "Great guts, Kat, how did you come by that?" I ask him.

"Ginger was glad I took it. I gave him three pieces of parachute-silk for it. Cold beans taste fine, too."

Patronizingly he gives the youngster a portion and says:

"Next time you come with your mess tin have a cigar or a chew of tobacco in your other hand. Get me?" Then he turns to us. "You get off scot free, of course."

We couldn't do without Katczinsky; he was a sixth sense. There are such people everywhere but one does not appreciate it at first. Every company has one or two. Katczinsky is the smartest I know. By trade he is a cobbler, I believe, but that hasn't anything to do with it; he understands all trades. It's a good thing to be friends with him, as Kropp and I are, and Haie Westhus too, more or less. But Haie is rather the executive arm, operating under Kat's orders when things come to blows. For that he has his qualifications.

For example, we land at night in some entirely unknown spot, a sorry hole, that has been eaten out to the very walls. We are quartered in a small dark factory adapted to the purpose. There are beds in it, or rather bunks—a couple of wooden beams over which wire netting is stretched.

Wire netting is hard. And there's nothing to put on it. Our waterproof sheets are too thin. We use our blankets to cover ourselves.

Kat looks at the place and then says to Haie Westhus: "Come with me." They go off to explore. Half an hour later they are back again with arms full of straw. Kat has found a horsebox with straw in it. Now we might sleep if we weren't so terribly hungry.

Kropp asks an artilleryman who has been some time in this neighborhood: "Is there a canteen anywhere abouts?"

"Is there a what?" he laughs. "There's nothing to be had here. You won't find so much as a crust of bread here."

"Aren't there any inhabitants here at all then?"

He spits. "Yes, a few. But they hang round the cookhouse and beg."

"That's a bad business!—Then we'll have to pull in our belts and wait till the rations come up in the morning."

But I see Kat has put on his cap. "Where to, Kat?" I ask.

"Just to explore the place a bit." He strolls off. The artilleryman grins scornfully. "Go ahead and explore. But don't strain yourself in carrying what you find."

Disappointed we lie down and consider whether we couldn't have a go at the iron rations. But it's too risky; so we try to get a wink of sleep.

Kropp divides a cigarette and hands me half. Tjaden gives an account of his national dish—broad beans and bacon. He despises it when not flavored with bog-myrtle, and, "for God's sake, let it all be cooked together, not the potatoes, the beans, and the bacon separately." Someone growls that he will pound Tjaden into bog-myrtle if he doesn't shut up. Then all becomes quiet in the big room—only the candles flickering from the necks of a couple of bottles and the artilleryman spitting every now and then.

We are just dozing off when the door opens and Kat appears. I think I must be dreaming; he has two loaves of bread under his arm and a bloodstained sandbag full of horse flesh in his hand.

The artilleryman's pipe drops from his mouth. He feels the bread. "Real bread, by God, and still hot too?"

Kat gives no explanation. He has the bread, the rest doesn't matter. I'm sure that if he were planted down in the middle of the desert, in half an hour we would have gathered together a supper of roast meat, dates, and wine.

"Cut some wood," he says curtly to Haie.

Then he hauls out a frying pan from under his coat, and a handful of salt as well as a lump of fat from his pocket. He has thought of everything. Haie makes a fire on the floor. It lights up the empty room of the factory. We climb out of bed.

The artilleryman hesitates. He wonders whether to praise Kat and so perhaps gain a little for himself. But Katczinsky doesn't even see him, he might as well be thin air. He goes off cursing.

Kat knows the way to roast horse flesh so that it's tender. It shouldn't be put straight into the pan, that makes it tough. It should be boiled first in a little water. With our knives we squat round in a circle and fill our bellies.

That is Kat. If for one hour in a year something eatable were to be had in some one place only, within that hour, as if moved by a vision, he would put on his cap, go out and walk directly there, as though following a compass, and find it.

He finds everything—if it is cold, a small stove and wood, hay and straw, a table and chairs—but above all food. It is uncanny; one would think he conjured it out of the air. His masterpiece was four boxes of lobster. Admittedly he would rather have had a good beef steak.

We have settled ourselves on the sunny side of the hut. There is a smell of tar, of summer, and of sweaty feet. Kat sits beside me. He likes to talk. Today we have done an hour's saluting drill because Tjaden failed to salute a major smartly enough. Kat can't get it out of his head.

"You take it from me, we are losing the war because we can salute too well," he says.

Kropp stalks up, with his breeches rolled up and his feet bare. He lays out his washed socks to dry on the grass. Kat turns his eyes to heaven, lets off a mighty fart, and says metitatively: "Every little bean must be heard as well as seen."

The two begin to argue. At the same time they lay a bottle of beer on the result of an air-fight that's going on above us. Katczinsky won't budge from the opinion which as an old Front-hog, he rhymes:

> *Give 'em all the same grub and all the same pay*
> *And the war would be over and done in a day.*

Kropp on the other hand is a thinker. He proposes that a declaration of war should be a kind of popular festival with entrance tickets and bands, like a bull fight. Then in the arena the ministers and generals of the two countries, dressed in bathing drawers and armed with clubs, can have it out among themselves. Whoever survives, his country wins. That would be much simpler and more just than this arrangement, where the wrong people do the fighting.

The subject is dropped. Then the conversation turns to drill.

A picture comes before me. Burning midday in the barrack yard. The heat hangs over the square. The barracks are deserted. Every thing sleeps. All one hears is the drummers practicing; they have installed themselves somewhere and practice brokenly, dully, monotously. What concord! Midday heat, barrack square, and drummers beating!

The windows of the barracks are empty and dark. From some of them trousers are hanging to dry. The rooms are cool and one looks toward them longingly.

O dark, musty platoon huts, with the iron bedsteads, the checkered bedding, the lockers and the stools! Even you can become the object of desire; out here you have a faint resemblance to home; your rooms, full of the smell of stale food, sleep, smoke, and clothes.

Katczinsky paints it all in lively colors. What would we not give to be able to return to it! Farther back than that our thoughts dare not go.

Those early morning hours of instruction—"What are the parts of the 98 rifle?"—the midday hours of physical training—"Pianist forward! By the right, quick march. Report to the cookhouse for potato peeling."

We indulge in reminiscences. Kropp laughs suddenly and says: "Change at Löhne!"

That was our corporal's favorite game. Löhne is a railway junction. In order that our fellows going on shouldn't get lost there, Himmelstoss used to practice the change in the barrack room. We had to learn that at Löhne, to reach the branch-line, we must pass through a subway. The beds represented the subway and each man stood at attention on the left side of his bed. Then came the command: "Change at Löhne!" and like lightning everyone scrambled under the bed to the opposite side. We practiced this for hours on end.

Meanwhile the German airplane has been shot down. Like a comet it bursts into a streamer of smoke and falls headlong. Kropp has lost the bottle of beer. Disgruntled he counts out the money from his wallet.

"Surely Himmelstoss was a very different fellow as a postman," say I, after Albert's disappointment has subsided. "Then how does it come that he's such a bully as a drill-sergeant?"

The question revives Kropp, more particularly as he hears there's no more beer in the canteen. "It's not only Himmelstoss, there are lots of them. As sure as they get a stripe or a star they become different men, just as though they'd swallowed concrete."

"That's the uniform," I suggest.

"Roughly speaking it is," says Kat, and prepares for a long speech; "but the root of the matter lies somewhere. For instance, if you train a dog to eat potatoes and then afterward put a piece of meat in front of him, he'll snap at it, it's his nature. And if you give a man a little bit of authority he behaves just the same way, he snaps at it too. The things are precisely the same. In himself man is essentially a beast, only he butters it over like a slice of bread with a little decorum. The army is based on that; one man must always have power over the other. The mischief is merely that each one has much too much power. A non-com. can torment a private, a lieutenant a non-com., a captain a lieutenant, until he goes mad. And because they know they can, they all soon aquire the habit more or less. Take a simple case: we are marching back from the parade ground dog-tired. Then comes the order to sing. We sing spiritlessly, for it is all we can do to trudge along with our rifles. At once the company is turned about and has to do another hour's drill as punishment. On the march back the order to sing is given again, and once more we start. Now what's the use of all that? It's simply that the company commander's head has been turned by having so much power. And nobody blames him. On the contrary, he is praised for being strict. That, of course, is only a trifling instance, but it holds also in very different affairs. Now I ask you: Let a man be whatever you like in peacetime, what occupation is there in which he can behave like that without getting a crack on the nose? He can only do that in the army. It goes to the heads of them all, you see. And the more insignificant a man has been in civil life the worse it takes him."

"They say, of course, there must be discipline," ventures Kropp meditatively.

"True," growls Kat, "they always do. And it may be so; still it oughtn't to become an abuse. But you try to explain that to a black-smith or a laborer or a workman, you try to make that clear to a peasant—and that's what most of them are here. All he sees is that he has been put through the mill and sent to the front, but he knows well enough what he must do and what not. It's simply amazing, I tell you, that the ordinary tommy sticks it all up here in the front line. Simply amazing!"

No one protests. Everyone knows that drill ceases only in the front line and begins again a few miles behind, with all the absurdi-ties of saluting and parade. It is an Iron law that the soldier must be employed under every circumstance.

Here Tjaden comes up with a flushed face. He is so excited that he stutters. Beaming with satisfaction he stammers out: "Himmels-toss is on his way. He's coming to the front!"

Tjaden has a special grudge against Himmelstoss, because of the way he educated him in the barracks. Tjaden wets his bed, he does it at night in his sleep. Himmelstoss maintained that it was sheer laziness and invented a method worthy of himself for curing Tjaden.

He hunted up another piss-a-bed, named Kindervater, from a neighboring unit, and quartered him with Tjaden. In the huts there were the usual bunks, one above the other in pairs, with matresses or wire netting. Himmelstoss put these two so that one occupied the upper and the other the lower bunk. The man underneath of course had a vile time. The next night they were changed over and the lower one put on top so that he could retaliate. That was Himmelstoss's system of self-education.

The idea was low but not ill-conceived. Unfortunately it accomplished nothing because the first assumption was wrong: it was not laziness in either of them. Anyone who looked at their sallow skin could see that. The matter ended in one of them always sleeping on the floor, where he frequently caught cold.

Meanwhile Haie sits down beside us. He winks at me and rubs his paws thoughtfully. We once spent the finest day of our army life together—the day before we left for the front. We had been allotted to one of the recently formed regiments, but were first to be sent back for equipment to the garrison, not to the reinforcement depot, or course, but to another barracks. We were due to leave the next morning early. In the evening we prepared ourselves to square accounts with Himmelstoss.

We had sworn for weeks past to do this. Kropp had even gone so far as to propose entering the postal service in peacetime in order to be Himmelstoss's superior when he became a postman again. He reveled in the thought of how he would grind him. It was this that made it impossible for him to crush us altogether—we always reckoned that later, at the end of the war, we would have our revenge on him.

In the meantime we decided to give him a good hiding. What could he do to us anyhow if he didn't recognize us and we left early in the morning?

We knew which pub he used to visit every evening. Returning to the barracks he had to go along a dark, uninhabited road. There we waited for him behind a pile of stones. I had a bed-cover with me. We trembled with suspense, hoping he would be alone. At last we heard his footstep, which we recognized easily, so often had we heard it in the mornings as the door flew open and he bawled: "Get up!"

"Alone?" whispered Kropp.

"Alone."

I slipped round the pile of stones with Tjaden.

Himmelstoss seemed a little elevated; he was singing. His belt buckle gleamed. He came on unsuspectingly.

We seized the bed-cover, made a quick leap, threw it over his head from behind and pulled it round him so that he stood there in a white sack unable to raise his arms. The singing stopped. The next moment Haie Westhus was there, and spreading his arms he shoved us back in order to be first in. He put himself in position with evident satisfaction, raised his arm like a signal-mast and his hand like a coal shovel and fetched such a blow on the white sack as would have felled an ox.

Himmelstoss was thrown down, he rolled five yards and started to yell. But we were prepared for that and had brought a cushion. Haie squatted down, laid the cushion on his knees, felt where Himmelstoss's head was and pressed it down on the pillow. Immediately his voice was muffled. Haie let him get a gasp of air every so often, when he would give a mighty yell that was immediately hushed.

Tjaden unbuttoned Himmelstoss's braces and pulled down his trousers, holding the whip meantime in his teeth. Then he stood up and set to work.

It was a wonderful picture: Himmelstoss on the ground; Haie bending over him with a fiendish grin and his mouth open with bloodlust, Himmelstoss's head on his knees; then the convulsed striped drawers, the knock knees, executing at every blow most original movements in the lowered breeches, and towering over them like a woodcutter the indefatigable Tjaden. In the end we had to drag him away to get our turn.

Finally Haie stood Himmelstoss on his feet again and gave one last personal remonstrance. As he stretched out his right arm preparatory to giving him a box on the ear he looked as if he were going to reach down a star.

Himmelstoss toppled over. Haie stood him up again, made ready and fetched him a second, well-aimed beauty with the left hand. Himmelstoss yelled and made off on all fours. His striped postman's backside gleamed in the moonlight.

We disappeared at full speed.

Haie looked round once again and said wrathfully, satisfied and rather mysteriously:

"Revenge is black pudding."

Himmelstoss ought to have been pleased; his saying that we should each educate one another had borne fruit for himself. We had become successful students of his method.

He never discovered whom he had to thank for the business. At any rate he scored a bedcover out of it; for when we returned a few hours later to look for it, it was no longer to be found.

That evening's work made us more or less content to leave next morning. And an old buffer was pleased to describe us as "young heroes."

4

We have to go up on wiring fatigue. The motor lorries roll up after dark. We climb in. It is a warm evening and the twilight seems like a canopy under whose shelter we feel drawn together. Even the stingy Tjaden gives me a cigarette and then a light.

We stand jammed in together, shoulder to shoulder, there is no room to sit. But we do not expect that. Müller is in a good mood for once; he is wearing his new boots.

The engines drone, the lorries bump and rattle. The roads are worn and full of holes. We dare not show a light so we lurch along and are often almost pitched out. That does not worry us, however. It can happen if it likes; a broken arm is better than a hole in the guts, and many a man would be thankful enough for such a chance of finding his home way again.

Beside us stream the munition-columns in long files. They are making the pace, they overtake us continually. We joke with them and they answer back.

A wall becomes visible, it belongs to a house which lies on the side of the road. I suddenly prick up my ears. Am I deceived? Again I hear distinctly the cackle of geese. A glance at Katczinsky—a glance from him to me; we understand one another.

"Kat, I hear some aspirants for the frying pan over there."

He nods. "It will be attended to when we come back. I have their number."

Of course Kat has their number. He knows all about every leg of goose within a radius of fifteen miles.

The lorries arrive at the artillery lines. The gun-emplacements are camouflaged with bushes against aerial observation, and look like a kind of military Feast of the Tabernacles. These branches might seem gay and cheerful were not cannon embowered there.

The air becomes acrid with the smoke of the guns and the fog. The fumes of powder taste bitter on the tongue. The roar of the guns makes our lorry stagger, the reverberation rolls raging away to the rear, everything quakes. Our faces change imperceptibly. We are not, indeed, in the front line, but only in the reserves, yet in every face can be read: This is the front, now we are within its embrace.

It is not fear. Men who have been up as often as we have become thick skinned. Only the young recruits are agitated. Kat explains to them: "That was a twelve-inch. You can tell by the report; now you'll hear the burst."

But the muffled thud of the burst does not reach us. It is swallowed up in the general murmur of the front. Kat listens: "There'll be a bombardment tonight."

We all listen. The front is restless. "The Tommies are firing already," says Kropp.

The shelling can be heard distinctly. It is the English batteries to the right of our section. They are beginning an hour too soon. According to us they start punctually at ten o'clock.

"What's got them?" says Müller, "their clocks must be fast."

"There'll be a bombardment, I tell you. I can feel it in my bones." Kat shrugs his shoulders.

Three guns open fire close beside us. The burst of flame shoots across the fog, the guns roar and boom. We shiver and are glad to think that we shall be back in the huts early in the morning.

Our faces are neither paler nor more flushed than usual; they are not more tense nor more flabby—and yet they are changed. We feel that in our blood a contact has shot home. That is no figure of speech; it is fact. It is the front, the consciousness of the front, that makes this contact. The moment that the first shells whistle over and the air is rent with the explosions there is suddenly in our veins, in our hands, in our eyes a tense waiting, a watching, a heightening alertness, a strange sharpening of the senses. The body with one bound is in full readiness.

It often seems to me as though it were the vibrating, shuddering air that with a noiseless leap springs upon us; or as though the front itself emitted an electric current which awakened unknown nerve centers.

Every time it is the same. We start out for the front plain soldiers, either cheerful or gloomy: then come the first gun-emplacements and every word of our speech has a new ring.

When Kat stands in front of the hut and says: "There'll be a bombardment," that is merely his own opinion; but if he says it here, then the sentence has the sharpness of a bayonet in the moonlight, it cuts clean through the thought, it thrusts nearer and speaks to this unknown thing that is awakened in us, a dark meaning—"There'll be a bombardment." Perhaps it is our inner and most secret life that shivers and falls on guard.

To me the front is a mysterious whirlpool. Though I am in still water far away from its center, I feel the whirl of the vortex sucking me slowly, irresistibly, inescapably into itself.

From the earth, from the air, sustaining forces pour into us—mostly from the earth. To no man does the earth mean so much as to the soldier. When he presses himself down upon her long and powerfully, when he buries his face and his limbs deep in her from the fear of death by shell-fire, then she is his only friend, his brother, his mother; he stifles his terror and his cries in her silence and her security; she shelters him and releases him for ten seconds to live, to run, ten seconds of life; receives him again and often for ever.

Earth!—Earth!—Earth!

Earth with thy folds, and hollows, and holes, into which a man may fling himself and crouch down. In the spasm of terror, under the hailing of annihilation, in the bellowing death of the explosions, O Earth, thou grantest us the great resisting surge of new-won life. Our being, almost utterly carried away by the fury of the storm, streams back through our hands from thee, and we, they redeemed ones, bury ourselves in thee, and through the long minutes in a mute agony of hope bite into thee with our lips!

At the sound of the first droning of the shells we rush back, in one part of our being, a thousand years. By the animal instinct that is awakened in us we are led and protected. It is not conscious; it is far quicker, much more sure, less fallible, than consciousness. One cannot explain it. A man is walking along without thought or heed;—suddenly he throws himself down on the ground and a storm of fragments flies harmlessly over him;—yet he cannot remember either to have heard the shell coming or to have thought of flinging himself down. But had he not abandoned himself to the impulse he would now be a heap of mangled flesh. It is this other, this second sight in us, that has thrown us to the ground and saved us, without our knowing how. If it were not so, there would not be one man alive from Flanders to the Vosges.

We march up, moody or good tempered soldiers—we reach the zone where the front begins and become on the instant human animals.

An indigent looking wood receives us. We pass by the soup-kitchens. Under cover of the wood we climb out. The lorries turn back. They are to collect us again in the morning before dawn.

Mist and the smoke of guns lie breast high over the fields. The moon is shining. Along the road troops file. Their helmets gleam softly in the moonlight. The heads and the rifles stand out above the white mist, nodding heads, rocking barrels.

Farther on the mist ends. Here the heads become figures; coats, trousers, and boots appear out of the mist as from a milky pool. They become a column. The column marches on, straight ahead, the figures resolve themselves into a block, individuals are no longer recognizable, the dark wedge presses onward, fantastically topped by the heads and the weapons floating on the milky pool. A column—not men at all.

Guns and munition wagons are moving along a cross-road. The backs of the horses shine in the moonlight, their movements are beautiful, they toss their heads, and their eyes gleam. The guns and the wagons float past the dim background of the moonlit landscape, the riders in their steel helmets resemble knights of a forgotten time; it is strangely beautiful and arresting.

We push on to the pioneer dump. Some of us load our shoulders with pointed and twisted iron stakes; others thrust smooth iron rods through rolls of wire and go off with them. The burdens are awkward and heavy.

The ground becomes more broken. From ahead come warnings: "Look out, deep shell-hole on the left"—"Mind, trenches"——

Our eyes peer out, our feet and our sticks feel in front of us before they take the weight of the body. Suddenly the line halts; I bump my face against the roll of wire carried by the man in front and curse.

There are some shell-smashed lorries in the road. Another order: "Cigarettes and pipes out." We are near the line.

In the meantime it has become pitch dark. We skirt a small wood and then have the front line immediately before us.

An uncertain red glow spreads along the skyline from one end to the other. It is in perpetual movement, punctuated with the bursts of flame from the nozzles of the batteries. Balls of light rise up high above it, silver and red spheres which explode and rain down in showers of red, white, and green stars. French rockets go up, which unfold a silk parachute to the air and drift slowly down. They light up everything as bright as day, their light shines on us and we see our shadows sharply outlined on the ground. They hover for the space of a minute before they burn out. Immediately fresh ones shoot up in the sky, and again green, red, and blue stars.

"Bombardment," says Kat.

The thunder of the guns swells to a single heavy roar and then breaks up again into separate explosions. The dry bursts of the machine guns rattle. Above us the air teems with invisible swift movement, with howls, pipings, and hisses. They are smaller shells;—and amongst them, booming through the night like an organ, go the great coal boxes and the heavies. They have a hoarse, distant bellow like a rutting stag and make their way high above the howl and whistle of the smaller shells. It reminds me of flocks of wild geese when I hear them. Last autumn the wild geese flew day after day across the path of the shells.

The searchlights begin to sweep the dark sky. They slide along it like gigantic tapering rulers. One of them pauses, and quivers a little. Immediately a second is beside him, a black insect is caught between them and tries to escape—the airman. He hesitates, is blinded and falls.

At regular intervals we ram in the iron stakes. Two men hold a roll and the others spool off the barbed wire. It is that awful stuff with close-set, long spikes. I am not used to unrolling it and tear my hand.

After a few hours it is done. But there is still some time before the lorries come. Most of us lie down and sleep. I try also, but it has turned too chilly. We know we are not far from the sea because we are constantly waked by the cold.

Once I fall fast asleep. Then wakening suddenly with a start I do not know where I am. I see the stars, I see the rockets, and for a moment have the impression that I have fallen asleep at a garden fête. I don't know whether it is morning or evening, I lie in the pale cradle of the twilight, and listen for soft words which will come, soft and near—am I crying? I put my hand to my eyes, it is so fantastic, am I a child? Smooth skin;—it lasts only a second, then I recognize the silhouette of Katczinsky. The old veteran, he sits quietly and smokes his pipe—a covered pipe of course. When he sees I am awake, he says: "That gave you a fright. It was only a nose-cap, it landed in the bushes over there."

I sit up, I feel myself strangely alone. It's good Kat is there. He gazes thoughtfully at the front and says:

"Mighty fine fireworks if they weren't so dangerous."

One lands behind us. Some recruits jump up terrified. A couple of minutes later another comes over, nearer this time. Kat knocks out his pipe. "We're in for it."

Then it begins in earnest. We crawl away as well as we can in our haste. The next lands fair amongst us. Two fellows cry out. Green rockets shoot up on the skyline. Barrage. The mud flies high, fragments whizz past. The crack of the guns is heard long after the roar of the explosions.

Beside us lies a fair-headed recruit in utter terror. He has buried his face in his hands, his helmet has fallen off. I fish hold of it and try to put it back on his head. He looks up, pushes the helmet off and like a child creeps under my arm, his head close to my breast. The little shoulders heave. Shoulders just like Kemmerich's. I let him be. So that the helmet should be of some use I stick it on his behind;—not for a jest, but out of consideration, since that is his highest part. And though there is plenty of meat there, a shot in it can be damned painful. Besides, a man has to lie for months on his belly in the hospital, and afterward he would be almost sure to have a limp.

It's got someone pretty badly. Cries are heard between the explosions.

At last it grows quiet. The fire has lifted over us and is now dropping on the reserves. We risk a look. Red rockets shoot up to the sky. Apparently there's an attack coming.

Where we are it is still quiet. I sit up and shake the recruit by the shoulder. "All over, kid! It's all right this time."

He looks round him dazedly. "You'll get used to it soon," I tell him.

He sees his helmet and puts it on. Gradually he comes to. Then suddenly he turns fiery red and looks confused. Cautiously he reaches his hand to his behind and looks at me dismally.

I understand at once: Gun-shy. That wasn't the reason I had stuck his helmet over it. "That's no disgrace," I reassure him: "Many's the man before you has had his pants full after the first bombardment. Go behind that bush there and throw your underpants away. Get along——"

He goes off. Things become quieter, but the cries do not cease. "What's up, Albert?" I ask.

"A couple of columns over there got it in the neck."

The cries continued. It is not men, they could not cry so terribly.

"Wounded horses," says Kat.

It's unendurable. It is the moaning of the world, it is the martyred creation, wild with anguish, filled with terror, and groaning.

We are pale. Detering stands up. "God! For God's sake! Shoot them."

He is a farmer and very fond of horses. It gets under his skin. Then as if deliberately the fire dies down again. The screaming of the beasts becomes louder. One can no longer distinguish whence in this now quiet silvery landscape it comes; ghostly, invisible, it is everywhere, between heaven and earth it rolls on immeasurably. Detering raves and yells out: "Shoot them! Shoot them, can't you? Damn you again!"

"They must look after the men first," says Kat quietly.

We stand up and try to see where it is. If we could only see the animals we should be able to endure it better. Müller has a pair of glasses. We see a dark group, bearers with stretchers, and larger black clumps moving about. Those are the wounded horses. But not all of them. Some gallop away in the distance, fall down, and then run on farther. The belly of one is ripped open, the guts trail out. He becomes tangled in them and falls, then he stands up again.

Detering raises up his gun and aims. Kat hits it in the air. "Are you mad——?"

Detering trembles and throws his rifle on the ground.

We sit down and hold our ears. But this appalling noise, these groans and screams penetrate, they penetrate everywhere.

We can bear almost anything. But now the sweat breaks out on us. We must get up and run no matter where, but where these cries can no longer be heard. And it is not men, only horses.

From the dark group stretchers move off again. Then single shots crack out. The black heap convulses and then sinks down. At last! But still it is not the end. The men cannot overtake the wounded beasts which fly in their pain, their wide open mouths full of anguish. One of the men goes down on one knee, a shot—one horse drops—another. The last one props itself on its forelegs and drags itself round in a circle like a merry-go-round; squatting, it drags round in circles on its stiffened forelegs, apparently its back is broken. The soldier runs up and shoots it. Slowly, humbly, it sinks to the ground.

We take our hands from our ears. The cries are silenced. Only a long-drawn, dying sigh still hangs on the air.

Then only again the rockets, the singing of the shells and the stars there—most strange.

Detering walks up and down cursing: "Like to know what harm they've done." He returns to it once again. His voice is agitated, it sounds almost dignified as he says: "I tell you it is the vilest baseness to use horses in the war."

We go back. It is time we returned to the lorries. The sky has become brighter. Three o'clock in the morning. The breeze is fresh and cool, the pale hour makes our faces look gray.

We trudge onward in single file through the trenches and shell-holes and come again to the zone of mist. Katczinsky is restive, that's a bad sign.

"What's up, Kat?" says Kropp.

"I wish I were back home." Home—he means the huts.

"We'll soon be out of it, Kat."

He is nervous. "I don't know, I don't know——"

We come to the communication trench and then to the open fields. The little wood reappears; we know every foot of ground here. There's the cemetery with the mounds and the black crosses.

That moment it breaks out behind us, swells, roars, and thunders. We duck down—a cloud of flame shoots up a hundred yards ahead of us.

The next minute under a second explosion part of the wood rises slowly in the air, three or four trees sail up and then crash to pieces. The shells begin to hiss like safety valves—heavy fire——

"Take cover!" yells somebody—"Cover!"

The fields are flat, the wood is too distant and dangerous—the only cover is the graveyard and the mounds. We stumble across in the dark and as though he had been spat there every man lies glued behind a mound.

Not a moment too soon. The dark goes mad. It heaves and raves. Darknesses blacker than the night rush on us with giant strides, over us and away. The flames of the explosions light up the graveyard.

There is no escape anywhere. By the light of the shells I try to get a view of the fields. They are a surging sea, daggers of flame from the explosions leap up like fountains. It is impossible for anyone to break through it.

The wood vanishes, it is pounded, crushed, torn to pieces. We must stay here in the graveyard.

The earth bursts before us. It rains clods. I feel a smack. My sleeve is torn away by a splinter. I shut my fist. No pain. Still that does not reassure me: wounds don't hurt till afterward. I feel the arm all over. It is grazed but sound. Now a crack on the skull, I begin to lose consciousness. Like lightning the thought comes to me: Don't faint! I sink down in the black broth and immediately come up to the top again. A splinter slashes into my helmet, but has already traveled so far that it does not go through. I wipe the mud out of my eyes. A hole is torn up in front of me. Shells hardly ever land in the same hole twice, I'll get into it. With one lunge, I shoot as flat as a fish over the ground; there it whistles again, quickly I crouch together, claw for cover, feel something on the left, shove in beside it, it gives way, I groan, the earth leaps, the blast thunders in my ears, I creep under the yielding thing, cover myself with it, draw it over me, it is wood, cloth, cover, cover, miserable cover against the whizzing splinters.

I open my eyes—my fingers grasp a sleeve, an arm. A wounded man? I yell to him—no answer—a dead man. My hand gropes farther, splinters of wood—now I remember again that we are lying in the graveyard.

But the shelling is stronger than everything. It wipes out the sensibilities, I merely crawl still farther under the coffin, it shall protect me, though Death himself lies in it.

Before me gapes the shell-hole. I grasp it with my eyes as with fists. With one leap I must be in it. There, I get a smack in the face, a hand clamps onto my shoulder—has the dead man waked up?— The hand shakes me, I turn my head, in the second of light I stare into the face of Katczinsky, he has his mouth wide open and is yelling. I hear nothing, he rattles me, comes nearer, in a momentary lull his voices reaches me: "Gas—Gaas—Gaaas—Pass it on."

I grab for my gas mask. Some distance from me there lies someone. I think of nothing but this: That fellow there must know: Gaaas—Gaaas—

I call, I lean toward him, I swipe at him with the satchel, he doesn't see—once again, again—he merely ducks—it's a recruit—I look at Kat desperately, he has his mask on—I pull out mine, too, my helmet falls to one side, it slips over my face, I reach the man, his satchel is on the side nearest me, I seize the mask, pull it over his head, he understands, I let go and with a jump drop into the shell-hole.

The dull thud of the gas-shells mingles with the crashes of the light explosives. A bell sounds between the explosions, gongs, and metal clappers warning everyone—Gas—Gas—Gaas.

Someone plumps down behind me, another. I wipe the goggles of my mask clear of the moist breath. It is Kat, Kropp, and someone else. All four of us lie there in heavy, watchful suspense and breathe as lightly as possible.

These first minutes with the mask decide between life and death: is it airtight? I remember the awful sights in the hospital: the gas patients who in day-long suffocation cough up their burned lungs in clots.

Cautiously, the mouth applied to the valve, I breathe. The gas still creeps over the ground and sinks into all hollows. Like a big, soft jellyfish it floats into our shell-hole and lolls there obscenely. I nudge Kat, it is better to crawl out and lie on top than to stay where the gas collects most. But we don't get as far as that; a second bombardment begins. It is no longer as though shells roared; it is the earth itself raging.

With a crash something black bears down on us. It lands close beside us; a coffin thrown up.

I see Kat move and I crawl across. The coffin has hit the fourth man in our hole on his outstretched arm. He tries to tear off his gas mask with the other hand. Kropp seizes him just in time, twists the hand sharply behind his back and holds it fast.

Kat and I proceed to free the wounded arm. The coffin lid is loose and bursts open, we are easily able to pull it off, we toss the corpse out, it slides down to the bottom of the shell-hole, then we try to loosen the under part.

Fortunately the man swoons and Kropp is able to help us. We no longer have to be careful, but work away till the coffin gives with a sigh before the spade that we have dug in under it.

It has grown lighter. Kat takes a piece of the lid, places it under the shattered arm, and we wrap all our bandages round it. For the moment we can do no more.

Inside the gas mask my head booms and roars—it is nigh bursting. My lungs are tight, they breathe always the same hot, used-up air, the veins on my temples are swollen. I feel I am suffocating.

A gray light filters through to us. I climb out over the edge of the shell-hole. In the dirty twilight lies a leg torn clean off; the boot is quite whole, I take that all in at a glance. Now something stands up a few yards distant. I polish the windows, in my excitement they are immediately dimmed again. I peer through them, the man there no longer wears his mask.

I wait some seconds—he has not collapsed—he looks around and makes a few paces—rattling in my throat I tear my mask off too and fall down, the air streams into me like cold water, my eyes are bursting the wave sweeps over me and extinguishes me.

The shelling has ceased, I turn toward the crater beckoning to the others. They take off their masks. We lift up the wounded man, one taking his splinted arm. And so we stumble off hastily.

The graveyard is a mass of wreckage. Coffins and corpses lie strewn about. They have been killed once again; but each of them that was flung up saved one of us.

The hedge is destroyed, the rails of the light railway are torn up and rise stiffly in the air in great arches. Someone lies in front of us. We stop; Kropp goes on alone with the wounded man.

The man on the ground is a recruit. His hip is covered with blood; he is so exhausted that I feel for my water bottle where I have rum and tea. Kat restrains my hand and stoops over him.

"Where's it got you comrade?"

His eyes move. He is too weak to answer.

We slit open his trousers carefully. He groans. "Gently, gently, it is much better——"

If he has been hit in the stomach he oughtn't to drink anything. There's no vomiting, that's a good sign. We lay the hip bare. It is one mass of mince-meat and bone splinters. The joint has been hit. This lad won't walk any more.

I wet his temples with a moistened finger and give him a swig. His eyes move again. We see now that the right arm is bleeding as well.

Kat spreads out two wads of dressing as wide as possible so that they will cover the wound. I look for something to bind loosely round it. We have nothing more, so I slip up the wounded man's trouser leg still farther in order to use a piece of his underpants as a bandage. But he is wearing none. I now look at him closely. He is the fair-headed boy of a little while ago.

In the meantime Kat has taken a bandage from a dead man's pocket and we carefully bind the wound. I say to the youngster who looks at us fixedly: "We're going for a stretcher now——"

Then he opens his mouth and whispers: "Stay here——"

"We'll be back again soon," says Kat. "We are only going to get a stretcher for you."

We don't know if he understands. He whimpers like a child and plucks at us: "Don't go away——"

Kat looks around and whispers: "Shouldn't we just take a revolver and put an end to it?"

The youngster will hardly survive the carrying, and at the most he will only last a few days. What he has gone through so far is nothing to what he's in for till he dies. Now he is numb and feels nothing. In an hour he will become one screaming bundle of intolerable pain. Every day that he can live will be a howling torture. And to whom does it matter whether he has them or not——

I nod. "Yes, Kat, we ought to put him out of his misery."

He stands still a moment. He has made up his mind. We look round—but we are no longer alone. A little group is gathering, from the shell-holes and trenches appear heads.

We get a stretcher.

Kat shakes his head. "Such a kid——" He repeats it. "Young innocents——"

Our losses are less than was to be expected—five killed and eight wounded. It was in fact quite a short bombardment. Two of our dead lie in the upturned graves. We merely throw the earth in on them.

We go back. We trot off silently in single file one behind the other. The wounded are taken to the dressing-station. The morning is cloudy. The bearers make a fuss about numbers and tickets, the wounded whimper. It begins to rain.

An hour later we reach our lorries and climb in. There is more room now than there was.

The rain becomes heavier. We take out waterproof sheets and spread them over our heads. The rain rattles down, and flows off at the sides in streams. The lorries bump through the holes, and we rock to and fro in a half-sleep.

Two men in the front of the lorry have long forked poles. They watch for telephone wires which hang crosswise over the road so low that they might easily pull our heads off. The two fellows take them at the right moment on their poles and lift them over behind us. We hear their call "Mind—wire—," dip the knee in a half-sleep and straighten up again.

Monotonously the lorries sway, monotonously come the calls, monotonously falls the rain. It falls on our heads and on the heads of the dead up in the line, on the body of the little recruit with the wound that is so much too big for his hip; it falls on Kemmerich's grave; it falls in our hearts.

An explosion sounds somewhere. We wince, our eyes become tense, our hands are ready to vault over the side of the lorry into the ditch by the road.

Nothing happens—only the monotonous cry: "Mind—wire,"— our knees bend—we are again half asleep.

5

Killing each separate louse is a tedious business when a man has hundreds. The little beasts are hard and the everlasting cracking with one's fingernails very soon becomes wearisome. So Tjaden has rigged up the lid of a boot-polish tin with a piece of wire over the lighted stump of a candle. The lice are simply thrown into this little pan. Crack! and they're done for.

We sit around with our shirts on our knees, our bodies naked to the warm air and our hands at work. Haie has a particularly fine brand of louse: they have a red cross on their heads. He suggests that he brought them back from the hospital at Thourhout, where they attended personally on a surgeon general. He says he means to use the fat that slowly accumulates in the tin-lid for polishing his boots, and roars with laughter for half an hour at his own joke.

But he gets little response today; we are too preoccupied with another affair.

The rumor has materialized. Himmelstoss has come. He appeared yesterday; we've already heard the well-known voice. He seems to have overdone it with a couple of young recruits on the ploughed field at home and unknown to him the son of the local magistrate was watching. That cooked his goose.

He will get some surprises here. Tjaden has been meditating for hours what to say to him. Haie gazes thoughtfully at his great paws and winks at me. The thrashing was the high water mark of his life. He tells me he often dreams of it. Kropp and Müller are amusing themselves. From somewhere or other, probably the pioneer cook-house, Kropp has bagged for himself a mess-tin full of beans. Müller squints hungrily into it but checks himself and says: "Albert, what would you do if it were suddenly peacetime again?"

"There won't be any peacetime," says Albert bluntly.

"Well, but if—" persists Müller, "what would you do?"

"Clear out of this!" growls Kropp.

"Of course. And then what?"

"Get drunk," says Albert.

"Don't talk rot, I mean seriously—"

"So do I," says Kropp, "what else should a man do?"

Kat becomes interested. He levies tribute on Kropp's tin of beans, swallows some, then considers for a while and says: "You might get drunk first, of course, but then you'd take the next train for home and mother. Peacetime, man, Albert——"

He fumbles in his oil-cloth pocketbook for a photograph and suddenly shows it all round. "My old woman!" Then he puts it back and swears: "Damned lousy war——"

"It's all very well for you to talk," I tell him. "You've got a wife and children."

"True," he nods, "and I have to see to it that they've something to eat."

We laugh. "They won't lack for that, Kat, you'd scrounge it from somewhere."

Müller is insatiable and gives himself no peace. He wakes Haie Westhus out of his dream. "Haie, what would you do if it was peacetime?"

"Give you a kick in the backside for the way you talk," I say. "How does it come about exactly?"

"How does the cowshit come on the roof?" retorts Müller laconically, and turns to Haie Westhus again.

It is too much for Haie. He shakes his freckled head:

"You mean when the war's over?"

"Exactly. You've said it."

"Well, there'd be women of course, eh?"—Haie licks his lips. "Sure."

"By Jove, yes," says Haie, his face smiling, "then I'd grab some good buxom dame, some real kitchen wench with plenty to get hold of, you know, and jump straight into bed. Just you think, boys, a real feather bed with a spring mattress; I wouldn't put trousers on again for a week."

Everyone is silent. The picture is too good. Our flesh creeps. At last Müller pulls himself together and says:

"And then what?"

A pause. Then Haie explains rather awkwardly: "If I were a non-com. I'd stay with the Prussians and serve out my time."

"Haie, you've got a screw loose, surely!" I say.

"Have you ever dug peat?" he retorts good-naturedly. "You try it."

Then he pulls a spoon out of the top of his boot and reaches over into Kopp's mess-tin.

"It can't be worse than digging trenches," I ventured.

Haie chews and grins: "It lasts longer though. And there's no getting out of it either."

"But, man, surely it's better at home."

"Some ways," says he, and with open mouth sinks into a daydream.

You can see what he is thinking. There is the mean little hut on the moors, the hard work on the heath from morning till night in the heat, the miserable pay, the dirty laborer's clothes.

"In the army in peacetime you've nothing to trouble about," he goes on, "your food's found every day, or else you kick up a row; you've a bed, every week clean underwear like a perfect gent, you do your non-com.'s duty, you have a good suit of clothes; in the evening you're a free man and go off to the pub."

Haie is extraordinarily set on his idea. He's in love with it.

"And when your twelve years are up you get your pension and become the village bobby, and you can walk about the whole day."

He's already sweating on it. "And just you think how you'd be treated. Here a dram, there a pint. Everybody wants to be well in with a bobby."

"You'll never be a non-com. though, Haie," interrupts Kat.

Haie looks at him sadly and is silent. His thoughts still linger over the clear evenings in autumn, the Sundays in the heather, the village bells, the afternoons and evenings with the servant girls, the fried bacon and barley, the carefree hours in the ale-house——

He can't part with all these dreams so abruptly; he merely growls: "What silly questions you do ask."

He pulls his shirt over his head and buttons up his tunic.

"What would you do, Tjaden!" asks Kropp.

Tjaden thinks of one thing only. "See to it that Himmelstoss didn't get past me."

Apparently he would like most to have him in a cage and sail into him with a club every morning. To Kropp he says warmly: "If I were in your place I'd see to it that I became a lieutenant. Then you could grind him till the water in his backside boils."

"And you, Detering!" asks Müller like an inquisitor. He's a born schoolmaster with all his questions.

Detering is sparing with his words. But on this subject he speaks. He looks at the sky and says only the one sentence: "I would go straight on with the harvesting."

Then he gets up and walks off.

He is worried. His wife has to look after the farm. They've already taken away two more of his horses. Every day he reads the papers that come, to see whether it is raining in his little corner of Oldenburg. They haven't brought in the hay yet.

At this moment Himmelstoss appears. He comes straight up to our group. Tjaden's face turns red. He stretches his length on the grass and shuts his eyes in excitement.

Himmelstoss is a little hesitant, his gait becomes slower. Then he marches up to us. No one makes any motion to stand up. Kropp looks up at him with interest.

He continues to stand in front of us and wait. As no one says anything he launches a "Well!"

A couple of seconds go by. Apparently Himmelstoss doesn't quite know what to do. He would like most to set us all on the run again. But he seems to have learned already that the front line isn't a parade ground. He tries it on though, and by addressing himself to one instead of to all of us hopes to get some response. Kropp is nearest, so he favors him.

"Well, you here too?"

But Albert's no friend of his. "A bit longer than you, I fancy," he retorts.

The red mustache twitches: "You don't recognize me any more, what?"

Tjaden now opens his eyes. "I do though."

Himmelstoss turns to him: "Tjaden, isn't it?"

Tjaden lifts his head. "And do you know what you are?"

Himmelstoss is disconcerted. "Since when have we become so familiar? I don't remember that we ever slept in the gutter together?"

He has no idea what to make of the situation. He didn't expect this open hostility. But he is on his guard: he has already had some rot dinned into him about getting a shot in the back.

The question about the gutter makes Tjaden so mad that he becomes almost witty: "No you slept there by yourself."

Himmelstoss begins to boil. But Tjaden gets in ahead of him. He must bring off his insult: "Wouldn't you like to know what you are? A dirty hound, that's what you are. I've been wanting to tell you that for a long time."

The satisfaction of months shines in his dull pig's eyes as he spits out: "Dirty hound!"

Himmelstoss lets fly too, now. "What's that, you muck-rake, you dirty peat-stealer? Stand up there, bring your heels together when your superior officer speaks to you."

Tjaden waves him off. "You take a run and jump at yourself, Himmelstoss."

Himmelstoss is a raging book of army regulations. The Kaiser couldn't be more insulted. "Tjaden, I command you, as your superior officer: Stand up!"

"Anything else you would like?" asks Tjaden.

"Will you obey my order or not?"

Tjaden replies, without knowing it, in the well-known classical phrase.

At the same time he ventilates his backside.

"I'll have you court-martialed," storms Himmelstoss.

We watch him disappear in the direction of the Orderly Room. Haie and Tjaden burst into a regular peat-digger's bellow. Haie laughs so much that he dislocates his jaw, and suddenly stands there helpless with his mouth wide open. Albert has to put it back again by giving it a blow with his fist.

Kat is troubled: "If he reports you, it'll be pretty serious."

"Do you think he will?" asks Tjaden.

"Sure to," I say.

"The least you'll get will be five days close arrest," says Kat.

That doesn't worry Tjaden. "Five days clink are five days rest."

"And if they send you to the Fortress?" urges the thoroughgoing Müller.

"Well, for the time being the war will be over so far as I am concerned."

Tjaden is a cheerful soul. There aren't any worries for him. He goes off with Haie and Leer so that they won't find him in the first flush of excitement.

Müller hasn't finished yet. He tackles Kropp again.

"Albert, if you were really at home now, what would you do?"

Kropp is contented now and more accommodating:

"How many of us were there in the class exactly?"

We count up: out of twenty, seven are dead, four wounded, one in a madhouse. That makes twelve.

"Three of them are lieutenants," says Müller. "Do you think they would still let Kantorek sit on them?"

We guess not: we wouldn't let ourselves be sat on for that matter.

"What do you mean by the three-fold theme in 'William Tell'?" says Kropp reminiscently, and roars with laughter.

"What was the purpose of the Poetic League of Göttingen?" asked Müller suddenly and earnestly.

"How many children has Charles the Bald?" I interrupt gently.

"You'll never make anything of your life, Bämer," croaks Müller.

"When was the battle of Zana?" Kropp wants to know.

"You lack the studious mind, Kropp, sit down, three minus——" I say.

"What offices did Lycurgus consider the most important for the state?" asks Müller, pretending to take off his pince-nez.

"Does it go: 'We Germans fear God and none else in the whole world,' or 'We, the Germans, fear God and——'" I submit.

"How many inhabitants has Melbourne?" asks Müller.

"How do you expect to succeed in life if you don't know that?" I ask Albert hotly.

Which he caps with: "What is meant by Cohesion?"

We remember mighty little of all that rubbish. Anyway, it has never been the slightest use to us. At school nobody ever taught us how to light a cigarette in a storm of rain, nor how a fire could be made with wet wood—nor that it is best to stick a bayonet in the belly because there it doesn't get jammed, as it does in the ribs.

Müller says thoughtfully: "What's the use? We'll have to go back and sit on the forms again."

I consider that out of the question. "We might take a special exam."

"That needs preparation. And if you do get through, what then? A student's life isn't any better. If you have no money, you have to work like the devil."

"It's a bit better. But it's rot all the same, everything they teach you."

Kropp supports me: "How can a man take all that stuff seriously when he's once been out here?"

"Still you must have an occupation of some sort," insists Müller, as though he were Kantorek himself.

Albert cleans his nails with a knife. We are surprised at this delicacy. But it is merely pensiveness. He puts the knife away and continues: "That's just it. Kat and Detering and Haie will go back to their jobs because they had them already. Himmelstoss too. But we never had any. How will we ever get used to one after this, here?"—he makes a gesture toward the front.

"What we'll want is a private income, and then we'll be able to live by ourselves in a wood," I say, but at once feel ashamed of this absurd idea.

"But what will really happen when we go back?" wonders Müller, and even he is troubled.

Kropp gives a shrug. "I don't know. Let's get back first, then we'll find out."

We are all utterly at a loss. "What could we do?" I ask.

"I don't want to do anything," replies Kropp wearily. "You'll be dead one day, so what does it matter? I don't think we'll ever go back."

"When I think about it, Albert," I say after a while rolling over on my back, "when I hear the word 'peacetime,' it goes to my head: and if it really came, I think I would do some unimaginable thing— something, you know, that it's worth having lain here in the muck for. But I can't even imagine anything. All I do know is that this business about professions and studies and salaries and so on—it makes me sick, it is and always was disgusting. I don't see anything at all, Albert."

All at once everything seems to me confused and hopeless.

Kropp feels it too. "It will go pretty hard with us all. But nobody at home seems to worry much about it. Two years of shells and bombs—a man won't peel that off as easy as a sock."

We agree that it's the same for everyone; not only for us here, but everywhere, for everyone who is of our age; to some more, and to others less. It is the common fate of our generation.

Albert expresses it: "The war has ruined us for everything."

He is right. We are not youth any longer. We don't want to take the world by storm. We are fleeing. We fly from ourselves. From our life. We were eighteen and had begun to love life and the world; and we had to shoot it to pieces. The first bomb, the first explosion, burst in our hearts. We are cut off from activity, from striving, from progress. We believe in such things no longer, we believe in the war.

The Orderly Room shows signs of life. Himmelstoss seems to have stirred them up. At the head of the column trots the fat sergeant major. It is queer that almost all of the regular sergeant majors are fat.

Himmelstoss follows him, thirsting for vengeance. His boots gleam in the sun.

We get up.

"Where's Tjaden?" the sergeant puffs.

No one knows, of course. Himmelstoss glowers at us wrathfully. "You know very well. You won't say, that's the fact of the matter. Out with it!"

Fatty looks round enquiringly; but Tjaden is not to be seen. He tries another way.

"Tjaden will report at the Orderly Room in ten minutes."

Then he steams off with Himmelstoss in his wake.

"I have a feeling that next time we go up wiring I'll be letting a bundle of wire fall on Himmelstoss's leg, hints Kropp.

"We'll have quite a lot of jokes with him," laughs Müller.—

That is our sole ambition: to knock the conceit out of a postman.

I go into the hut and put Tjaden wise. He disappears.

Then we change our possy and lie down again to play cards. We know how to do that: to play cards, to swear, and to fight. Not much for twenty years;—and yet too much for twenty years.

Half an hour later Himmelstoss is back again. Nobody pays any attention to him. He asks for Tjaden. We shrug our shoulders.

"Then you'd better find him," he persists. "Haven't you been to look for him?"

Kropp lies back on the grass and says: "Have you ever been out here before?"

"That's none of your business," retorts Himmelstoss. "I expect an answer."

"Very good," says Kropp, getting up. "See up there where those little white clouds are. Those are anti-aircraft. We were over there yesterday. Five dead and eight wounded. And that's a mere nothing. Next time, when you go up with us, before they die the fellows will come up to you, click their heels, and ask stiffly: 'Please may I go? Please may I hop it? We've been waiting here a long time for someone like you.'"

He sits down again and Himmelstoss disappears like a comet.

"Three days C.B.," conjectures Kat.

"Next time I'll let fly," I say to Albert.

But that is the end. The case comes up for trial in the evening. In the Orderly Room sits our Lieutenant, Bertink, and calls us in one after another.

I have to appear as a witness and explain the reason of Tjaden's insubordination.

The story of the bed-wetting makes an impression. Himmelstoss is recalled and I repeat my statement.

"Is that right?" Bertink asks Himmelstoss.

He tries to evade the question, but in the end has to confess, for Kropp tells the same story.

"Why didn't someone report the matter, then?" asks Bertink.

We are silent: he must know himself how much use it is in reporting such things. It isn't usual to make complaints in the army. He understands it all right though, and lectures Himmelstoss, making it plain to him that the front isn't a parade ground. Then comes Tjaden's turn, he gets a long sermon and three days' open arrest. Bertink gives Kropp a wink and one day's open arrest. "It can't be helped," he says to him regretfully. He is a decent fellow.

Open arrest is quite pleasant. The clink was once a fowl-house; there we can visit the prisoners, we know how to manage it. Close arrest would have meant the cellar.

They used to tie us to a tree, but that is forbidden now. In many ways we are treated quite like men.

An hour later after Tjaden and Kropp are settled in behind their wire netting we make our way into them. Tjaden greets us crowing. Then we play skat far into the night. Tjaden wins of course, the lucky wretch.

When we break it up Kat says to me: "What do you say to some roast goose?"

"Not bad," I agree.

We climb up on a munition wagon. The ride costs us two cigarettes. Kat has marked the spot exactly. The shed belongs to a regimental headquarters. I agree to get the goose and receive my instructions. The outhouse is behind the wall and the door shuts with just a peg.

Kat hoists me up. I rest my foot in his hands and climb over the wall. Kat keeps watch below.

I wait a few moments to accustom my eyes to the darkness. Then I recognize the shed. Softly I steal across, lift the peg, pull it out and open the door.

I distinguish two white patches. Two geese, that's bad: if I grab one the other will cackle. Well, both of them—if I'm quick, it can be done.

I make a jump. I catch hold of one and the next instant the second. Like a madman I bash their heads against the wall to stun them. But I haven't quite enough weight. The beasts cackle and strike out with their feet and wings. I fight desperately, but Lord! what a kick a goose has! They struggle and I stagger about. In the dark these white patches are terrifying. My arms have grown wings and I'm almost afraid of going up into the sky, as though I held a couple of captive balloons in my fists.

Then the row begins; one of them gets his breath and goes off like an alarmclock. Before I can do anything, something comes in from outside; I feel a blow, lie outstretched on the floor, and hear awful growls. A dog. I steal a glance to the side, he makes a snap at my throat. I lie still and tuck my chin into my collar.

It's a bull dog. After an eternity he withdraws his head and sits down beside me. But if I make the least movement he growls. I consider. The only thing to do is to get hold of my small revolver, and that too before anyone arrives. Inch by inch I move my hand toward it.

I have the feeling that it lasts an hour. The slightest movement and then an awful growl; I lie still, then try again. When at last I have the revolver my hand starts to tremble. I press it against the ground and say over to myself: Jerk the revolver up, fire before he has a chance to grab, and then jump up.

Slowly I take a deep breath and become calmer. Then I hold my breath, whip up the revolver, it cracks, the dog leaps howling to one side, I make for the door of the shed and fall head over heels over one of the scuttering geese.

At full speed I seize it again, and with a swing toss it over the wall and clamber up. No sooner am I on top than the dog is up again as lively as ever and springs at me. Quickly I let myself drop. Ten paces away stands Kat with the goose under his arm. As soon as he sees me we run.

At last we can take a breather. The goose is dead, Kat saw to that in a moment. We intend to roast it at once so that nobody will be any wiser. I fetch a dixie and wood from the hut and we crawl into a small deserted lean-to which we use for such purposes. The single window space is heavily curtained. There is a sort of hearth, an iron plate set on some bricks. We kindle a fire.

Kat plucks and cleans the goose. We put the feathers carefully to one side. We intend to make two cushions out of them with the inscription: "Sleep soft under shell-fire." The sound of the gun-fire from the front penetrates into our refuge. The glow of the fire lights up our faces, shadows dance on the wall. Sometimes a heavy crash and the lean-to shivers. Airplane bombs. Once we hear a stifled cry. A hut must have been hit.

Airplanes drone; the tack-tack of machine-guns breaks out. But no light that could be observed shows from us.

We sit opposite one another, Kat and I, two soldiers in shabby coats, cooking a goose in the middle of the night. We don't talk much, but I believe we have a more complete communion with one another than even lovers have.

We are two men, two minute sparks of life; outside is the night and the circle of death. We sit on the edge of it crouching in danger, the grease drips from our hands, in our hearts we are close to one another, and the hour is like the room: flecked over with the lights and shadows of our feelings cast by a quiet fire. What does he know of me or I of him? Formerly we should not have had a single thought in common—now we sit with a goose between us and feel in unison, are so intimate that we do not even speak.

It takes a long time to roast a goose, even when it is young and fat. So we take turns. One bastes it while the other lies down and sleeps. A grand smell gradually fills the hut.

The noises without increase in volume, pass into my dream and yet linger in my memory. In a half sleep, I watch Kat dip and raise the ladle. I love him, his shoulders, his angular, stooping figure—and at the same time I see behind him woods and stars, and a clear voice utters words that bring me peace, to me, a soldier in big boots, belt, and knapsack, taking the road that lies before him under the high heaven, quickly forgetting and seldom sorrowful, forever pressing on under the wide night sky.

A little soldier and a clear voice, and if anyone were to caress him he would hardly understand, this soldier with the big boots and the shut heart, who marches because he is wearing big boots, and has forgotten all else but marching. Beyond the skyline is a country with flowers, lying so still that he would like to weep. There are sights there that he has not forgotten, because he never possessed them—perplexing, yet lost to him. Are not his twenty summers there?

Is my face wet, and where am I? Kat stands before me, his gigantic, stooping shadow falls upon me, like home. He speaks gently, he smiles and goes back to the fire.

Then he says: "It's done."

"Yes, Kat."

I stir myself. In the middle of the room shines the brown goose. We take out our collapsible forks and our pocketknives and each cuts off a leg. With it we have army bread dipped in gravy. We eat slowly and with gusto.

"How does it taste, Kat?"

"Good! And yours?"

"Good, Kat."

We are brothers and press on one another the choicest pieces. Afterward I smoke a cigarette and Kat a cigar. There is still a lot left.

"How would it be, Kat if we took a bit to Kropp and Tjaden?"

"Sure," says he.

We carve off a portion and wrap it up carefully in newspaper. The rest we thought of taking over to the hut. Kat laughs, and simply says: "Tjaden."

I agree, we will have to take it all.

So we go off to the fowl-house to waken them. But first we pack away the feathers.

Kropp and Tjaden take us for magicians. Then they get busy with their teeth. Tjaden holds a wing in his mouth with both hands like a mouth-organ, and gnaws. He drinks the gravy from the pot and smacks his lips:

"May I never forget you!"

We go to our hut. Again there is the lofty sky with the stars and the oncoming dawn, and I pass beneath it, a soldier with big boots and a full belly, a little soldier in the early morning—but by my side, stooping and angular, goes Kat, my comrade.

The outlines of the huts are upon us in the dawn like a dark, deep sleep.

6

There are rumors of an offensive. We go up to the front two days earlier than usual. On the way we pass a shelled schoolhouse. Stacked up against its longer side is a high double wall of yellow, unpolished, brand new coffins. They still smell of resin, and pine, and the forest. There are at least a hundred.

"That's a good preparation for the offensive," says Müller astonished.

"They're for us," growls Detering.

"Don't talk rot," says Kat to him angrily.

"You be thankful if you get so much as a coffin," grins Tjaden, "they'll slip you a waterproof sheet for your old Aunt Sally of a carcass."

The others jest too, unpleasant jests, but what else can a man do?—The coffins are really for us. The organization surpasses itself in that kind of thing.

Ahead of us everything is shimmering. The first night we try to get our bearings. When it is fairly quiet we can hear the transports behind the enemy lines rolling ceaselessly until dawn. Kat says that they do not go back and are bringing up troops—troops, munitions, and guns.

The English artillery has been strengthened, that we can detect at once. There are at least four more batteries of nine-inch guns to the right of the farm, and behind the poplars they have put in trenchmortars. Besides these they have brought up a number of those little French beasts with instantaneous fuses.

We are now in low spirits. After we have been in the dugouts two hours our own shells begin to fall in the trench. This is the third time in four weeks. If it were simply a mistake in aim no one would say anything, but the truth is that the barrels are worn out. The shots are often so uncertain that they land within our own lines. Tonight two of our men were wounded by them.

The front is a cage in which we must await fearfully whatever may happen. We lie under the network of arching shells and live in a suspense of uncertainty. Over us, Chance hovers. If a shot comes, we can duck, that is all; we neither know nor can determine where it will fall.

It is this Chance that makes us indifferent. A few months ago I was sitting in a dugout playing skat; after a while I stood up and went to visit some friends in another dugout. On my return nothing more was to be seen of the first one, it had been blown to pieces by a direct hit. I went back to the second and arrived just in time to lend a hand digging it out. In the interval it had been buried.

It is just as much a matter of chance that I am still alive as that I might have been hit. In a bomb-proof dugout I may be smashed to atoms and in the open may survive ten hours' bombardment unscathed. No soldier outlives a thousand chances. But every soldier believes in Chance and trusts his luck.

We must look out for our bread. The rats have become much more numerous lately because the trenches are no longer in good condition. Detering says it is a sure sign of a coming bombardment.

The rats here are particularly repulsive, they are so fat—the kind we all call corpse-rats. They have shocking, evil, naked faces, and it is nauseating to see their long, nude tails.

They seem to be mighty hungry. Almost every man has had his bread gnawed. Kropp wrapped his in his waterproof sheet and put it under his head, but he cannot sleep because they run over his face to get at it. Detering meant to outwit them: he fastened a thin wire to the roof and suspended his bread from it. During the night when he switched on his pocket-torch he saw the wire swing to and fro. On the bread was riding a fat rat.

At last we put a stop to it. We cannot afford to throw the bread away, because then we should have nothing left to eat in the morning, so we carefully cut off the bits of bread that the animals have gnawed.

The slices we cut off are heaped together in the middle of the floor. Each man takes out his spade and lies down prepared to strike. Detering, Kropp, and Kat hold their pocket-torches ready.

After a few minutes we hear the first shuffling and tugging. It grows, now it is the sound of many little feet. Then the torches switch on and every man strikes at the heap, which scatters with a rush. The result is good. We toss the bits of rat over the parapet and again lie in wait.

Several times we repeat the process. At last the beasts get wise to it, or perhaps they have scented the blood. They return no more. Nevertheless, before morning the remainder of the bread on the floor has been carried off.

In the adjoining sector they attacked two large cats and a dog, bit them to death and devoured them.

Next day there was an issue of Edamer cheese. Each man gets almost a quarter of a cheese. In one way that is all to the good, for Edamer is tasty—but in another way it is vile, because the fat red balls have long been a sign of a bad time coming. Our forebodings increase as rum is served out. We drink it of course; but are not greatly comforted.

During the day we loaf about and make war on the rats. Ammunition and hand grenades become more plentiful. We overhaul the bayonets—that is to say, the ones that have a saw on the blunt edge. If the fellows over there catch a man with one of those he's killed at sight. In the next sector some of our men were found whose noses were cut off and their eyes poked out with their own saw-bayonets. Their mouths and noses were stuffed with sawdust so that they suffocated.

Some of the recruits have bayonets of this sort; we take them away and give them the ordinary kind.

But the bayonet has practically lost its importance. It is usually the fashion now to charge with bombs and spades only. The sharpened spade is a more handy and many-sided weapon; not only can it be used for jabbing a man under the chin, but it is much better for striking with because of its greater weight; and if one hits between the neck and shoulder it easily cleaves as far down as the chest. The bayonet frequently jams on the thrust and then a man has to kick hard on the other fellow's belly to pull it out again; and in the interval he may easily get one himself. And what's more the blade often gets broken off.

At night they send over gas. We expect the attack to follow and lie with our masks on, ready to tear them off as soon as the first shadow appears.

Dawn approaches without anything happening—only the ever-lasting, nerve-wracking roll behind the enemy lines, trains, trains, lorries, lorries; but what are they concentrating? Our artillery fires on it continually, but still it does not cease.

We have tired faces and avoid each other's eyes. "It will be like the Somme," says Kat gloomily. "There we were shelled steadily for seven days and nights." Kat has lost all his fun since we have been here, which is bad, for Kat is an old front hog, and can smell what is coming. Only Tjaden seems pleased with the good rations and the rum; he thinks we might even go back to rest without anything happening at all.

It almost looks like it. Day after day passes. At night I squat in the listening-post. Above me the rockets and parachute lights shoot up and float down again. I am cautious and tense, my heart thumps. My eyes turn again and again to the luminous dial of my watch; the hands will not budge. Sleep hangs on my eyelids, I work my toes in my boots in order to keep awake. Nothing happens till I am relieved;—only the everlasting rolling over there. Gradually we grow calmer and play skat and poker continually. Perhaps we will be lucky.

All day the sky is hung with observation balloons. There is a rumor that the enemy are going to put tanks over and use low-flying planes for the attack. But that interests us less than what we hear of the new flamethrowers.

We wake up in the middle of the night. The earth booms. Heavy fire is falling on us. We crouch into corners. We distinguish shells of every calibre.

Each man lays hold of his things and looks again every minute to reassure himself that they are still there. The dugout heaves, the night roars and flashes. We look at each other in the momentary flashes of light, and with pale faces and pressed lips shake our heads.

Every man is aware of the heavy shells tearing down the parapet, rooting up the embankment and demolishing the upper layers of concrete. When a shell lands in the trench we note how the hollow, furious blast is like a blow from the paw of a raging beast of prey. Already by morning a few of the recruits are green and vomiting. They are too inexperienced.

Slowly the gray light trickles into the post and pales the flashes of the shells. Morning is come. The explosion of mines mingles with the gunfire. That is the most dementing convulsion of all. The whole region where they go up becomes one grave.

The reliefs go out, the observers stagger in, covered with dirt, and trembling. One lies down in silence in the corner and eats, the other, an older man of the new draft, sobs; twice he has been flung over the parapet by the blast of the explosions without getting any more than shellshock.

The recruits are eyeing him. We must watch them, these things are catching, already some lips begin to quiver. It is good that it is growing daylight; perhaps the attack will come before noon.

The bombardment does not diminish. It is falling in the rear too. As far as one can see spout fountains of mud and iron. A wide belt is being raked.

The attack does not come, but the bombardment continues. We are gradually benumbed. Hardly a man speaks. We cannot make ourselves understood.

Our trench is almost gone. At many places it is only eighteen inches high, it is broken by holes, and craters, and mountains of earth. A shell lands square in front of our post. At once it is dark. We are buried and must dig ourselves out. After an hour the entrance is clear again, and we are calmer because we have had something to do.

Our Company Commander scrambles in and reports that two dugouts are gone. The recruits calm themselves when they see him. He says that an attempt will be made to bring up food this evening.

That sounds reassuring. No one had thought of it except Tjaden. Now the outside world seems to draw a little nearer: if food can be brought up, think the recruits, then it can't really be so bad.

We do not disabuse them; we know that food is as important as ammunition and only for that reason must be brought up.

But it miscarries. A second party goes out, and it also turns back. Finally Kat tries, and even he reappears without accomplishing anything. No one gets through, not even a fly is small enough to get through such a barrage.

We pull in our belts tighter and chew every mouthful three times as long. Still the food does not last out; we are damnably hungry. I take out a scrap of bread, eat the white and put the crust back in my knapsack; from time to time I nibble at it.

The night is unbearable. We cannot sleep, but stare ahead of us and doze. Tjaden regrets that we wasted the gnawed pieces of bread on the rats. We would gladly have them again to eat now. We are short of water, too, but not seriously yet.

Toward morning, while it is still dark, there is some excitement. Through the entrance rushes in a swarm of fleeing rats that try to storm the walls. Torches light up the confusion. Everyone yells and curses and slaughters. The madness and despair of many hours unloads itself in this outburst. Faces are distorted, arms strike out, and the beasts scream; we just stop in time to avoid attacking one another.

The onslaught has exhausted us. We lie down to wait again. It is a marvel that our post has had no casualties so far. It is one of the less deep dugouts.

A corporal creeps in; he has a loaf of bread with him. Three people have had the luck to get through during the night and bring some provisions. They say the bombardment extends undiminished as far as the artillery lines. It is a mystery where the enemy gets all his shells.

We wait and wait. By midday what I expected happens. One of the recruits has a fit. I have been watching him for a long time, grinding his teeth and opening and shutting his fists. These hunted, protruding eyes, we know them too well. During the last few hours he has had merely the appearance of calm. He had collapsed like a rotten tree.

Now he stands up, stealthily creeps across the floor, hesitates a moment and then glides toward the door. I intercept him and say: "Where are you going?"

"I'll be back in a minute," says he, and tries to push past me.

"Wait a bit, the shelling will stop soon."

He listens for a moment and his eyes become clear. Then again he has the glowering eyes of a mad dog, he is silent, he shoves me aside.

"One minute, lad," I say. Kat notices. Just as the recruit shakes me off Kat jumps in and we hold him.

Then he begins to rave: "Leave me alone, let me go out, I will go out!"

He won't listen to anything and hits out, his mouth is wet and pours out words, half choked, meaningless words. It is a case of claustrophobia, he feels as though he is suffocating here and wants to get out at any price. If we let him go he would run about everywhere regardless of cover. He is not the first.

Though he raves and his eyes roll, it can't be helped, we have to give him a hiding to bring him to his senses. We do it quickly and mercilessly, and at last he sits down quietly. The others have turned pale; let's hope it deters them. This bombardment is too much for the poor devils, they have been sent straight from a recruiting depot into a barrage that is enough to turn an old soldier's hair gray.

After this affair the sticky, close atmosphere works more than ever on our nerves. We sit as if in our graves waiting only to be closed in.

Suddenly it howls and flashes terrifically, the dugout cracks in all its joints under a direct hit, fortunately only a light one that the concrete blocks are able to withstand. It rings metallically, the walls reel, rifles, helmets, earth, mud, and dust fly everywhere. Sulphur fumes pour in.

If we were in one of those light dugouts that they have been building lately instead of this deeper one, none of us would be alive.

But the effect is bad enough even so. The recruit starts to rave again and two others follow suit. One jumps up and rushes out, we have truble with the other two. I start after one who escapes and wonder whether to shoot him in the leg—then it shrieks again, I fling myself down and when I stand up the wall of the trench is plastered with smoking splinters, lumps of flesh, and bits of uniform. I scramble back.

The first recruit seems actually to have gone insane. He butts his head against the wall like a goat. We must try tonight to take him to the rear. Meanwhile we bind him, but in such a way that in case of attack he can be released at once.

Kat suggests a game of skat: it is easier when a man has something to do. But it is no use, we listen for every explosion that comes close, miscount the tricks, and fail to follow suit. We have to give it up. We sit as though in a boiler that is being belabored from without on all sides.

Night again. We are deadened by the strain—a deadly tension that scrapes along one's spine like a gapped knife. Our legs refuse to move, our hands tremble, our bodies are a thin skin stretched painfully over repressed madness, over an almost irresistible, bursting roar. We have neither flesh nor muscles any longer, we dare not look at one another for fear of some miscalculable thing. So we shut our teeth—it will end—it will end—perhaps we will come through.

Suddenly the nearer explosions cease. The shelling continues but it has lifted and falls behind us, our trench is free. We seize the hand grenades, pitch them out in front of the dugout and jump after them. The bombardment has stopped and a heavy barrage now falls behind us. The attack has come.

No one would believe that in this howling waste there could still be men; but steel helmets now appear on all sides out of the trench, and fifty yards from us a machine gun is already in position and barking.

The wire entanglements are torn to pieces. Yet they offer some obstacle. We see the storm troops coming. Our artillery opens fire. Machine guns rattle, rifles crack. The charge works its way across. Haie and Kropp begin with the hand grenades. They throw as fast as they can, others pass them, the handles with the strings already pulled. Haie throws seventy-five yards, Kropp sixty, it has been measured, the distance is important. The enemy as they run cannot do much before they are within forty yards.

We recognize the smooth distorted faces, the helmets; they are French. They have already suffered heavily when they reach the remnants of the barbed wire entanglements. A whole line has gone down before our machine guns; then we have a lot of stoppages and they come nearer.

I see one of them, his face upturned, fall into a wire cradle. His body collapses, his hands remain suspended as though he were praying. Then his body drops clean away and only his hands with the stumps of his arms, shot off, now hang in the wire.

The moment we are about to retreat three faces rise up from the ground in front of us. Under one of the helmets a dark pointed beard and two eyes that are fastened on me. I raise my hand, but I cannot throw into those strange eyes; for one mad moment the whole slaughter whirls like a circus around me, and these two eyes alone are motionless; then the head rises up, a hand, a movement, and my hand grenade flies through the air and into him.

We make for the rear, pull wire cradles into the trench and leave bombs behind us with the strings pulled, which ensures us a fiery retreat. The machine guns are already firing from the next position.

We have become wild beasts. We do not fight, we defend ourselves against annihilation. It is not against men that we fling our bombs, what do we know of men in this moment when Death is hunting us down—now, for the first time in three days we can see his face, now for the first time in three days we can oppose him; we feel a mad anger. No longer do we lie helpless, waiting on the scaffold, we can destroy and kill, to save ourselves, to save ourselves and to be revenged.

We crouch behind every corner, behind every barrier of barbed wire, and hurl heaps of explosives at the feet of the advancing enemy before we run. The blast of the hand grenades impinges powerfully on our arms and legs; crouching like cats we run on, overwhelmed by this wave that bears us along, that fills us with ferocity, turns us into thugs, into murderers, into God only knows what devils; this wave that multiplies our strength with fear and madness and greed of life, seeking and fighting for nothing but our deliverance. If your own father came over with them you would not hesitate to fling a bomb at him.

The forward trenches have been abandoned. Are they still trenches? They are blown to pieces, annihilated—there are only broken bits of trenches, holes linked by cracks, nests of craters, that is all. But the enemy's casualties increase. They did not count on so much resistance.

It is nearly noon. The sun blazes hotly, the sweat stings in our eyes, we wipe it off on our sleeves and often blood with it. At last we reach a trench that is in a somewhat better condition. It is manned and ready for the counterattack, it receives us. Our guns open in full blast and cut off the enemy attack.

The lines behind us stop. They can advance no farther. The attack is crushed by our artillery. We watch. The fire lifts a hundred yards and we break forward. Beside me a lance-corporal has his head torn off. He runs a few steps more while the blood spouts from his neck like a fountain.

It does not come quite to hand-to-hand fighting; they are driven back. We arrive once again at our shattered trench and pass on beyond it.

Oh, this turning back again! We reach the shelter of the reserves and yearn to creep in and disappear;—but instead we must turn round and plunge again into the horror. If we were not automata at that moment we would continue lying there, exhausted, and without will. But we are swept forward again, powerless, madly savage and raging; we will kill, for they are still our mortal enemies, their rifles and bombs are aimed against us, and if we don't destroy them, they will destroy us.

The brown earth, the torn, blasted earth, with a greasy shine under the sun's rays; the earth is the background of this restless, gloomy world of automatons, our gasping is the scratching of a quill, our lips are dry, our heads are debauched with stupor—thus we stagger forward, and into our pierced and shattered souls bores the torturing image of the brown earth with the greasy sun and the convulsed and dead soldiers, who lie there—it can't be helped—who cry and clutch at our legs as we spring away over them.

We have lost all feeling for one another. We can hardly control ourselves when our glance lights on the form of some other man. We are insensible, dead men, who through some trick, some dreadful magic, are still able to run and to kill.

A young Frenchman lags behind, he is overtaken, he puts up his hands, in one he still holds his revolver—does he mean to shoot or to give himself!—a blow from a spade cleaves through his face. A second sees it and tries to run farther; a bayonet jabs into his back. He leaps in the air, his arms thrown wide, his mouth wide open, yelling; he staggers, in his back the bayonet quivers. A third throws away his rifle, cowers down with his hands before his eyes. He is left behind with a few other prisoners to carry off the wounded.

Suddenly in the pursuit we reach the enemy line.

We are so close on the heels of our retreating enemies that we reach it almost at the same time as they. In this way we suffer few casualties. A machine gun barks, but is silenced with a bomb. Nevertheless, the couple of seconds has sufficed to give us five stomach wounds. With the butt of his rifle Kat smashes to pulp the face of one of the unwounded machine gunners. We bayonet the others before they have time to get out their bombs. Then thirstily we drink the water they have for cooling the gun.

Everywhere wire-cutters are snapping, planks are thrown across the entanglements, we jump through the narrow entrances into the trenches. Haie strikes his spade into the neck of a gigantic Frenchman and throws the first hand grenade; we duck behind a breastwork for a few seconds, then the straight bit of trench ahead of us is empty. The next throw whizzes obliquely over the corner and clears a passage; as we run past we toss handfuls down into the dugouts, the earth shudders, it crashes, smokes and groans, we stumble over slippery lumps of flesh, over yielding bodies; I fall into an open belly on which lies a clean, new officer's cap.

The fight ceases. We lose touch with the enemy. We cannot stay here long but must retire under cover of our artillery to our own position. No sooner do we know this than we dive into the nearest dugouts, and with the utmost haste seize on whatever provisions we can see, especially the tins of corned beef and butter, before we clear out.

We get back pretty well. There is no further attack by the enemy. We lie for an hour panting and resting before anyone speaks. We are so completely played out that in spite of our great hunger we do not think of the provisions. Then gradually we become something like men again.

The corned beef over there is famous along the whole front. Occasionally it has been the chief reason for a flying raid on our part, for our nourishment is generally very bad; we have a constant hunger.

We bagged five tins altogether. The fellows over there are well looked after; they fare magnificently, as against us, poor starving wretches, with our turnip jam; they can get all the meat they want. Haie has scored a thin loaf of white French bread, and stuck it behind his belt like a spade. It is a bit bloody at one corner, but that can be cut off.

It is a good thing we have something decent to eat at last; we still have a use for all our strength. Enough to eat is just as valuable as a good dugout; it can save our lives; that is the reason we are so greedy for it.

Tjaden has captured two water bottles full of cognac. We pass them round.

The evening benediction begins. Night comes, out of the craters rise the mists. It looks as though the holes were full of ghostly secrets. The white vapour creeps painfully round before it ventures to steal away over the edge. Then long streaks stretch from crater to crater.

It is chilly. I am on sentry and stare into the darkness. My strength is exhausted as always after an attack, and so it is hard for me to be alone with my thoughts. They are not properly thoughts; they are memories which in my weakness haunt me and strangely move me.

The parachute lights soar upward—and I see a picture, a summer evening, I am in the cathedral cloister and look at the tall rose trees that bloom in the middle of the little cloister garden where the monks lie buried. Around the walls are the stone carvings of the Stations of the Cross. No one is there. A great quietness rules in this blossoming quadrangle, the sun lies warm on the heavy gray stones, I place my hand upon them and feel the warmth. At the right-hand corner the green cathedral spire ascends into the pale blue sky of the evening. Between the glowing columns of the cloister is the cool darkness that only churches have, and I stand there and wonder whether, when I am twenty, I shall have experienced the bewildering emotions of love.

The image is alarmingly near; it touches me before it dissolves in the light of the next starshell.

I lay hold of my rifle to see that it is in trim. The barrel is wet, I take it in my hands and rub off the moisture with my fingers.

Between the meadows behind our town there stands a line of old poplars by a stream. They were visible from a great distance, and although they grew on one bank only, we called them the poplar avenue. Even as children we had a great love for them, they drew us vaguely thither, we played truant the whole day by them and listened to their rustling. We sat beneath them on the bank of the stream and let our feet hang in the bright, swift waters. The pure fragrance of the water and the melody of the wind in the poplars held our fancies. We loved them dearly, and the image of those days still makes my heart pause in its beating.

It is strange that all the memories that come have these two qualities. They are always completely calm, that is predominant in them; and even if they are not really calm, they become so. They are soundless apparitions that speak to me, with looks and gestures silently, without any word—and it is the alarm of their silence that forces me to lay hold of my sleeve and my rifle lest I should abandon myself to the liberation and allurement in which my body would dilate and gently pass away into the still forces that lie behind these things.

They are quiet in this way, because quietness is so unattainable for us now. At the front there is no quietness and the curse of the front reaches so far that we never pass beyond it. Even in the remote depots and rest areas the droning and the muffled noise of shelling is always in our ears. We are never so far off that it is no more to be heard. But these last few days it has been unbearable.

Their stillness is the reason why these memories of former times do not awaken desire so much as sorrow—a vast, inapprehensible melancholy. Once we had such desires—but they return not. They are past, they belong to another world that is gone from us. In the barracks they called forth a rebellious, wild craving for their return; for then we were still bound to us, we belonged to them and they to us, even though we were already absent from them. They appeared in the soldiers' songs which we sang as we marched between the glow of the dawn and the black silhouettes of the forests to drill on the moor, they were a powerful remembrance that was in us and came from us.

But here in the trenches they are completely lost to us. They arise no more; we are dead and they stand remote on the horizon, they are a mysterious reflection, an apparition, that haunts us, that we fear and love without hope. They are strong and our desire is strong—but they are unattainable, and we know it.

And even if these scenes of our youth were given back to us we would hardly know what to do. The tender, secret influence that passed from them into us could not rise again. We might be amongst them and move in them; we might remember and love them and be stirred by the sight of them. But it would be like gazing at the photograph of a dead comrade; those are his features, it is his face, and the days we spent together take on a mournful life in the memory; but the man himself it is not.

We could never regain the old intimacy with those scenes. It was not any recognition of their beauty and their significance that attracted us, but the communism, the feeling of a comradeship with the things and events of our existence, which cut us off and made the world of our parents a thing incomprehensible to us—for then we surrendered ourselves to events and were lost in them, and the least little thing was enough to carry us down the stream of eternity. Perhaps it was only the privilege of our youth, but as yet we recognized no limits and saw nowhere an end. We had that thrill of expectation in the blood which united us with the course of our days.

Today we would pass through the scenes of our youth like travelers. We are burned up by hard facts; like tradesmen we understand distinctions, and like butchers, necessities. We are no longer untrubled—we are indifferent. We might exist there; but should we really live there?

We are forlorn like children, and experienced like old men, we are crude and sorrowful and superficial—I believe we are lost.

My hands grow cold and my flesh creeps; and yet the night is warm. Only the mist is cold, this mysterious mist that trails over the dead and sucks from them their last, creeping life. By morning they will be pale and green and their blood congealed and black.

Still the parachute-rockets shoot up and cast their pitiless light over the stony landscape, which is full of craters and frozen lights like a moon. The blood beneath my skin brings fear and restlessness into my thoughts. They become feeble and tremble, they want warmth and life. They cannot persist without solace, without illusion, they are disordered before the naked picture of despair.

I hear the rattle of the mess tins and immediately feel a strong desire for warm food; it would do me good and comfort me. Painfully I force myself to wait until I am relieved.

Then I go into the dugout and find a mug of barley. It is cooked in fat and tastes good, I eat it slowly. I remain quiet, though the others are in a better mood, for the shelling has died down.

The days go by and the incredible hours follow one another as a matter of course. Attacks alternate with counterattacks and slowly the dead pile up in the field of craters between the trenches. We are able to bring in most of the wounded that do not lie too far off. But many have long to wait and we listen to them dying.

For one of them we search two days in vain. He must be lying on his belly and unable to turn over. Otherwise it is hard to understand why we cannot find him; for it is only when a man has his mouth close to the ground that it is impossible to gauge the direction of his cry.

He must have been badly hit—one of those nasty wounds neither so severe that they exhaust the body at once and a man dreams on in a half-swoon, nor so light that a man endures the pain in the hope of becoming well again. Kat thinks he has either a broken pelvis or a shot through the spine. His chest cannot have been injured otherwise he would not have such strength to cry out. And if it were any other kind of wound it would be possible to see him moving.

He grows gradually hoarser. The voice is so strangely pitched that it seems to be everywhere. The first night some of our fellows go out three times to look for him. But when they think they have located him and crawl across, the next time they hear the voice it seems to come from somewhere else altogether.

We search in vain until dawn. We scrutinize the field all day with glasses, but discover nothing. On the second day the calls are fainter; that will be because his lips and mouth have become dry.

Our Company Commander has promised next turn of leave with three days extra to anyone who finds him. This is a powerful inducement, but we would do all that is possible without that for his cry is terrible. Kat and Kropp even go out in the afternoon, and Albert gets the lobe of his ear shot off in consequence. It is to no purpose, they come back without him.

It is easy to understand what he cries. At first he called only for help—the second night he must have had some delirium, he talked with his wife and his children, we often detected the name Elise. Today he merely weeps. By evening the voice dwindles to a croaking. But it persists still through the whole night. We hear it so distinctly because the wind blows toward our line. In the morning when we suppose he must already have long gone to his rest, there comes across to us one last gurgling rattle.

The days are hot and the dead lie unburied. We cannot fetch them all in, if we did we should not know what to do with them. The shells will bury them. Many have their bellies swollen up like balloons. They hiss, belch, and make movements. The gases in them make noises.

The sky is blue and without clouds. In the evening it grows sultry and the heat rises from the earth. When the wind blows toward us it brings the smell of blood, which is very heavy and sweet. This deathly exhalation from the shell-holes seems to be a mixture of chloroform and putrefaction, and fills us with nausea and retching.

The nights become quiet and the hunt for copper driving bands and the silken parachutes of the French star-shells begins. Why the driving bands are so desirable no one knows exactly. The collectors merely assert that they are valuable. Some have collected so many that they will stoop under the weight of them when we go back.

But Haie at least gives a reason. He intends to give them to his girl to supplement her garters. At this the Friesians explode with mirth. They slap their knees: "By Jove though, he's a wit, Haie is, he's got brains." Tjaden especially can hardly contain himself; he takes the largest of the rings in his hand and every now and then puts his legs through it to show how much slack there is.

"Haie, man, she must have legs like, legs——" his thoughts mount somewhat higher "and a behind too she must have, like a— like an elephant!"

He cannot get over it. "I wish I could play hothand with her once, my hat——"

Haie beams, proud that his girl should receive so much appreciation.

"She's a nice bit," he says with self-satisfaction.

The parachutes are turned to more practical uses. According to the size of the bust three or perhaps four will make a blouse. Kropp and I use them as handkerchiefs. The others send them home. If the women could see at what risk these bits of rag are often obtained, they would be horrified.

Kat surprises Tjaden endeavoring with perfect equanimity to knock the driving band off a dud. If anyone else had tried it the thing would have exploded, but Tjaden always has his luck with him.

One morning two butterflies play in front of our trench. They are brimstone-butterflies, with red spots on their yellow wings. What can they be looking for here? There is not a plant nor a flower for miles. They settle on the teeth of a skull. The birds too are just as carefree, they have long since accustomed themselves to the war. Every morning larks ascend from No Man's Land. A year ago we watched them nesting; the young ones grew up too.

We have a spell from the rats in the trench. They are in No Man's Land—we know what for. They grow fat; when we see one we have a crack at it. At night we hear again the rolling behind the enemy lines. All day we have only the normal shelling, so that we are able to repair the trenches. There is always plenty of amusement, the airmen see to that. There are countless fights for us to watch every day.

Battle planes don't trouble us, but the observation planes we hate like the plague; they put the artillery to us. A few minutes after they appear, shrapnel and high explosives begin to drop on us. We lose eleven men in one day that way, and five of them stretcher-bearers. Two are smashed so that Tjaden remarks you could scrape them off the wall of the trench with a spoon and bury them in a mess tin. Another has the lower part of his body and his legs torn off. Dead, his chest leans against the side of the trench, his face is lemon-yellow, in his beard still burns a cigarette. It glows until it dies out on his lips.

We put the dead in a large shell-hole. So far there are three layers, one on top of the other.

Suddenly the shelling begins to pound again. Soon we are sitting up once more with the rigid tenseness of blank anticipation.

Attack, counterattack, charge, repulse—these are words, but what things they signify! We have lost a good many men, mostly recruits. Reinforcements have again been sent up to our sector. They are one of the new regiments, composed almost entirely of young fellows just called up. They have had hardly any training, and are sent into the field with only a theoretical knowledge. They do know what a hand grenade is, it is true, but they have very little idea of cover, and what is most important of all, have no eye for it. A fold in the ground has to be quite eighteen inches high before they can see it.

Although we need reinforcement, the recruits give us almost more trouble than they are worth. They are helpless in this grim fighting area, they fall like flies. Modern trench warfare demands knowledge and experience; a man must have a feeling for the contours of the ground, an ear for the sound and character of the shells, must be able to decide beforehand where they will drop, how they will burst, and how to shelter from them.

The young recruits of course know none of these things. They get killed simply because they hardly can tell shrapnel from high-explosive, they are mown down because they are listening anxiously to the roar of the big coal boxes falling in the rear, and miss the light, piping whistle of the low spreading daisy-cutters. They flock together like sheep instead of scattering, and even the wounded are shot down like hares by the airmen.

Their pale turnip faces, their pitiful clenched hands, the fine courage of these poor devils, the desperate charges and attacks made by the poor brave wretches, who are so terrified that they dare not cry out loudly, but with battered chests, with torn bellies, arms and legs only whimper softly for their mothers and cease as soon as one looks at them.

Their sharp, downy, dead faces have the awful expressionlessness of dead children.

It brings a lump into the throat to see how they go over, and run and fall. A man would like to spank them, they are so stupid, and to take them by the arm and lead them away from here where they have no business to be. They wear gray coats and trousers and boots, but for most of them the uniform is far too big, it hangs on their limbs, their shoulders are too narrow, their bodies too slight; no uniform was ever made to these childish measurements.

Between five and ten recruits fall to every old hand.

A surprise gas-attack carries off a lot of them. They have not yet learned what to do. We found one dugout full of them, with blue heads and black lips. Some of them in a shell-hole took off their masks too soon; they did not know that the gas lies longest in the hollows; when they saw others on top without masks they pulled theirs off too and swallowed enough to scorch their lungs. Their condition is hopeless, they choke to death with haemorrhages and suffocation.

In one part of the trench I suddenly ran into Himmelstoss. We dive into the same dugout. Breathless we are all lying one beside the other waiting for the charge.

When we run out again, although I am very excited, I suddenly think: "Where's Himmelstoss?" Quickly I jump back into the dugout and find him with a small scratch lying in a corner pretending to be wounded. His face looks sullen. He is in a panic; he is new to it too. But it makes me mad that the young recruits should be out there and he here.

"Get out!" I spit.

He does not stir, his lips quiver, his mustache twitches.

"Out!" I repeat.

He draws up his legs, crouches back against the wall, and shows his teeth like a cur.

I seize him by the arm and try to pull him up. He barks.

This is too much for me. I grab him by the neck and shake him like a sack, his head jerks from side to side.

"You lump, will you get out—you hound, you skunk, sneak out of it, would you?" His eye becomes glassy, I knock his head against the wall—"You cow"—I kick him in the ribs—"You swine"—I push him toward the door and shove him out head first.

Another wave of our attack has just come up. A lieutenant is with them. He sees us and yells: "Forward, forward, join in, follow." And the word of command does what all my banging could not. Himmelstoss hears the order, looks round him as if awakened, and follows on.

I come after and watch him go over. Once more he is the smart Himmelstoss of the parade ground, he has even outstripped the lieutenant and is far ahead.

Bombardment, barrage, curtain fire, mines, gas, tanks, machine guns, hand grenades—words, words, but they hold the horror of the world.

Our faces are encrusted, our thoughts are devastated, we are weary to death; when the attack comes we shall have to strike many of the men with our fists to waken them and make them come with us—our eyes are burned, our hands are torn, our knees bleed, our elbows are raw.

How long has it been? Weeks—months—years? Only days. We see time pass in the colorless faces of the dying, we cram food into us, we run, we throw, we shoot, we kill, we lie about, we are feeble and spent, and nothing supports us but the knowledge that there are still feebler, still more spent, still more helpless ones there who, with staring eyes, look upon us as gods that escape death many times.

In the few hours of rest we teach them. "There, see that waggle-top? That's a mortar coming. Keep down, it will go clean over. But if it comes this way, then run for it. You can run from a mortar."

We sharpen their ears to the malicious, hardly audible buzz of the smaller shells that are not easily distinguishable. They must pick them out from the general din by their insect-like hum—we explain to them that these are far more dangerous than the big ones that can be heard long beforehand.

We show them how to take cover from aircraft, how to stimulate a dead man when one is overrun in an attack, how to time hand grenades so that they explode half a second before hitting the ground; we teach them to fling themselves into holes as quick as lightning before the shells with instantaneous fuses; we show them how to clean up a trench with a handful of bombs; we explain the difference between the fuse length of the enemy bombs and our own; we put them wise to the sound of gas shells;—show them all the tricks that can save them from death.

They listen, they are docile—but when it begins again, in their excitement they do everything wrong.

Haie Westhus drags off with a great wound in his back through which the lung pulses at every breath. I can only press his hand; "It's all up, Paul," he groans and he bites his arm because of the pain.

We see men living with their skulls blown open; we see soldiers run with their two feet cut off, they stagger on their splintered stumps into the next shell-hole; a lance-corporal crawls a mile and a half on his hands dragging his smashed knee after him; another goes to the dressing station and over his clasped hands bulge his intestines; we see men without mouths, without jaws, without faces; we find one man who has held the artery of his arm in his teeth for two hours in order not to bleed to death. The sun goes down, night comes, the shells whine, life is at an end.

Still the little piece of convulsed earth in which we lie is held. We have yielded no more than a few hundred yards of it as a prize to the enemy. But on every yard there lies a dead man.

We have just been relieved. The wheels roll beneath us, we stand dully, and when the call "Mind—wire" comes, we bend our knees. It was summer when we came up, the trees were still green, now it is autumn and the night is gray and wet. The lorries stop, we climb out—a confused heap, a remnant of many names. On either side stand people, dark, calling out the numbers of the brigades, the battalions. And at each call a little group separates itself off, a small handful of dirty, pallid soldiers, a dreadfully small handful, and a dreadfully small remnant.

Now someone is calling the number of our company, it is, yes, the Company Commander, he has come through, then; his arm is in a sling. We go over to him and I recognize Kat and Albert, we stand together, lean against each other, and look at one another.

And we hear the number of our company called again and again. He will call a long time, they do not hear him in the hospitals and shell-holes.

Once again: "Second Company, this way!" And then more softly: "Nobody else, Second Company?"

He is silent, and then huskily he says: "Is that all?" he gives the order: "Number!"

The morning is gray, it was still summer when we came up, and we were one hundred and fifty strong. Now we freeze, it is autumn, the leaves rustle, the voices flutter out wearily: "One—two—three—four——" and cease at thirty-two. And there is a long silence before the voice asks: "Anyone else?"—and waits and then says softly: "In squads——" and then breaks off and is only able to finish: "Second Company——" with difficulty: "Second Company—march easy!"

A line, a short line trudges off into the morning.

Thirty-two men.

7

They have taken us farther back than usual to a field depot so that we can be reorganized. Our company needs more than a hundred reinforcements.

In the meantime, when we are off duty, we loaf around. After a couple of days Himmelstoss comes up to us. He has had the bounce knocked out of him since he has been in the trenches and wants to get on good terms with us. I am willing, because I saw how he brought Haie Westhus in when he was hit in the back. Besides he's decent enough to treat us in the canteen when we are out of funds. Only Tjaden is still reserved and suspicious.

But he is won over, too, when Himmelstoss tells us that he is taking the place of the sergeant-cook who has gone on leave. As a proof he produces on the spot two pounds of sugar for us and a half-pound of butter specially for Tjaden. He even sees to it that we are detailed the next two or three days to the cookhouse for potato and turnip peeling. The grub he gives us there is real officers' fare.

Thus momentarily we have the two things a soldier needs for contentment: good food and rest. That's not much when one comes to think of it. A few years ago we would have despised ourselves terribly. But now we are almost happy. It is all a matter of habit—even the front line.

Habit is the explanation of why we seem to forget things so quickly. Yesterday we were under fire, today we act the fool and go foraging through the countryside, tomorrow we go up to the trenches again. We forget nothing really. But so long as we have to stay here in the field, the front line days, when they are past, sink down in us like a stone; they are too grievous for us to be able to reflect on them at once. If we did that, we should have been destroyed long ago. I soon found out this much:—terror can be endured so long as a man simply ducks;—but it kills, if a man thinks about it.

Just as we turn into animals when we go up to the line, because that is the only thing which brings us through safely, so we turn into wags and loafers when we are resting. We can do nothing else, it is a sheer necessity. We want to live at any price; so we cannot burden ourselves with feelings which, though they might be ornamental enough in peacetime, would be out of place here. Kemmerich is dead, Haie Westhus is dying, they will have a job with Hans Kramer's body at the Judgment Day, piecing it together after a direct hit; Martens has no legs anymore, Meyer is dead, Max is dead, Beyer is dead, Hämmerling is dead, there are a hundred and twenty wounded men lying somewhere or other; it is a damnable business, but what has it to do with us now—we live. If it were possible for us to save them, then it would be seen how much we cared—we would have a shot at it though we went under ourselves; for we can be damned quixotic when we like; fear we do not know much about—terror of death, yes; but that is a different matter, that is physical.

But our comrades are dead, we cannot help them, they have their rest—and who knows what is waiting for us? We will make ourselves comfortable and sleep, and eat as much as we can stuff into our bellies, and drink and smoke so that hours are not wasted. Life is short.

The terror of the front sinks deep down when we turn our back upon it; we make grim, coarse jests about it, when a man dies, then we say he has nipped off his turd, and so we speak of everything; that keeps us from going mad; as long as we take it that way we maintain our own resistance.

But we do not forget. It's all rot that they put in the war news about the good humor of the troops, how they are arranging dances almost before they are out of the front line. We don't act like that because we are in a good humor: we are in a good humor because otherwise we should go to pieces. Even so we cannot hold out much longer; our humor becomes more bitter every month.

And this I know: all these things that now, while we are still in the war, sink down in us like a stone, after the war shall waken again, and then shall begin the disentanglement of life and death.

The days, the weeks, the years out here shall come back again, and our dead comrades shall then stand up again and march with us, our heads shall be clear, we shall have a purpose, and so we shall march, our dead comrades beside us, the years at the Front behind us:—against whom, against whom?

Some time ago there was an army theater in these parts. Colored posters of the performances are still sticking on a hoarding. With wide eyes Kropp and I stand in front of it. We can hardly credit that such things still exist. A girl in a light summer dress, with a red patent-leather belt about her hips! She is standing with one hand on a railing and with the other she holds a straw hat. She wears white stockings and white shoes, fine buckle shoes with high heels. Behind her smiles the blue sea with white horses, at the side is a bright bay. She is a lovely girl with a delicate nose, red lips, and slender legs, wonderfully clean and well cared for, she certainly bathes twice a day and never has any dirt under her nails. At most perhaps a bit of sand from the beach.

Beside her stands a man in white trousers, a blue jacket, and sailor's cap; but he interests us much less.

The girl on the poster is a wonder to us. We have quite forgotten that there are such things, and even now we hardly believe our eyes.

We have seen nothing like it for years, nothing like it for happiness, beauty and joy. That is peacetime, that is as it should be; we feel excited.

"Just look at those thin shoes though, she couldn't march many miles in those," I say, and then begin to feel silly, for it is absurd to stand in front of the picture like this and think of nothing but marching.

"How old would she be?" Kropp asks.

"About twenty-two at the most," I hazard.

"Then she would be older than us! She is not more than seventeen, let me tell you!"

It gives us goose flesh.

"That would be good, Albert, what do you think?"

He nods. "I have some white trousers at home too."

"White trousers," say I, "but a girl like that——"

We look askance at one another. There's not much to boast of here—two ragged, stained, and dirty uniforms. It is hopeless to compete.

So we proceed to tear the young man with the white trousers off the hoarding, taking care not to damage the girl. That is something toward it.

"We could go and get deloused, anyway," Kropp then suggests.

I am not very enthusiastic because it doesn't do one's clothes any good and a man is lousy again inside two hours. But when we have considered the picture once more, I declare myself willing. I go even farther.

"We might see if we could get a clean shirt as well——"

"Socks might be better," says Albert, not without reason.

"Yes, socks too perhaps. Let's go and explore a bit."

Then Leer and Tjaden stroll up; they look at the poster and immediately the conversation becomes smutty. Leer was the first of our class to have intercourse, and he gave stirring details of it. After his fashion he enjoys himself over the picture, and Tjaden supports him nobly.

It does not distress us exactly. Who isn't smutty is no soldier; it merely does not suit us at the moment, so we edge away and march off to the delousing station with the same feeling as if it were a swell gentlemen's outfitters.

The houses in which we are billeted lie near the canal. On the other side of the canal there are ponds flanked with poplars;—on the other side of the canal there are women too.

The houses on our side have been abandoned. On the other side though one occasionally sees inhabitants.

In the evening we go swimming. Three women come strolling along the bank. They walk slowly and don't look away, although we have no bathing suits.

Leer calls out to them. They laugh and stop to watch us. We fling remarks at them in broken French, anything that comes into our heads, hastily and all jumbled together, anything to detain them. They are not specially wonderful pieces, but then where are such to be had about here?

There is one slim little brunette, her teeth gleam when she laughs. She has quick movements, her dress swings loosely about her legs. Although the water is cold we are very jovial and do our best to interest them so that they will stay. We try to make jokes and they answer with things we cannot understand; we laugh and beckon. Tjaden is more crafty. He runs into the house, gets a loaf of army bread and holds it up.

That produces a great effect. They nod and beckon us to come over. But we don't dare to do that. It is forbidden to cross to the opposite bank. There are sentries on all the bridges. It's impossible without a pass. So we indicate that they should come over to us; but they shake their heads and point to the bridge. They are not allowed to pass either. They turn back and walk slowly down the canal, keeping along the tow-path all the way. We accompany them swimming. After a few hundred yards they turn off and point to a house that stands a little distance away among the trees and shrubbery.

Leer asks if they live there.

They laugh—sure, that's their house.

We call out to them that we would like to come, sometime when the guards cannot see us. At night. Tonight.

They raise their hands, put them together, rest their faces on them and shut their eyes. They understand. The slim brunette does a two-step. The blonde girl twitters: "Bread—good——"

Eagerly we assure them that we will bring some with us. And other tasty bits too, we roll our eyes and try to explain with our hands. Leer nearly drowns trying to demonstrate a sausage. If it were necessary we would promise them a whole quartermaster's store. They go off and frequently turn and look back. We climb out on the bank on our side of the canal and watch to see whether they go into the house, for they might easily have been lying. Then we swim back.

No one can cross the bridge without leave, so we will simply have to swim over tonight. We are full of excitement. We cannot last out without a drink, so we go to the canteen where there is beer and a kind of punch.

We drink punch and tell one another lying tales of our experiences. Each man gladly believes the other man's story, only waiting impatiently till he can cap it with a taller one. Our hands are fidgety, we smoke countless cigarettes, until Kropp says: "We might as well take them a few cigarettes too." So we put some inside our caps to keep them.

The sky turns apple-green. There are four of us, but only three can go; we must shake off Tjaden, so ply him with rum and punch until he rocks. As it turns dark we go to our billets, Tjaden in the center. We are glowing and full of a lust for adventure.

The little brunette is mine, we have settled all that.

Tjaden drops on his sack of straw and snores. Once he wakes up and grins so craftily that we are alarmed and begin to think he is cheating, and that we have given him the punch to no purpose. Then he drops back again and sleeps on.

We each get hold of a whole army loaf and wrap it up in newspaper. The cigarettes we put in too, as well as three good rations of liver sausage that were issued to us this evening. That makes a decent present.

We stow the things carefully in our boots; we have to take them to protect our feet against treading on wire and broken glass on the other bank. As we must swim for it we can take no other clothes. But it is not far and quite dark.

We make off with our boots in our hands. Swiftly we slip into the water, lie on our backs and swim, holding the boots with their contents up over our heads.

We climb out carefully on the opposite bank, take out the packages and put on our boots. We put the things under our arms. And so, all wet and naked, clothed only in our boots, we break into a trot. We find the house at once. It lies among the trees. Leer trips over a root and skins his elbows.

"No matter," he says gaily.

The windows are shuttered. We slip round the house and try to peer through the cracks. Then we grow impatient. Suddenly Kropp hesitates:

"What if there's a Major with them?"

"Then we just clear off," grins Leer, "he can try to read our regimental numbers here," and smacks his behind.

The door of the courtyard stands open. Our boots made a great clatter. The house door opens, a chink of light shines through and a woman cries out in a scared voice.

"Ssh, ssh! camerade—bon ami—" we say, and show our packages protestingly.

The other two are now on the scene, the door opens and the light floods over us. They recognize us and all three burst into laughter at our appearance. They rock and sway in the doorway, they laugh so much. How supple their movements are.

"*Un moment*—" They disappear and throw us bits of clothing which we gladly wrap round ourselves. Then we are allowed in. A small lamp burns in their room, which is warm and smells a little of perfume. We unwrap our parcels and hand them over to the women. Their eyes shine, it is obvious that they are hungry.

Then we all become rather embarrassed. Leer makes the gestures of eating, and then they come to life again and bring out plates and knives and fall to on the food, and they hold up every slice of livered sausage and admire it before they eat it, and we sit proudly by.

They overwhelm us with their chatter;—we understand very little of it, but we listen and the words sound friendly. No doubt we all look very young. The little brunette strokes my hair and says what all French women say: "*La guerre—grand malheur—pauvres garçons——*"

I hold her arm tightly and press my lips into the palm of her hand. Her fingers close round my face. Close above me are her bewildering eyes, the soft brown of her skin and her red lips. Her mouth speaks words I do not understand. Nor do I fully understand her eyes; they seem to say more than we anticipated when we came here.

There are other rooms adjoining. In passing I see Leer, he has made a great hit with the blonde. He's an old hand at the game. But I—I am lost in remoteness, in weakness, and in a passion to which I yield myself trustingly. My desires are strangely compounded of yearning and misery. I feel giddy, there is nothing here that a man can hold on to. We have left our boots at the door, they have given us slippers instead, and now nothing remains to recall for me the assurance and self-confidence of the soldier; no rifle, no belt, no tunic, no cap. I let myself drop into the unknown, come what may—yet, in spite of all, I feel somewhat afraid.

The little brunette contracts her brows when she is thinking; but when she talks they are still. And often sound does not quite become a word but suffocates or floats away over me half finished; an arch, a pathway, a comet. What have I known of it—what do I know of it?—The words of this foreign tongue, that I hardly understand, they caress me to a quietness, in which the room grows dim, and dissolves in the half light, only the face above me lives and is clear.

How various is a face; but an hour ago it was strange and it is now touched with a tenderness that comes, not from it, but from out of the night, the world and the blood, all these things seem to shine in it together. The objects in the room are touched by it and transformed, they become isolated, and I feel almost awed at the sight of my clear skin when the light of the lamp falls upon it and the cool, brown hand passes over it.

How different this is from the conditions in the soldiers' brothels, to which we are allowed to go, and where we have to wait in long queues. I wish I never thought of them; but desire turns my mind to them involuntarily and I am afraid for it might be impossible ever to be free of them again.

But then I feel the lips of the little brunette and press myself against them, my eyes close, I want it all to fall from me, war and terror and grossness; in order to awaken young and happy; I think of the picture of the girl on the poster and, for a moment, believe that my life depends on winning her. And if I press ever deeper into the arms that embrace me, perhaps a miracle may happen. . . .

So, after a time we find ourselves reassembled again. Leer is in high spirits. We pull on our boots and take our leave warmly. The night air cools our hot bodies. The rustling poplars loom large in the darkness. The moon floats in the heavens and in the waters of the canal. We do not run, we walk beside one another with long strides.

"That was worth a ration loaf," says Leer.

I cannot trust myself to speak, I am not in the least happy.

Then we hear footsteps and dodge behind a shrub.

The steps come nearer, close by us. We see a naked soldier, in boots, just like ourselves; he has a package under his arm, and gallops onward. It is Tjaden in full course. He has disappeared already.

We laugh. In the morning he will curse us.

Unobserved, we arrive again at our sacks of straw.

I am called to the Orderly Room. The Company Commander gives me a leave-pass and a travel-pass and wishes me a good journey. I look to see how much leave I have got. Seventeen days—fourteen days leave and three days for traveling. It is not enough and I ask whether I cannot have five days for traveling. Bertinck points to my pass. There I see that I am not to return to the front immediately. After my leave I have to report for a course of training to a camp on the moors.

The others envy me. Kat gives me good advice, and tells me I ought to try to get a base job. "If you're smart, you'll hang on to it."

I would rather not have gone for another eight days; we are to stay here that much longer and it is good here.

Naturally I have to stand the others drinks at the canteen. We are all a little bit drunk. I become gloomy: I will be away for six weeks—that is lucky, of course, but what may happen before I get back? Shall I meet all these fellows again? Already Haie and Kemmerich have gone—who will the next be?

As we drink, I look at each of them in turn. Albert sits beside me and smokes, he is cheerful, we have always been together;—opposite squats Kat, with his drooping shoulders, his broad thumb, and calm voice—Müller with the projecting teeth and the booming laugh; Tjaden with his mousey eyes;—Leer who has grown a full beard and looks at least forty.

Over us hangs a dense cloud of smoke. Where would a soldier be without tobacco? The canteen is his refuge, and beer is far more than a drink, it is a token that a man can move his limbs and stretch in safety. We do it ceremonially, we stretch our legs out in front of us and spit deliberately, that is the only way. How it all rises up before a man when he is going away the next morning!

At night we go again to the other side of the canal. I am almost afraid to tell the little brunette that I am going away, and when I return we will be far from here; we will never see one another again. But she merely nods and takes no special notice. At first I am at a loss to understand, then it suddenly dawns on me. Yes, Leer is right: if I were going up to the front, then she would have called me again "pauvre garçon"; but merely going on leave—she does not want to hear about that, that is not nearly so interesting. May she go to the devil with her chattering talk. A man dreams of a miracle and wakes up to loaves of bread.

Next morning, after I have been deloused, I go the rail head. Albert and Kat come with me. At the halt we learn that it will be a couple of hours yet before the train leaves. The other two have to go back to duty. We take leave of one another.

"Good luck, Kat: good luck, Albert."

They go off and wave once or twice. Their figures dwindle. I know their every step and movement; I would recognize them at any distance. Then they disappear. I sit down on my pack and wait.

Suddenly I become filled with a consuming impatience to be gone.

I lie down on many a station platform; I stand before many a soup kitchen; I squat on many a bench;—then at last the landscape becomes disturbing, mysterious, and familiar. It glides past the western windows with its villages, their thatched roofs like caps, pulled over the whitewashed, half-timbered houses, its cornfields, gleaming like mother-of-pearl in the slanting light, its orchards, its barns and old lime trees.

The names of the stations begin to take on meaning and my heart trembles. The train stamps and stamps onward. I stand at the window and hold on to the frame. These names mark the boundaries of my youth.

Smooth meadows, fields, farmyards; a solitary team moves against the skyline along the road that runs parallel to the horizon—a barrier, before which peasants stand waiting, girls waving, children playing on the embankment, roads, leading into the country, smooth roads without artillery.

It is evening, and if the train did not rattle I should cry out. The plain unfolds itself.

In the distance, the soft, blue silhouette of the mountain ranges begins to appear. I recognize the characteristic outline of the Dolbenberg, a jagged comb, springing up precipitously from the limits of the forests. Behind it should lie the town.

But now the sun streams through the world, dissolving everything in its golden-red light, the train swings round one curve and then another;—far away, in a long line one behind the other, stand the poplars, unsubstantial, swaying and dark, fashioned out of shadow, light, and desire.

The field swings round as the train encircles it, and the intervals between the trees diminish; the trees become a block and for a moment I see one only—then they reappear from behind the foremost tree and stand out a long line against the sky until they are hidden by the first houses.

A street-crossing. I stand by the window, I cannot drag myself away. The others put their baggage ready for getting out. I repeat to myself the name of the street that we cross over— Bremerstrasse—Bremerstrasse—

Below there are cyclists, lorries, men; it is a gray street and a gray subway;—it affects me as though it were my mother.

Then the train stops, and there is the station with noise and cries and signboards. I pick up my pack and fasten the straps, I take my rifle in my hand and stumble down the steps.

On the platform I look round; I know no one among all the people hurrying to and fro. A Red Cross sister offers me something to drink. I turn away, she smiles at me too foolishly, so obsessed with her own importance: "Just look, I am giving a soldier coffee!"—She calls me "Comrade," but I will have none of it.

Outside in front of the station the stream roars alongside the street, it rushes foaming from the sluices of the mill bridge. There stands the old, square watchtower, in front of it the great mottled lime tree and behind it the evening.

Here we have often sat—how long ago it was—we have passed over this bridge and breathed the cool, acid smell of the stagnant water; we have leaned over the still water on this side of the lock, where the green creepers and weeds hang from the piles of the bridge;—and on hot days we rejoiced in the spouting foam on the other side of the lock and told tales about our school teachers.

I pass over the bridge, I look right and left; the water is as full of weeds as ever, and it still shoots over in gleaming arches; in the tower building laundresses still stand with bare arms as they used to over the clean linen, and the heat from the ironing pours out through the open windows. Dogs trot along the narrow street, before the doors of the houses people stand and follow me with their gaze as I pass by, dirty and heavy laden.

In this confectioner's we used to eat ices, and there we learned to smoke cigarettes. Walking down the street I know every shop, the grocer's, the chemist's, the baker's. Then at last I stand before the brown door with its worn latch and my hand grows heavy. I open the door and a strange coolness comes out to meet me, my eyes are dim.

The stairs creak under my boots. Upstairs a door rattles, someone is looking over the railing. It is the kitchen door that was opened, they are cooking potato-cakes, the house reeks of it, and today of course is Saturday; that will be my sister leaning over. For a moment I am shy and lower my head, then I take off my helmet and look up. Yes, it is my eldest sister.

"Paul," she cries, "Paul——"

I nod, my pack bumps against the banisters; my rifle is so heavy.

She pulls a door open and calls: "Mother, mother, Paul is here."

I can go no further—mother, mother, Paul is here.

I lean against the wall and grip my helmet and rifle. I hold them as tight as I can, but I cannot take another step, the staircase fades before my eyes, I support myself with the butt of my rifle against my feet and clench my teeth fiercely, but I cannot speak a word, my sister's call has made me powerless, I can do nothing, I struggle to make myself laugh, to speak, but no word comes, and so I stand on the steps, miserable, helpless, paralyzed, and against my will the tears run down my cheeks.

My sister comes back and says: "Why, what is the matter?"

Then I pull myself together and stagger on to the landing. I lean my rifle in a corner, I set my pack against the wall, place my helmet on it and fling down my equipment and baggage. Then I say fiercely: "Bring me a handkerchief."

She gives me one from the cupboard and I dry my face. Above me on the wall hangs the glass case with the colored butterflies that once I collected.

Now I hear my mother's voice. It comes from the bedroom.

"Is she in bed?" I ask my sister.

"She is ill——" she replies.

I go into her, give her my hand and say as calmly as I can: "Here I am, Mother."

She lies still in the dim light. Then she asks anxiously:

"Are you wounded?" and I feel her searching glance.

"No, I have got leave."

My mother is very pale. I am afraid to make a light.

"Here I lie now," says she, "and cry instead of being glad."

"Are you sick, Mother?" I ask.

"I am going to get up a little today," she says and turns to my sister, who is continually running to the kitchen to watch that the food does not burn: "And put out that jar of preserved whortleberries—you like that, don't you?" she asks me.

"Yes, Mother, I haven't had any for a long time."

"We might almost have known you were coming," laughs my sister, "there is just your favorite dish, potato-cakes, and even whortleberries to go with them too."

"And it is Saturday," I add.

"Sit here beside me," says my mother.

She looks at me. Her hands are white and sickly and frail compared with mine. We say very little and I am thankful that she asks nothing. What ought I to say? Everything I could have wished for has happened. I have come out of it safely and sit here beside her. And in the kitchen stands my sister preparing supper and singing.

"Dear boy," says my mother softly.

We were never very demonstrative in our family; poor folk who toil and are full of cares are not so. It is not their way to protest what they already know. When my mother says to me "dear boy," it means much more than when another uses it. I know well enough that the jar of whortleberries is the only one they have had for months, and that she has kept it for me; and the somewhat stale cakes that she gives me too. She must have got them cheap some time and put them all by for me.

I sit by her bed, and through the window the chestnut trees in the beer garden opposite glow in brown and gold. I breathe deeply and say over to myself:—"You are at home, you are at home." But a sense of strangeness will not leave me, I cannot feel at home amongst these things. There is my mother, there is my sister, there my case of butterflies, and there the mahogany piano—but I am not myself there. There is a distance, a veil between us.

I go and fetch my pack to the bedside and turn out the things I have brought—a whole Edamer cheese, that Kat provided me with, two loaves of army bread, three-quarters of a pound of butter, two tins of livered sausage, a pound of dripping and a little bag of rice.

"I suppose you can make some use of that——"

They nod.

"It is pretty bad for food here?" I enquire.

"Yes, there's not much. Do you get enough out there?"

I smile and point to the things I have brought.

"Not always quite as much as that, of course, but we fare reasonably well."

Erna takes away the food. Suddenly my mother seizes hold of my hand and asks falteringly: "Was it very bad out there, Paul?"

Mother, what should I answer to that! You would not understand, you could never realize it. And you shall never realize it. Was it bad, you ask.—You, Mother,—I shake my head and say: "No, Mother, not so very. There are always a lot of us together so it isn't so bad."

"Yes, but Heinrich Bredemeyer was here just lately and said it was terrible out there now, with the gas and all the rest of it."

It is my mother who says that. She says: "With the gas and all the rest of it." She does not know what she is saying, she is merely anxious for me. Should I tell her how we once found three enemy trenches with their garrison all stiff as though stricken with apoplexy? against the parapet, in the dugouts, just where they were, the men stood and lay about, with blue faces, dead.

"No Mother, that's only talk," I answer, "there's not very much in what Bredemeyer says. You see for instance, I'm well and fit——"

Before my mother's tremulous anxiety I recover my composure. Now I can walk about and talk and answer questions without fear of having suddenly to lean against the wall because the world turns soft as rubber and my veins become brimstone.

My mother wants to get up. So I go for a while to my sister in the kitchen. "What is the matter with her?" I ask.

She shrugs her shoulders. "She has been in bed some months now, but we did not want to write and tell you. Several doctors have been to see her. One of them said it is probably cancer again."

I go to the district commandant to report myself. Slowly I wander through the streets. Occasionally someone speaks to me. I do not delay long for I have little inclination to talk.

On the way back from the barracks a loud voice calls out to me. Still lost in thought I turn round and find myself confronted by a Major. "Can't you salute?" he blusters.

"Sorry, Major," I say in embarrassment, "I didn't notice you."

"Don't you know how to speak properly?" he roars.

I would like to hit him in the face, but control myself, for my leave depends on it. I click my heels and say: "I did not see you, Herr Major."

"Then keep your eyes open," he snorts. "What is your name?" I give it.

His fat red face is furious. "What regiment?"

I give him full particulars. Even yet he has not had enough. "Where are you quartered?"

But I have had more than enough and say: "Between Langemark and Bixschoote."

"Eh?" he asks, a bit stupefied.

I explain to him that I arrived on leave only an hour or two since, thinking that he would then trot along. But not at all. He gets even more furious: "You think you can bring your front line manners here, what? Well, we don't stand for that sort of thing. Thank God, we have discipline here!"

"Twenty paces backward, double march!" he commands.

I am mad with rage. But I cannot say anything to him; he could put me under arrest if he liked. So I double back, and then march up to him. Six paces from him I spring to a stiff salute and maintain it until I am six paces behind him.

He calls me back again and affably gives me to understand that for once he is pleased to put mercy before justice. I pretend to be duly grateful. "Now, dismiss!" he says. I turn about smartly and march off.

That ruins the evening for me. I go back home and throw my uniform into a corner; I had intended to change it in any case. Then I take out my civilian clothes from the wardrobe and put them on.

I feel awkward. The suit is rather tight and short, I have grown in the army. Collar and tie give me some trouble. In the end my sister ties the bow for me. But how light the suit is, it feels as though I had nothing on but a shirt and underpants.

I look at myself in the glass. It is a strange sight. A sunburned, overgrown candidate for confirmation gazes at me in astonishment.

My mother is pleased to see me wearing civilian clothes; it makes me less strange to her. But my father would rather I kept my uniform on so that he could take me to visit his acquaintances.

But I refuse.

It is pleasant to sit quietly somewhere, in the beer garden for example, under the chestnuts by the skittle-alley. The leaves fall down on the table and on the ground, only a few, the first. A glass of beer stands in front of me, I've learned to drink in the army. The glass is half empty, but there are a few good swigs ahead of me, and besides I can always order a second and a third if I wish to. There are no bugles and no bombardments, the children of the house play in the skittle-alley, and the dog rests his head against my knee. The sky is blue, between the leaves of the chestnuts rises the green spire of St. Margaret's Church.

This is good, I like it. But I cannot get on with the people. My mother is the only one who asks no questions. Not so my father. He wants me to tell him about the front; he is curious in a way that I find stupid and distressing; I no longer have any real contact with him. There is nothing he likes more than just hearing about it. I realize he does not know that a man cannot talk of such things; I would do it willingly, but it is too dangerous for me to put these things into words. I am afraid they might then become gigantic and I be no longer able to master them. What would become of us if everything that happens out there were quite clear to us?

So I confine myself to telling him a few amusing things. But he wants to know whether I have ever had a hand-to-hand fight. I say "No," and get up and go out.

But that does not mend matters. After I have been startled a couple of times in the street by the screaming of the tramcars, which resembles the shriek of a shell coming straight for one, somebody taps me on the shoulder. It is my German-master, and he fastens on me with the usual question: "Well, how are things out there? Terrible, terrible, eh? Yes, it is dreadful, but we must carry on. And after all, you do at least get decent food out there, so I hear. You look well, Paul, and fit. Naturally it's worse here. Naturally. The best for our soldiers every time, that goes without saying."

He drags me along to a table with a lot of others. They welcome us, a headmaster shakes hands with me and says: "So you come from the front? What is the spirit like out there? Excellent, eh? Excellent?"

I explain that no one would be sorry to be back home.

He laughs uproariously. "I can well believe it! But first you have to give the Froggies a good hiding. Do you smoke? Here, try one. Waiter, bring a beer as well for our young warrior."

Unfortunately I have accepted the cigar, so I have to remain. And they are all so dripping with good will that it is impossible to object. All the same I feel annoyed and smoke like a chimney as hard as I can. In order to make at least some show of appreciation I toss off the beer in one gulp. Immediately a second is ordered; people know how much they are indebted to the soldiers. They argue about what we ought to annex. The headmaster with the steel watch chain wants to have at least the whole of Belgium, the coal areas of France, and a slice of Russia. He produces reasons why we must have them and is quite inflexible until at last the others give in to him. Then he begins to expound just whereabouts in France the breakthrough must come, and turns to me: "Now, shove ahead a bit out there with your everlasting trench warfare—Smash through the johnnies and then there will be peace."

I reply that in our opinion a breakthrough may not be possible. The enemy may have too many reserves. Besides, the war may be rather different from what people think.

He dismisses the idea loftily and informs me I know nothing about it. "The details, yes," says he, "but this relates to the whole. And of that you are not able to judge. You see only your little sector and so cannot have any general survey. You do your duty, you risk your lives, that deserves the highest honor—every man of you ought to have the Iron Cross—but first of all the enemy line must be broken through in Flanders and then rolled up from the top."

He blows his nose and wipes his beard. "Completely rolled up they must be, from the top to the botton. And then to Paris."

I would like to know just how he pictures it to himself, and pour the third glass of beer into me. Immediately he orders another.

But I break away. He stuffs a few more cigars into my pocket and sends me off with a friendly slap. "All of the best! I hope we will soon hear something worth while from you."

I imagined leave would be different from this. Indeed, it was different a year ago. It is I of course that have changed in the interval. There lies a gulf between that time and today. At that time I still knew nothing about the war, we had only been in quiet sectors. But now I see that I have been crushed without knowing it. I find I do not belong here any more, it is a foreign world. Some of these people ask questions, some ask no questions, but one can see that the latter are proud of themselves for their silence; they often say with a wise air that these things cannot be talked about. They plume themselves on it.

I prefer to be alone, so that no one troubles me. For they all come back to the same thing, how badly it goes and how well it goes; one thinks it is this way, another that; and yet they are always absorbed in the things that go to make up their existence. Formerly I lived in just the same way myself, but now I feel no contact here.

They talk too much for me. They have worries, aims, desires, that I cannot comprehend. I often sit with one of them in the little beer garden and try to explain to him that this is really the only thing: just to sit quietly, like this. They understand of course, they agree, they may even feel it so too, but only with words, only with words, yes that is it—they feel it, but always with only half of themselves, the rest of their being is taken up with other things, they are so divided in themselves that none feels it with his whole essence; I cannot even say myself exactly what I mean.

When I see them here, in their rooms, in their offices, about their occupations, I feel an irresistible attraction in it, I would like to be here too and forget the war; but also it repels me, it is so narrow, how can that fill a man's life, he ought to smash it to bits; how can they do it, while out at the front the splinters are whining over the shell-holes and star-shells go up, the wounded are carried back on waterproof sheets and comrades crouch in the trenches.—They are different men here, men I cannot properly understand, whom I envy and despise. I must think of Kat and Albert and Müller and Tjaden, what will they be doing? No doubt they are sitting in the canteen, or perhaps swimming—soon they will have to go up to the front line again.

In my room behind the table stands a brown leather sofa. I sit down on it.

On the walls are pinned countless pictures that I once used to cut out of the newspapers. In between are drawings and postcards that have pleased me. In the corner is a small iron stove. Against the wall opposite stand the bookshelves with my books.

I used to live in this room before I was a soldier. The books I bought gradually with the money I earned by coaching. Many of them are secondhand, all the classics for example, one volume in blue cloth boards cost one mark twenty pfennig. I bought them complete because it was thoroughgoing, I did not trust the editors of selections to choose all the best. So I purchased only "collected works." I read most of them with laudable zeal, but few of them really appealed to me. I preferred the other books, the moderns, which were of course much dearer. A few I came by not quite honestly, I borrowed and did not return them because I did not want to part with them.

One shelf is filled with school books. They are not so well cared for, they are badly thumbed, and pages have been torn out for certain purposes. Then below are periodicals, papers, and letters all jammed in together with drawings and rough sketches.

I want to think myself back into that time. It is still in the room, I feel it at once, the walls having preserved it. My hands rest on the arms of the sofa; now I make myself at home and draw up my legs so that I sit comfortably in the corner, in the arms of the sofa. The little window is open, through it I see the familiar picture of the street with the rising spire of the church at the end. There are a couple of flowers on the table. Penholders, a shell as a paper weight, the ink-well—here nothing is changed.

It will be like this too. If I am lucky, when the war is over and I come back here for good. I will sit here just like this and look at my room and wait.

I feel excited; but I do not want to be, for that is not right. I want that quiet rapture again. I want to feel the same powerful, nameless urge that I used to feel when I turned to my books. The breath of desire that then arose from the colored backs of the books, shall fill me again, melt the heavy, dead lump of lead that lies somewhere in me and waken again the impatience of the future, the quick joy in the world of thought, it shall bring back again the lost eagerness of my youth. I sit and wait.

It occurs to me that I must go and see Kemmerich's mother;—I might visit Mittelstaedt too, he should be at the barracks. I look out of the window;—beyond the picture of the sunlit street appears a range of hills, distant and light; it changes to a clear day in autumn, and I sit by the fire with Kat and Albert and eat potatoes baked in their skins.

But I do not want to think of that, I sweep it away. The room shall speak, it must catch me up and hold me, I want to feel that I belong here, I want to hearken and know when I go back to the front that the war will sink down, be drowned utterly in the great homecoming tide, know that it will then be past forever, and not gnaw us continually, that it will have none but an outward power over us.

The backs of the books stand in rows. I know them all still, I remember arranging them in order. I implore them with my eyes: Speak to me—take me up—take me, Life of my Youth—you who are carefree, beautiful—receive me again—

I wait, I wait.

Images float through my mind, but they do not grip me, they are mere shadows and memories.

Nothing—nothing—

My disquietude grows.

A terrible feeling of foreignness suddenly rises up in me. I cannot find my way back, I am shut out though I entreat earnestly and put forth all my strength.

Nothing stirs; listless and wretched, like a condemned man, I sit there and the past withdraws itself. And at the same time I fear to importune it too much, because I do not know what might happen then. I am a soldier, I must cling to that.

Wearily I stand up and look out of the window. Then I take one of the books, intending to read, and turn over the leaves. But I put it away and take out another. There are passages in it that have been marked. I look, turn over the pages, take up fresh books. Already they are piled up beside me. Speedily more join the heap, papers, magazines, letters.

I stand there dumb. As before a judge.

Dejected.

Words, Words, Words—they do not reach me.

Slowly I place the books back in the shelves.

Nevermore.

Quietly, I go out of the room.

Still I do not give up hope. I do not indeed go to my room any more, but comfort myself with the thought that a few days are not enough to judge by. Afterwards—later on—there is plenty of time for that.

So I go over to see Mittelstaedt in the barracks, and we sit in his room; there is an atmosphere about it that I do not like but with which I am quite familiar.

Mittelstaedt has some news ready for me that electrifies me on the spot. He tells me Kantorek has been called up as a territorial.

"Just think of it," says he, and takes out a couple of good cigars, "I come back here from the hospital and bump right into him. He stretches out his paw to me and bleats: 'Hullo Mittelstaedt, how are you?'—I look at him and say: 'Territorial Kantorek, business is business and schnapps is schnapps, you ought to know that well enough. Stand to attention when you speak to a superior officer.' You should have seen his face! A cross between a dud and a pickled cucumber. He tried once again to chum up. So I snubbed him a bit harder. Then he brought up his biggest guns and asked confidentially: 'Would you like me to use my influence so that you can take an emergency-exam?' He was trying to remind me of those things, you know. Then I got mad, and I reminded him of something instead. 'Territorial Kantorek, two years ago you preached us into enlisting; and among us there was one, Joseph Behm, who didn't want to enlist. He was killed three months before he would have been called up in the ordinary way. If it had not been for you he would have lived just that much longer. And now: Dismiss. You will hear from me later.' It was easy to get put in charge of his company. First thing I did was to take him to the stores and fit him out with suitable equipment. You will see in a minute."

We go to the parade ground. The company has fallen in, Mittelstaedt stands them at ease and inspects.

Then I see Kantorek and am scarcely able to stifle my laughter. He is wearing a faded blue tunic. On the back and in the sleeves there are big dark patches. The tunic must have belonged to a giant. The black, worn breeches are just as much too short; they reach barely halfway down his calf. The boots, tough old clod-hoppers, with turned-up toes and laces at the side are much too big for him. But as a compensation the cap is too small, a terribly dirty, mean little pillbox. The whole rig-out is just pitiful.

Mittelstaedt stops in front of him: "Territorial Kantorek, do you call those buttons polished? You seem as though you can never learn. Inadequate, Kantorek, quite inadequate——"

It makes me bubble with glee. In school Kantorek used to chasten Mittelstaedt with exactly the same expression—"Inadequate, Mittelstaedt, quite inadequate."

Mittelstaedt continues to upbraid him: "Look at Boettcher now, there's a model for you to learn from."

I can hardly believe my eyes. Boettcher is there too, Boettcher, our school porter. And he is a model! Kantorek shoots a glance at me as if he would like to eat me. But I grin at him innocently, as though I do not recognize him any more.

Nothing could look more ludicrous than his forage-cap and his uniform. And this is the object before whom we used to stand in anguish as he sat up there enthroned at his desk, spearing at us with his pencil for our mistakes in those irregular French verbs with which afterward we made so little headway in France. That is barely two years ago—and now here stands Territorial Kantorek, the spell quite broken, with bent knees, arms like pothooks, unpolished buttons and that ludicrous rig-out—an impossible soldier. I cannot reconcile this with the menacing figure at the schoolmaster's desk. I wonder what I, the old soldier, would do if this skinful of woe ever dared to say to me again: "Bäumer, give the imperfect of 'aller.'"

The Mittelstaedt makes them practice skirmishing, and as a favor appoints Kantorek squad leader.

Now, in skirmishing the squad leader has always to keep twenty paces in front of his squad; if the order comes "On the march, about turn," the line of skirmishers simply turns about, but the squad leader, who now finds himself suddenly twenty paces in the rear of the line, has to rush up at the double and take his position again twenty paces in front of the squad. That makes altogether forty paces double march. But no sooner has he arrived than the order "On the march, about turn," comes again and he once more has to race at top speed another forty paces to the other side. In this way the squad has merely made the turnabout and a couple of paces, while the squad leader dashes backward and forward like a fart on a curtain pole. That is one of Himmelstoss' well-worn recipes.

Kantorek can hardly expect anything else from Mittelstaedt, for he once messed up the latter's chance of promotion, and Mittelstaedt would be a big fool not to make the best of such a good opportunity as this before he goes back to the front again. A man might well die easier after the army has given him just one such stroke of luck.

In the meantime Kantorek is dashing up and down like a wild boar. After a while Mittelstaedt stops the skirmish and begins the very important exercise of creeping.

On hands and knees, carrying his gun in regulation fashion, Kantorek shoves his absurd figure over the sand immediately in front of us. He is breathing hard, and his panting is music.

Mittelstaedt encourages Kantorek the territorial with quotations from Kantorek the schoolmaster. "Territorial Kantorek, we have the good fortune to live in a great age, we must brace ourselves and triumph over hardship."

Kantorek sweats and spits out a dirty piece of wood that has lodged in his teeth.

Mittelstaedt stoops down and says reproachfully: "And in the trifles never lose sight of the great adventure, Territorial Kantorek!"

It amazes me that Kantorek does not explode with a bang, especially when, during physical exercises, Mittelstaedt copies him to perfection, seizing him by the seat of his trousers as he is pulling himself up on the horizontal bar so that he can just raise his chin above the beam, and then starts to give him good advice. That is exactly what Kantorek used to do to him at school.

The extra fatigues are next detailed off. "Kantorek and Boettcher, bread fatigue! Take the handcart with you."

A few minutes later the two set off together pushing the barrow. Kantorek in a fury walks with his head down. But the porter is delighted to have scored light duty.

The bakehouse is away at the other end of the town, and the two must go there and back through the whole length of it.

"They've done that a couple of times already," grins Mittelstaedt. "People have begun to watch for them coming."

"Excellent," I say, "but hasn't he reported you yet?"

"He did try. Our C.O. laughed like the deuce when he heard the story. He hasn't any time for schoolmasters. Besides, I'm sweet with his daughter."

"He'll mess up the examination for you."

"I don't care," says Mittelstaedt calmly. "Besides, his complaint came to nothing because I could show that he had had hardly anything but light duty."

"Couldn't you polish him up a bit?" I ask.

"He's too stupid, I couldn't be bothered," answers Mittelstaedt contemptuously.

What is leave?—A pause that only makes everything after it so much worse. Already the sense of parting begins to intrude itself. My mother watches me silently; I know she counts the days; every morning she is sad. It is one day less. She has put away my pack, she does not want to be reminded by it.

The hours pass quickly if a man broods. I pull myself together, and go with my sister to the slaughterhouse to get a pound or two of bones. That is a great favor and people line up early in the morning and stand waiting. Many of them faint.

We have no luck. After waiting by turns for three hours the queue disperses. The bones have not lasted out.

It is a good thing that I get my rations. I bring them to my mother and in that way we all get something decent to eat.

The days grow ever more strained and my mother's eyes more sorrowful. Four days left now. I must go and see Kemmerich's mother.

I cannot write that down. This quaking, sobbing woman who shakes me and cries out on me: "Why are you living then, when he is dead?"—who drowns me in tears and calls out: "What are you there for at all, child, when you——"—who drops into a chair and wails: "Did you see him? Did you see him then? How did he die?"

I tell her he was shot through the heart and died instantaneously. She looks at me, she doubts me: "You lie. I know better. I have felt how terrribly he died. I have heard his voice at night, I have felt his anguish—tell the truth, I want to know it, I must know it."

"No," I say, "I was beside him. He died at once."

She pleads with me gently: "Tell me. You must tell me. I know you want to comfort me, but don't you see, you torment me far more than if you told me the truth? I cannot bear the uncertainty. Tell me how it was and even though it will be terrible, it will be far better than what I have to think if you don't."

I will never tell her, she can make mincemeat out of me first. I pity her, but she strikes me as rather stupid all the same. Why doesn't she stop worrying? Kemmerich will stay dead whether she knows about it or not. When a man has seen so many dead he cannot understand any longer why there should be so much anguish over a single individual. So I say rather impatiently: "He died immediately. He felt absolutely nothing at all. His face was quite calm."

She is silent. Then says slowly: "Will you swear it?"

"Yes."

"By everything that is sacred to you?"

Good God, what is there that is sacred to me?—such things change pretty quickly with us.

"Yes, he died at once."

"Are you willing never to come back yourself, if it isn't true?"

"May I never come back if he wasn't killed instantaneously."

I would swear to anything. But she seems to believe me. She moans and weeps steadily. I have to tell how it happened, so I invent a story and I almost believe it myself.

As I leave she kisses me and gives me a picture of him. In his recruit's uniform he leans on a round rustic table with legs made of birch branches. Behind him a wood is painted on a curtain, and on the table stands a mug of beer.

It is the last evening at home. Everyone is silent. I go to bed early, I seize the pillow, press it against myself and bury my head in it. Who knows if I will ever lie in a feather bed again?

Late in the night my mother comes into my room. She thinks I am asleep, and I pretend to be so. To talk, to stay awake with one another, it is too hard.

She sits long into the night although she is in pain and often writhes. At last I can bear it no longer, and pretend I have just woken up.

"Go and sleep, Mother, you will catch cold here."

"I can sleep enough later," she says.

I sit up. "I don't go straight back to the front, Mother. I have to do four weeks at the training camp. I may come over from there on Sunday, perhaps.

She is silent. Then she asks gently: "Are you very much afraid?"

"No Mother."

"I would like to tell you to be on your guard against the women out in France. They are no good."

Ah! Mother, Mother! You still think I am a child—why can I not put my head in your lap and weep? Why have I always to be strong and self-controlled? I would like to weep and be comforted too, indeed I am little more than a child; in the wardrobe still hang short, boy's trousers—it is such a little time ago, why is it over?

"Where we are there aren't any women, Mother," I say as calmly as I can.

"And be very careful at the front, Paul."

Ah, Mother, Mother! Why do I not take you in my arms and die with you. What poor wretches we are!

"Yes Mother, I will."

"I will pray for you every day, Paul."

Ah! Mother, Mother! Let us rise up and go out, back through the years, where the burden of all this misery lies on us no more, back to you and me alone, Mother!

"Perhaps you can get a job that is not so dangerous."

"Yes, Mother, perhaps I can get into the cookhouse, that can easily be done."

"You do it then, and if the others say anything——"

"That won't worry me, Mother——"

She sighs. Her face is a white gleam in the darkness.

"Now you must go to sleep, Mother."

She does not reply. I get up and wrap my cover round her shoulders.

She supports herself on my arm, she is in pain. And so I take her to her room. I stay with her a little while.

"And you must get well again, Mother, before I come back."

"Yes, yes, my child."

"You ought not to send your things to me, Mother. We have plenty to eat out there. You can make much better use of them here."

How destitute she lies there in her bed, she that loves me more than all the world. As I am about to leave, she says hastily: "I have two pairs of underpants for you. They are all wool. They will keep you warm. You must not forget to put them in your pack."

Ah! Mother! I know what these underpants have cost you in waiting, and walking, and begging! Ah! Mother, Mother! how can it be that I must part from you? Who else is there that has any claim on me but you? Here I sit and there you are lying; we have so much to say, and we shall never say it.

"Good night, Mother."

"Good night, my child."

The room is dark. I hear my mother's breathing, and the ticking of the clock. Outside the window the wind blows and the chestnut trees rustle.

On the landing I stumble over my pack, which lies there already made up because I have to leave early in the morning.

I bite into my pillow. I grasp the iron rods of my bed with my fists. I ought never to have come here. Out there I was intelligent and often hopeless—I will never be able to be so again. I was a soldier, and now I am nothing but an agony for myself, for my mother, for everything that is so comfortless and without end.

I ought never to have come on leave.

8

I already know the camp on the moors. It was here that Himmelstoss gave Tjaden his education. But now I know hardly anyone here; as ever, all is altered. There are only a few people that I have occasionally met before.

I go through the routine mechanically. In the evenings I generally go to the Soldiers' Home, where the newspapers are laid out, but I do not read them; still there is a piano there that I am glad enough to play on. Two girls are in attendance, one of them is young.

The camp is surrounded with high barbed wire fences. If we come back late from the Soldiers' Home we have to show passes. But those who are on good terms with the guard can get through, of course.

Among the junipers and the birch trees on the moor we practice company drill each day. It is bearable if one expects nothing better. We advance at a run, fling ourselves down, and our panting breath moves the stalks of the grasses and the flowers of the heather to and fro. Looked at so closely one sees the fine sand is composed of millions of the tiniest pebbles, as clear as if they had been made in a laboratory. It is strangely inviting to dig one's hands into it.

But most beautiful are the woods with their line of birch trees. Their color changes with every minute. Now the stems gleam purest white, and between them airy and silken, hangs the pastel-green of the leaves; the next moment all changes to an opalescent blue, as the shivering breezes pass down from the heights and touch the green lightly away; and again in one place it deepens almost to black as a cloud passes over the sun. And this shadow moves like a ghost through the dim trunks and rides far out over the moor to the sky—then the birches stand out again like gay banners on white poles, with their red and gold patches of autumn-tinted leaves.

I often become so lost in the play of soft light and transparent shadow, that I almost fail to hear the commands. It is when one is alone that one begins to observe Nature and to love her. And here I have not much companionship, and do not even desire it. We are too little acquainted with one another to do more than joke a bit and play poker or nap in the evenings.

Alongside our camp is the big Russian prison camp. It is separated from us by a wire fence, but in site of this the prisoners come across to us. They seem nervous and fearful, though most of them are big fellows with beards—they look like meek, scolded, St. Bernard dogs.

They slink about our camp and pick over the garbage tins. One can imagine what they find there. With us food is pretty scarce and none too good at that—turnips cut into six pieces and boiled in water, and unwashed carrot tops—mouldy potatoes are tit-bits, and the chief luxury is a thin rice soup in which float little bits of beef sinew, but these are cut up so small that they take a lot of finding.

Everything gets eaten, notwithstanding, and if ever anyone is so well off as not to want all his share, there are a dozen others standing by ready to relieve him of it. Only the dregs that the ladle cannot reach are tipped out and thrown into the garbage tins. Along with that there sometimes go a few turnip peelings, mouldy bread crusts and all kinds of muck.

This thin, miserable, dirty garbage is the objective of the prisoners. They pick it out of the stinking tins greedily and go off with it under their blouses.

It is strange to see these enemies of ours so close up. They have faces that make one think—honest peasant faces, broad foreheads, broad noses, broad mouths, broad hands, and thick hair.

They ought to be put to threshing, reaping, and apple picking. They look just as kindly as our own peasants in Friesland.

It is distressing to watch their movements, to see them begging for something to eat. They are all rather feeble, for they only get enough nourishment to keep them from starving. Ourselves we have not had sufficient to eat for long enough. They have dysentery; furtively many of them display the blood-stained tails of their shirts. Their backs, their necks are bent, their knees sag, their heads droop as they stretch out their hands and beg in the few words of German that they know—beg with those soft, deep, musical voices, that are like warm stoves and cozy rooms at home.

Some men there are who give them a kick, so that they fall over;—but those are not many. The majority do nothing to them, just ignore them. Occasionally, when they are too groveling, it makes a man mad and then he kicks them. If only they would not look at one so—What great misery can be in two such small spots, no bigger than a man's thumb—in their eyes!

They come over to the camp in the evenings and trade. They exchange whatever they possess for bread. Often they have fair success, because they have very good boots and ours are bad. The leather of their knee boots is wonderfully soft, like suede. The peasants among us who get tit-bits sent from home can afford to trade. The price of a pair of boots is about two or three loaves of army bread, or a loaf of bread and a small, tough ham sausage.

But most of the Russians have long since parted with whatever things they had. Now they wear only the most pitiful clothing, and try to exchange little carvings and objects that they have made out of shell fragments and copper driving bands. Of course, they don't get much for such things, though they may have taken immense pains with them—they go for a slice or two of bread. Our peasants are hard and cunning when they bargain. They hold the piece of bread or sausage right under the nose of the Russian till he grows pale with greed and his eyes bulge and then he will give anything for it. The peasants wrap up their booty with the utmost solemnity, and then get out their big pocketknives, and slowly and deliberately cut off a slice of bread for themselves from their supply and with every mouthful take a piece of the good tough sausage and so reward themselves with a good feed. It is distressing to watch them take their afternoon meal thus; one would like to crack them over their thick pates. They rarely give anything away. How little we understand one another.

I am often on guard over the Russians. In the darkness one sees their forms move like sick storks, like great birds. They come close up to the wire fence and lean their faces against it; their fingers hook round the mesh. Often many stand side by side, and breathe the wind that comes down from the moors and the forest.

They rarely speak and then only a few words. They are more human and more brotherly toward one another, it seems to me, than we are. But perhaps that is merely because they feel themselves to be more unfortunate than us. Anyway the war is over so far as they are concerned. But to wait for dysentery is not much of a life either.

The territorials who are in charge of them say that they were much more lively at first. They used to have intrigues among themselves, as always happens, and it would often come to blows and knives. But now they are quite apathetic and listless; most of them do not masturbate any more, they are so feeble, though otherwise things come to such a pass that whole huts full of them do it.

They stand at the wire fence; sometimes one goes away and then another at once takes his place in the line. Most of them are silent; occasionally one begs a cigarette butt.

I see their dark forms, their beards move in the wind. I know nothing of them except that they are prisoners; and that is exactly what troubles me. Their life is obscure and guiltless;—if I could know more of them, what their names are, how they live, what they are waiting for, what their burdens are, then my emotion would have an object and might become sympathy. But as it is I perceive behind them only the suffering of the creature, the awful melancholy of life and the pitilessness of men.

A word of command has made these silent figures our enemies; a word of command might transform them into our friends. At some table a document is signed by some persons whom none of us knows, and then for years together that very crime on which formerly the world's condemnation and severest penalty fall, becomes our highest aim. But who can draw such a distinction when he looks at these quiet men with their childlike faces and apostles' beards. Any noncommissioned officer is more of an enemy to a recruit, any schoolmaster to a pupil, than they are to us. And yet we would shoot at them again and they at us if they were free.

I am frightened: I dare think this way no more. This way lies the abyss. It is not now the time but I will not lose these thoughts, I will keep them, shut them away until the war is ended. My heart beats fast: this is the aim, the great, the sole aim, that I have thought of in the trenches; that I have looked for as the only possibility of existence after this annihilation of all human feeling; this is a task that will make life afterward worthy of these hideous years.

I take out my cigarettes, break each one in half and give them to the Russians. They bow to me and then light the cigarettes. Now red points glow in every face. They comfort me; it looks as though there were little windows in dark village cottages saying that behind them are rooms full of peace.

The days go by. On a foggy morning another of the Russians is buried; almost every day one of them dies. I am on guard during the burial. The prisoners saying a chorale, they sing in parts, and it sounds almost as if there were no voices, but an organ far away on the moor.

The burial is quickly over.

In the evening they stand again at the wire fence and the wind comes down to them from the beech woods. The stars are cold.

I now know a few of those who speak a little German. There is a musician amongst them, he says he used to be a violinist in Berlin. When he hears that I can play the piano he fetches his violin and plays. The others sit down and lean their backs against the fence. He stands up and plays, sometimes he has that absent expression which violinists get when they close their eyes, or again he sways the instrument to the rhythm and smiles across to me.

He plays mostly folk songs and the others hum with him. They are like a country of dark hills that sing far down under the ground. The sound of the violin stands like a slender girl above it and is clear and alone. The voices cease and the violin continues alone. In the night it is so thin it sounds frozen; one must stand close up; it would be much better in a room—out here it makes a man grow sad.

Because I have already had a long leave I get none on Sundays. So the last Sunday before I go back to the front my father and eldest sister come over to see me. All day we sit in the Soldiers' Home. Where else could we go? We don't want to stay in the camp. About midday we go for a stroll on the moors.

The hours are a torture; we do not know what to talk about, so we speak of my mother's illness. It is now definitely cancer, she is already in the hospital and will be operated on shortly. The doctors hope she will recover, but we have never heard of cancer being cured.

"Where is she then?" I ask.

"In the Luisa Hospital," says my father.

"In which class?"

"Third. We must wait till we know what the operation costs. She wanted to be in the third herself. She said that then she would have some company. And besides it is cheaper."

"So she is lying there with all those people. If only she could sleep properly."

My father nods. His face is broken and full of furrows. My mother has always been sickly; and though she has only gone to the hospital when she has been compelled to, it has cost a great deal of money, and my father's life has been practically given up to it.

"If only I knew how much the operation costs," says he.

"Have you not asked?"

"Not directly. I cannot do that—the surgeon might take it amiss and that would not do; he must operate on Mother."

Yes, I think bitterly, that's how it is with us, and with all poor people. They don't dare ask the price, but worry themselves dreadfully beforehand about it; but the others, for whom it is not important, they settle the price first as a matter of course. And the doctor does not take it amiss from them.

"The dressings afterward are so expensive," says my father.

"Doesn't the Invalid's Fund pay anything toward it, then?" I ask.

"Mother has been ill too long."

"Have you any money at all?"

He shakes his head: "No, but I can do some overtime."

I know. He will stand at his desk folding and pasting and cutting until twelve o'clock at night. At eight o'clock in the evening he will eat some miserable rubbish they get in exchange for their food tickets, then he will take a powder for his headache and work on.

In order to cheer him up a bit I tell him a few stories, soldiers' jokes and the like, about generals and sergeant majors.

Afterward I accompany them both to the railway station. They give me a pot of jam and a bag of potato-cakes that my mother has made for me.

Then they go off and I return to the camp.

In the evening I spread the jam on the cakes and eat some. But I have no taste for them. So I go out to give them to the Russians. Then it occurs to me that my mother cooked them herself and that she was probably in pain as she stood before the hot stove. I put the bag back in my pack and take only two cakes to the Russians.

9

We travel for several days. The first airplanes appear in the sky. We roll on past transport lines. Guns, guns. The light railway picks us up. I search for my regiment. No one knows exactly where it lies. Somewhere or other I put up for the night, somewhere or other I receive provisions and a few vague instructions. And so with my pack and my rifle I set out again on the way.

By the time I come up they are no longer in the devastated place. I hear we have become one of the flying divisions that are pushed in wherever it is hottest. That does not sound cheerful to me. They tell me of heavy losses that we have been having. I inquire after Kat and Albert. No one knows anything of them.

I search farther and wander about here and there; it is a strange feeling. One night more and then another I camp out like a Red Indian. Then at last I get some definite information, and by the afternoon I am able to report to the Orderly Room.

The sergeant-major detains me there. The company comes back in two days' time. There is no object in sending me up now.

"What was it like on leave?" he asks, "pretty good, eh?"

"In parts," I say.

"Yes," he sighs, "yes, if a man didn't have to come away again. The second half is always rather messed up by that."

I loaf around until the company comes back in the early morning, gray, dirty, soured, and gloomy. Then I jump up, push in amongst them, my eyes searching. There is Tjaden, there is Müller blowing his nose, and there are Kat and Kropp. We arrange our sacks of straw side by side. I have an uneasy conscience when I look at them, and yet without any good reason. Before we turn in I bring out the rest of the potato-cakes and jam so that they can have some too.

The outer cakes are moldy, still it is possible to eat them. I keep those for myself and give the fresh one to Kat and Kropp.

Kat chews and says: "These are from your mother?"

I nod.

"Good," says he, "I can tell by the taste."

I could almost weep. I can hardly control myself any longer. But it will soon be all right again back here with Kat and Albert. This is where I belong.

"You've been lucky," whispers Kropp to me before we drop off to sleep, "they say we are going to Russia."

To Russia? It's not much of a war over there.

In the distance the front thunders. The walls of the hut rattle.

There's a great deal of polishing being done. We are ispected at every turn. Everything that is torn is exchanged for new. I score a spotless new tunic out of it and Kat, of course, an entire outfit. A rumor is going round that there may be peace, but the other story is more likely—that we are bound for Russia. Still, what do we need new things for in Russia? At least it leaks out—the Kaiser is coming to review us. Hence all the inspections.

For eight whole days one would suppose we were in a base camp, there is so much drill and fuss. Everyone is peevish and touchy, we do not take kindly to all this polishing, much less to the full-dress parades. Such things exasperate a soldier more than the front line.

At last the moment arrives. We stand to attention and the Kaiser appears. We are curious to see what he looks like. He stalks along the line, and I am really rather disappointed; judging from his pictures I imagined him to be bigger and more powerfully built, and above all to have a thundering voice.

He distributes Iron Crosses, speaks to this man and that. Then we march off.

Afterward we discuss it. Tjaden says with astonishment:

"So that is the All Highest! And everyone, bar nobody, has to stand up stiff in front of him!" He meditates: "Hindenburg too, he has to stand up stiff to him, eh?"

"Sure," says Kat.

Tjaden hasn't finished yet. He thinks for a while and then asks: "And would a king have to stand up stiff to an emperor?"

None of us is quite sure about it, but we don't suppose so. They are both so exalted that standing strictly to attention is probably not insisted on.

"What rot you do hatch out," says Kat. "The main point is that you have to stand stiff yourself."

But Tjaden is quite fascinated. His otherwise prosy fancy is blowing bubbles. "But look," he announces, "I simply can't believe that an emperor has to go to the latrine the same as I have."

"You can bet your boots on it."

"Four and a half-wit make seven," says Kat. "You've got a maggot in your brain, Tjaden, just you run along to the latrine quick, and get your head clear, so that you don't talk like a two-year-old."

Tjaden disappears.

"But what I would like to know," says Albert, "is whether there would not have been a way if the Kaiser had said No."

"I'm sure there would," I interject, "he was against it from the first."

"Well, if not him alone, then perhaps if twenty or thirty people in the world had said No."

"That's probable," I agree, "but they damned well said Yes."

"It's queer, when one thinks about it," goes on Kropp, "we are here to protect our fatherland. And the French are over there to protect their fatherland. Now who's in the right?"

"Perhaps both," say I without believing it.

"Yes, well now," pursues Albert, and I see that he means to drive me into a corner, "but our professors and parsons and newspapers say that we are the only ones that are right, and let's hope so;—but the French professors and parsons and newspapers say that the right is on their side, now what about that?"

"That I don't know," I say, "but whichever way is is there's war all the same and every month more countries coming in."

Tjaden reappears. He is still quite excited and again joins the conversation, wondering just how a war gets started.

"Mostly by one country badly offending another," answers Albert with a slight air of superiority.

The Tjaden pretends to be obtuse. "A country? I don't follow. A mountain in Germany cannot offend a mountain in France. Or a river, or a wood, or a field of wheat."

"Are you really as stupid as that, or are you just pulling my leg?" growls Kropp. "I don't mean that at all. One people offends the other——"

"Then I haven't any business here at all," replies Tjaden, "I don't feel myself offended."

"Well, let me tell you," says Albert sourly, "it doesn't apply to tramps like you."

"Then I can be going home right away," retorts Tjaden, and we all laugh.

"Ach, man! he means the people as a whole, the State——" exclaims Müller.

"State, State"—Tjaden snaps his fingers contemptuously, "Gendarmes, police, taxes, that's your State;—if that's what you are talking about, no, thank you."

"That's right," says Kat, "youve said something for once, Tjaden. State and home country, there's a big difference."

"But they go together," insists Kropp, "without the State there wouldn't be any home country."

"True, but just you consider, almost all of us are simple folk. And in France, too, the majority of men are laborers, workmen, or poor clerks. Now just why would a French blacksmith or a French shoemaker want to attack us? No, it is merely the rulers. I have never seen a Frenchman before I came here, and it will be just the same with the majority of Frenchmen as regards us. They weren't asked about it any more than we were."

"Then what exactly is the war for?" asks Tjaden.

Kat shrugs his shoulders. "There must be some people to whom the war is useful."

"Well, I'm not one of them," grins Tjaden.

"Not you, nor anybody else here."

"Who are they then?" persists Tjaden. "It isn't any use to the Kaiser either. He has everything he can want already."

"I'm not so sure about that," contradicts Kat, "he has not had a war up till now. And every full grown emperor requires at least one war, otherwise he would not become famous. You look in your school books."

"And generals too," adds Detering," "they become famous through war."

"Even more famous than emperors," adds Kat.

"There are other people back behind there who profit by the war, that's certain," growls Detering.

"I think it is more of a kind of fever," says Albert. "No one in particular wants it, and then all at once there it is. We didn't want the war, the others say the same thing—and yet half the world is in it all the same."

"But there are more lies told by the other side than by us," says I; "just think of those pamphlets the prisoners have on them, where it says that we eat Belgian children. The fellows who write those lies ought to go out and hang themselves. They are real culprits."

Müller gets up. "Anyway, it is better that the war is here instead of in Germany. Just you look at the shell-holes."

"True," assents Tjaden, "but no war at all would be better still."

He is quite proud of himself because he has scored for once over us volunteers. And his opinion is quite typical, here one meets it time and again, and there is nothing with which one can properly counter it, because that is the limit of their comprehension of the factors involved. The national feeling of the tommy resolves itself into this—here he is. But that is the end of it; everything else he criticizes from his own practical point of view.

Albert lies down on the grass and growls angrily: "The best thing is not to talk about the rotten business."

"It won't make any difference, that's sure," agrees Kat.

To make matters worse, we have to return almost all the new things and take back our old rags again. The good ones were merely for the inspection.

Instead of going to Russia, we go up the line again. On the way we pass through a devastated wood with the tree trunks shattered and the ground ploughed up.

At several places there are tremendous craters. "Great guns, something's hit that," I say to Kat.

"Trench mortars," he replies, and then points up at one of the trees.

In the branches dead men are hanging. A naked soldier is squatting in the fork of a tree, he still has his helmet on, otherwise he is entirely unclad. There is only half of him sitting up there, the top half, the legs are missing.

"What can that mean?" I ask.

"He's been blown out of his clothes," mutters Tjaden.

"It's funny," says Kat, "we have seen that several times now. If a mortar gets you it blows you clean out of your clothes. It's the concussion that does it."

I search around. And so it is. Here hang bits of uniform, and somewhere else is plastered a bloody mess that was once a human limb. Over there lies a body with nothing but a piece of the underpants on one leg and the collar of the tunic around its neck. Otherwise it is naked and the clothes are hanging up in the tree. Both arms are missing as though they had been pulled out. I discover one of them twenty yards off in a shrub.

The dead man lies on his face. There, where the arm wounds are, the earth is black with blood. Underfoot the leaves are scratched up as though the man had been kicking.

"That's no joke, Kat," says I.

"No more is a shell splinter in the belly," he replies, shrugging his shoulders.

"But don't get tender-hearted," says Tjaden.

All this can only have happened a little while ago, the blood is still fresh. As everybody we see there is dead we do not waste any more time, but report the affair at the next stretcher-bearers' post. After all it is not our business to take these stretcher-bearers' jobs away from them.

A patrol has to be sent out to discover just how strongly the enemy position is manned. Since my leave I feel a certain strange attachment to the other fellows, and so I volunteer to go with them. We agree on a plan, slip out through the wire and then divide and creep forward separately. After a while I find a shallow shell-hole and crawl into it. From here I peer forward.

There is moderate machine gun fire. It sweeps across from all directions, not very heavy, but always sufficient to make one keep down.

A parachute star-shell opens out. The ground lies stark in the pale light, and then the darkness shuts down again blacker than ever. In the trenches we were told there were black troops in front of us. That is nasty, it is hard to see them; they are very good at patrolling, too. And oddly enough they are often quite stupid; for instance, both Kat and Kropp were once able to shoot down a black enemy patrol because the fellows in their enthusiasm for cigarettes smoked while they were creeping about. Kat and Albert had simply to aim at the glowing ends of the cigarettes.

A bomb or something lands close beside me. I have not heard it coming and am terrified. At the same moment a senseless fear takes hold of me. Here I am alone and almost helpless in the dark—perhaps two other eyes have been watching me for a long while from another shell-hole in front of me, and a bomb lies ready to blow me to pieces. I try to pull myself together. It is not my first patrol and not a particularly risky one. But it is the first since my leave, and besides, the lie of the land is still rather strange to me.

I tell myself that my alarm is absurd, that there is probably nothing at all there in the darkness watching me, otherwise they would not be firing so low.

It is in vain. In whirling confusion my thoughts hum in my brain—I hear the warning voice of my mother, I see the Russians with the flowing beards leaning against the wire fence, I have a bright picture of a canteen with stools, of a cinema in Valenciennes;

tormented, terrified, in my imagination I see the gray, implacable muzzle of a rifle which moves noiselessly before me whichever way I try to turn my head. The sweat breaks out from every pore.

I still continue to lie in the shallow bowl. I look at the time; only a few minutes have passed. My forehead is wet, the sockets of my eyes are damp, my hands tremble, and I am panting softly. It is nothing but an awful spasm of fear, a simple animal fear of poking out my head and crawling on farther.

All my efforts subside like froth into the one desire to be able just to stay lying there. My limbs are glued to the earth. I make a vain attempt;—they refuse to come away. I press myself down on the earth, I cannot go forward, I make up my mind to stay lying there.

But immediately the wave floods over me anew, a mingled sense of shame, of remorse, and yet at the same time of security. I raise myself up a little to take a look round.

My eyes burn with staring into the dark. A star-shell goes up;—I duck down again.

I wage a wild and senseless fight, I want to get out of the hollow and yet slide back into it again; I say "You must, it is your comrades, it is not an idiotic command," and again: "What does it matter to me, I have only one life to lose——"

That is the result of all this leave, I plead in extenuation. But I cannot reassure myself; I become terribly faint. I raise myself slowly and reach forward with my arms, dragging my body after me and then lie on the edge of the shell-hole, half in and half out.

There I hear sounds and drop back. Suspicious sounds can be detected clearly despite the noise of the artillery fire. I listen; the sound is behind me. They are our people moving along the trench. Now I hear muffled voices. To judge by the tone that might be Kat talking.

At once a new warmth flows through me. These voices, these quiet words, these footsteps in the trench behind me recall me at a bound from the terrible loneliness and fear of death by which I had been almost destroyed. They are more to me than life, these voices, they are more than motherliness and more than fear; they are the strongest, most comforting thing there is anywhere: they are the voices of my comrades.

I am no longer a shuddering speck of existence, alone in the darkness;— I belong to them and they to me; we all share the same fear and the same life, we are nearer than lovers, in a simpler, a harder way; I could bury my face in them, in these voices, these words that have saved me and will stand by me.

Cautiously I glide out over the edge and snake my way forward. I shuffle along on all fours a bit farther, I keep track of my bearings, look around me and observe the distribution of the gunfire so as to be able to find my way back. Then I try to get in touch with the others.

I am still afraid, but it is an intelligent fear, an extraordinarily heightened caution. The night is windy and shadows flit hither and thither in the flicker of the gunfire. It reveals too little and too much. Often I pause, stock still, motionless, and always for nothing. Thus I advance a long way and then turn back in a wide curve. I have not established touch with the others. Every yard nearer our trench fills me with confidence—and with haste, too. It would be bad to get hit now.

Then a new fear lays hold of me. I can no longer remember the direction. Quiet, I squat in a shell-hole and try to locate myself. More than once it has happened that some fellow has jumped joyfully into a trench, only then to discover that it was the wrong one.

After a little time I listen again, but still I am not sure. The confusion of shell-holes now seems so bewildering that I can no longer tell in my agitation which way I should go. Perhaps I am crawling parallel to the lines, and that might go on forever. So I crawl round once again in a wide curve.

These damned rockets! They seem to burn for an hour, and a man cannot make the least movement without bringing the bullets whistling round.

But there is nothing for it, I must get out. Falteringly I work my way farther, I move off over the ground like a crab and rip my hands sorely on the jagged splinters, as sharp as razor blades. Often I think that the sky is becoming lighter on the horizon, but it may be merely my imagination. Then gradually I realize that to crawl in the right direction is a matter of life or death.

A shell crashes. Almost immediately two others. And then it begins in earnest. A bombardment. Machine guns rattle. Now there is nothing for it but to stay lying low. Apparently an attack is coming. Everywhere the rockets shoot up. Unceasing.

I lie huddled in a large shell-hole, my legs in the water up to the belly. When the attack starts I will let myself fall into the water, with my face as deep in the mud as I can keep it without suffocating. I must pretend to be dead.

Suddenly I hear the barrage lift. At once I slip down into the water, my helmet on the nape of my neck and my mouth just clear so that I can get a breath of air.

I lie motionless;—somewhere something clanks; it stamps and stumbles nearer—all my nerves became taut and icy. It clatters over me and away, the first wave has passed. I have but this one shattering thought: What will you do if someone jumps into your shell-hole?—Swiftly I pull out my little dagger, grasp it fast and bury it in my hand once again under the mud. If anyone jumps in here I will go for him. It hammers in my forehead; at once, stab him clean through the throat, so that he cannot call out; that's the only way; he will be just as frightened as I am; when in terror we fall upon one another, then I must be first.

Now our batteries are firing. A shell lands near me. That makes me savage with fury, all it needs now is to be killed by our own shells; I curse and grind my teeth in the mud; it is a raving frenzy; in the end all I can do is groan and pray.

The crash of the shells bursts in my ears. If our fellows make a counterraid I will be saved. I press my head against the earth and listen to the muffled thunder, like the explosions of quarrying—and raise it again and listen for the sounds on top.

The machine guns rattle. I know our barbed wire entanglements are strong and almost undamaged;—parts of them are charged with a powerful electric current. The rifle fire increases. They have not broken through; they have to retreat.

I sink down again, huddled, strained to the uttermost. The banging, the creeping, the clanging becomes audible. One single cry yelling amongst it all. They are raked with fire, the attack is repulsed.

Already it has become somewhat lighter. Steps hasten over me. The first. Gone. Again, another. The rattle of machine guns becomes an unbroken chain. Just as I am about to turn round a little, something heavy stumbles, and with a crash a body falls over me into the shell-hole, slips down, and lies across me—

I do not think at all, I make no decision—I strike madly at home, and feel only how the body suddenly convulses, then becomes limp, and collapses. When I recover myself, my hand is sticky and wet.

The man gurgles. It sounds to me as though he bellows, every gasping breath is like a cry, a thunder—but it is not only my heart pounding. I want to stop his mouth, stuff it with earth, stab him again, he must be quiet, he is betraying me; now at last I regain control of myself, but have suddenly become so feeble that I cannot any more lift my hand against him.

So I crawl away to the farthest corner and stay there, my eyes glued on him, my hand grasping the knife—ready, if he stirs, to spring at him again. But he won't do so any more, I can hear that already in his gurgling.

I can see him indistinctly. I have but one desire, to get away. If it is not soon it will be too light; it will be difficult enough now. Then as I try to raise up my head I see it is impossible already. The machine gunfire so sweeps the ground that I should be shot through and through before I could make one jump.

I test it once with my helmet, which I take off and hold up to find out the level of the shots. The next moment it is knocked out of my hand by a bullet. The fire is sweeping very low to the ground. I am not far enough from the enemy line to escape being picked off by one of the snipers if I attempt to get away.

The light increases. Burning I wait for our attack. My hands are white at the knuckles, I clench them so tightly in my longing for the fire to cease so that my comrades may come.

Minute after minute trickles away. I dare not look again at the dark figure in the shell-hole. With an effort I look past it and wait, wait. The bullets hiss, they make a steel net, never ceasing, never ceasing.

Then I notice my bloody hand and suddenly feel nauseated. I take some earth and rub the skin with it; now my hand is muddy and the blood cannot be seen any more.

The fire does not diminish. It is equally heavy from both sides. Our fellows have probably given me up for lost long ago.

It is early morning, clear and gray. The gurgling continues, I stop my ears, but soon take my fingers away again, because then I cannot hear the other sound.

The figure opposite me moves. I shrink together and involuntarily look at it. Then my eyes remain glued to it. A man with a small pointed beard lies there; his head is fallen to one side, one arm is halfbent, his head rests helplessly upon it. The other hand lies on his chest, it is bloody.

He is dead, I say to myself, he must be dead, he doesn't feel anything any more; it is only the body that is gurgling there. Then the head tries to raise itself, for a moment the groaning becomes louder, his forehead sinks back upon his arm. The man is not dead, he is dying, but he is not dead. I drag myself toward him, hesitate, support myself on my hands, creep a bit farther, wait, again a terrible journey. At last I am beside him.

Then he opens his eyes. He must have heard me, for he gazes at me with a look of utter terror. The body lies still, but in the eyes there is such an extraordinary expression of fright that for a moment I think they have power enough to carry the body off with them. Hundreds of miles away with one bound. The body is still perfectly still, without a sound, the gurgle has ceased, but the eyes cry out, yell, all the life is gathered together in them for one tremendous effort to flee, gathered together there in a dreadful terror of death, of me.

My legs give way and I drop on my elbows. "No, no," I whisper.

The eyes follow me. I am powerless to move so long as they are there.

Then his hand slips slowly from his breast, only a little bit, it sinks just a few inches, but this movement breaks the power of the eyes. I bend forward, shake my head and whisper: "No, no, no," I raise one hand, I must show him that I want to help him, I stroke his forehead.

The eyes shrink back as the hand comes, then they lose their stare, the eyelids droop lower, the tension is past. I open his collar and place his head more comfortably.

His mouth stands half open, it tries to form words. The lips are dry. My water bottle is not there. I have not brought it with me. But there is water in the mud, down at the bottom of the crater. I climb down, take out my handkerchief, spread it out, push it under and scoop up the yellow water that strains through into the hollow of my hand.

He gulps it down. I fetch some more. Then I unbutton his tunic in order to bandage him if it is possible. In any case I must do it, so that if the fellows over there capture me they will see that I wanted to help him, and so will not shoot me. He tries to resist, but his hand is too feeble. The shirt is stuck and will not come away, it is buttoned at the back. So there is nothing for it but to cut it open.

I look for the knife and find it again. But when I begin to cut the shirt the eyes open once more and the cry is in them again and the demented expression, so that I must close them, press them shut and whisper: "I want to help you, Comrade, camerade, camerade, camerade——" eagerly repeating the word, to make him understand.

There are three stabs. My field dressing covers them, the blood runs out under it, I press it tighter; there; he groans.

That is all I can do. Now we must wait, wait.

These hours. . . . The gurgling starts again—but how slowly a man dies! For this I know—he cannot be saved, I have, indeed, tried to tell myself that he will be, but at noon this pretence breaks down and melts before his groans. If only I had not lost my revolver crawling about, I would shoot him. Stab him I cannot.

By noon I am grouping on the outer limits of reason. Hunger devours me, I could almost weep for something to eat, I cannot struggle against it. Again and again I fetch water for the dying man and drink some myself.

This is the first time I have killed with my hands, whom I can see close at hand, whose death is my doing. Kat and Kropp and Müller have experienced it already, when they have hit someone; it happens to many, in hand-to-hand fighting especially—

But every gasp lays my heart bare. This dying man has time with him, he has an invisible dagger with which he stabs me: Time and my thoughts.

I would give much if he would but stay alive. It is hard to lie here and to have to see and hear him.

In the afternoon, about three, he is dead.

I breathe freely again. But only for a short time. Soon the silence is more unbearable than the groans. I wish the gurgling were there again, gasping hoarse, now whistling softly and again hoarse and loud.

It is mad, what I do. But I must do something. I prop the dead man up again so that he lies comfortably, although he feels nothing any more. I close his eyes. They are brown, his hair is black and a bit curly at the sides.

The mouth is full and soft beneath his mustache; the nose is slightly arched, the skin brownish; it is now not so pale as it was before, when he was still alive. For a moment the face seems almost healthy;—then it collapses suddenly into the strange face of the dead that I have so often seen, strange faces, all alike.

No doubt his wife still thinks of him; she does not know what happened. He looks as if he would have often written to her;—she will still be getting mail from him—Tomorrow, in a week's time—perhaps even a stray letter a month hence. She will read it, and in it he will be speaking to her.

My state is getting worse, I can no longer control my thoughts. What would his wife look like? Like the little brunette on the other side of the canal? Does she belong to me now? Perhaps by this act she becomes mine. I wish Kantorek were sitting here beside me. If my mother could see me——. The dead man might have had thirty more years of life if only I had impressed the way back to our trench more sharply on my memory. If only he had run two yards farther to the left, he might now be sitting in the trench over there and writing a fresh letter to his wife.

But I will get no further that way; for that is the fate of all of us: if Kemmerich's leg had been six inches to the right: Haie Westhus had bent his back three inches further forward—

The silence spreads. I talk and must talk. So I speak to him and to say to him: "Comrade, I did not want to kill you. If you jumped in here again, I would not do it, if you would be sensible too. But you were only an idea to me before, an abstraction that lived in my mind and called forth its appropriate response. It was that abstraction I stabbed. But now, for the first time, I see you are a man like me. I thought of your hand grenades, of your bayonet, of your rifle; now I see your wife and your face and our fellowship. Forgive me, comrade. We always see it too late. Why do they never tell us that you are poor devils like us, that your mothers are just as anxious as ours, and that we have the same fear of death, and the same dying and the same agony—Forgive me, comrade; how could you be my enemy? If we threw away these rifles and this uniform you could be my brother just like Kat and Albert. Take twenty years of my life, comrade, and stand up—take more, for I do not know what I can even attempt to do with it now."

It is quiet, the front is still except for the crackle of rifle fire. The bullets rain over, they are not fired haphazard, but shrewdly aimed from all sides. I cannot get out.

"I will write to your wife," I say hastily to the dead man, "I will write to her, she must hear it from me, I will tell her everything I have told you, she shall not suffer, I will help her, and your parents too, and your child——"

His tunic is half open. The pocketbook is easy to find. But I hesitate to open it. In it is the book with his name. So long as I do not know his name perhaps I may still forget him, time will obliterate it, this picture. But his name, it is a nail that will be hammered into me and never come out again. It has the power to recall this forever, it will always come back and stand before me.

Irresolutely I take the wallet in my hand. It slips out of my hand and falls open. Some pictures and letters drop out. I gather them up and want to put them back again, but the strain I am under, the uncertainty, the hunger, the danger, these hours with the dead man have made me desperate, I want to hasten the relief, to intensify and to end the torture, as one strikes an unendurably painful hand against the trunk of a tree, regardless of everything.

There are portraits of a woman and a little girl, small amateur photographs taken against an ivy-clad wall. Along with them are letters. I take them out and try to read them. Most of it I do not understand, it is so hard to decipher and I scarcely know any French. But each word I translate pierces me like a shot in the chest;—like a stab in the chest.

My brain is taxed beyond endurance. But I realize this much, that I will never dare to write to these people as I intended. Impossible. I look at the portraits once more; they are clearly not rich people. I might send them money anonymously if I earn anything later on. I seize upon that, it is at least something to hold on to. This dead man is bound up with my life, therefore I must do everything, promise everything in order to save myself; I swear blindly that I mean to live only for his sake and his family, with wet lips I try to placate him—and deep down in me lies the hope that I may buy myself off in this way and perhaps even get out of this; it is a little stratagem: if only I am allowed to escape, then I will see to it. So I open the book and read slowly:—Gérard Duval, compositor.

With the dead man's pencil I write the address on an envelope, then swiftly thrust everything back into his tunic.

I have killed the printer, Gérard Duval. I must be a printer, I think confusedly, be a printer, printer——

By afternoon I am calmer. My fear was groundless. The name trubles me no more. The madness passes. "Comrade," I say to the dead man, but I say it calmly, "today you, tomorrow me. But if I come out of it, comrade, I will fight against this, that has struck us both down; from you, taken life—and from me—? Life also. I promise you, comrade. It shall never happen again."

The sun strikes low, I am stupefied with exhaustion and hunger. Yesterday is like a fog to me, there is no hope of ever getting out of this. I fall into a doze and do not at first realize that evening is approaching. The twilight comes. It seems to me to come quickly now. One hour more. If it were summer, it would be three hours more. One hour more.

Now suddenly I begin to tremble; something might happen in the interval. I think no more of the dead man, he is of no consequence to me now. With one bound the lust to live flares up again and everything that has filled my thoughts goes down before it. Now, merely to avert any ill luck, I babble mechanically: "I will fulfil everything, fulfil everything I have promised you——" but already I know that I shall not do so.

Suddenly it occurs to me that my own comrades may fire on me as I creep up; they do not know I am coming. I will call out as soon as I can so that they will recognize me. I will stay lying in front of the trench until they answer me.

The first star. The front remains quiet. I breathe deeply and talk to myself in my excitement: "No foolishness now, Paul—Quiet, Paul, quiet—then you will be saved, Paul." When I use my Christian name it works as though someone else spoke it to me, it has more power.

The darkness grows. My excitement subsides, I wait cautiously until the first rocket goes up. Then I crawl out of the shell-hole. I have forgotten the dead man. Before me lies the oncoming night and the pale gleaming field. I fix my eyes on a shell-hole; the moment the light dies I scurry over into it, grope farther, spring into the next, duck down, scramble onward.

I come nearer. There, by the light of the rocket I see something move in the wire, then it stiffens and I lie still. Next time I see it again, yes, they are men from our trench. But I am suspicious until I recognize our helmets. Then I call. And immediately an answer rings out, my name: "Paul—Paul——"

I call again in answer. It is Kat and Albert who have come out with a stretcher to look for me.

"Are you wounded?"

"No, no——"

We drop into the trench. I ask for something to eat and wolf it down. Müller gives me a cigarette. In a few words I tell what happened. There is nothing new about it; it happens quite often. The night attack is the only unusual feature of the business. In Russia Kat once lay for two days behind the enemy lines before he could make his way back.

I do not mention the dead printer.

But by next morning I can keep it to myself no longer. I must tell Kat and Albert. They both try to calm me. "You can't do anything about it. What else could you have done? That is what you are here for."

I listen to them and feel comforted, reassured by their presence. It was mere drivelling nonsense that I talked out there in the shell-hole.

"Look there for instance," points Kat.

On the firestep stand some snipers. They rest their rifles with telescopic sights on the parapet and watch the enemy front. Once and again a shot cracks out.

Then we hear the cry: "That's found a billet!" "Did you see how he leapt in the air?" Sergeant Oellrich turns round proudly and scores his point. He heads the shooting list for today with three unquestionable hits.

"What do you say to that?" asks Kat.

I nod.

"If he keeps that up he will get a little colored bird for his buttonhole by this evening," says Albert.

"Or rather he will soon be made acting sergeant major," says Kat.

We look at one another. "I would not do it," I say.

"All the same," says Kat, "it's very good for you to see it just now."

Sergeant Oellrich returns to the firestep. The muzzle of his rifle searches to and fro.

"You don't need to lose any sleep over your affair," nods Albert.

And now I hardly understand it myself any more.

"It was only because I had to lie there with him so long," I say. "After all, war is war."

Oellrich's rifle cracks out sharply and dry.

10

We have dropped in for a good job. Eight of us have to guard a village that has been abandoned because it is being shelled too heavily.

In particular we have to watch the supply dump as that is not empty yet. We are supposed to provision ourselves from the same store. We are just the right people for that;—Kat, Albert, Müller, Tjaden, Detering, our whole gang is there. Haie is dead, though. But we are mighty lucky all the same, all the other squads have had more casualties than we have.

We select, as a dugout, a reinforced concrete cellar into which steps lead down from above. The entrance is protected by a separate concrete wall.

Now we develop an immense industry. This is an opportunity not only to stretch one's legs, but to stretch one's soul also. We make the best use of such opportunities. The war is too desperate to allow us to be sentimental for long. That is only possible so long as things are not going too badly. After all, we cannot afford to be anything but matter-of-fact. So matter-of-fact, indeed, that I often shudder when a thought from the days before the war comes momentarily into my head. But it does not stay long.

We have to take things as lightly as we can, so we make the most of every opportunity, and nonsense stands stark and immediate beside horror. It cannot be otherwise, that is how we hearten ourselves. So we zealously set to work to create an idyll—an idyll of eating and sleeping of course.

The floor is first covered with mattresses which we haul in from the houses. Even a soldier's behind likes to sit soft. Only in the middle of the floor is there any clear space. Then we furnish ourselves with blankets, and eiderdowns, luxurious soft affairs. There is plenty of everything to be had in the village. Albert and I find a mahogany bed which can be taken to pieces with a sky of blue silk and a lace coverlet. We sweat like monkeys moving it in, but a man cannot let a thing like that slip, and it would certainly be shot to pieces in a day or two.

Kat and I do a little patrolling through the houses. In very short time we have collected a dozen eggs and two pounds of fairly fresh butter. Suddenly there is a crash in the drawing room, and an iron stove hurtles through the wall past us and on, a yard from us out through the wall behind. Two holes. It comes from the house opposite where a shell has just landed. "The swine," grimaces Kat, and we continue our search. All at once we prick up our ears, hurry across, and suddenly stand petrified—there running up and down in a little sty are two live sucking pigs. We rub our eyes and look once again to make certain. Yes, they are still there. We seize hold of them—no doubt about it, two real young pigs.

This will make a grand feed. About twenty yards from our dugout there is a small house that was used as an officers' billet. In the kitchen is an immense fireplace with two ranges, pots, pans, and kettles—everything, even to a stack of small chopped wood in an outhouse—a regular cook's paradise.

Two of our fellows have been out in the fields all the morning hunting for potatoes, carrots and green peas. We are quite simply uppish and sniff at the tinned stuff in the supply dump, we want fresh vegetables. In the dining room there are already two heads of cauliflower.

The sucking pigs are slaughtered. Kat sees to them. We want to make potato cakes to go with the roast. But we cannot find a grater for the potatoes. However, the difficulty is soon got over. With a nail we punch a lot of holes in a pot lid and there we have a grater. Three fellows put on thick gloves to protect their fingers against the grater, two others peel the potatoes, and the business gets going.

Kat takes charge of the sucking pigs, the carrots, the peas, and the cauliflower. He even mixes a white sauce for the cauliflower. I fry the pancakes, four at a time. After ten minutes I get the knack of tossing the pan so that the pancakes which are done on one side sail up, turn in the air and are caught again as they come down. The sucking pigs are roasted whole. We all stand round them as before an altar.

In the meantime we receive visitors, a couple of wireless men, who are generously invited to the feed. They sit in the living room where there is a piano. One of them plays, the other sings "An der Weser." He sings feelingly, but with a rather Saxon accent. All the same it moves us as we stand at the fireplace preparing the good things.

Then we begin to realize we are in for trouble. The observation balloons have spotted the smoke from our chimney, and the shells start to drop on us. They are those damned spraying little daisy cutters that make only a small hole and scatter widely close to the ground. They keep dropping closer and closer all round us; still we cannot leave the grub in the lurch. A couple of splinters whizz through the top of the kitchen window. The roast is ready. But frying the pancakes is getting difficult. The explosions come so fast that the splinters strike again and again against the wall of the house and sweep in through the window. Whenever I hear a shell coming I drop down on one knee with the pan and the pancakes, and duck behind the wall of the window. Immediately afterward I am up again and going on with the frying.

The Saxon stops singing—a fragment has smashed the piano. At last everything is ready and we organize the transport of it back to the dugout. After the next explosion two men dash across the fifty yards to the dugout with the pots of vegetables. We see them disappear.

The next shot. Everyone ducks and then two more trot off, each with a big can of finest grade coffee, and reach the dugout before the next explosion.

Then Kat and Kropp seize the masterpiece—the big dish with the brown, roasted sucking pigs. A screech, a knee bend, and away they race over the fifty yards of open country.

A stay to finish my last four pancakes; twice I have to drop to the floor;—after all, it means four pancakes more, and they are my favorite dish.

Then I grab the plate with the great pile of cakes and squeeze myself behind the house door. A hiss, a crash, and I gallop off with the plate clamped against my chest with both hands. I am almost in, there is a rising screech, I bound, I run like a deer, sweep round the wall, fragments clatter against the concrete, I tumble down the cellar steps, my elbows are skinned, but I have not lost a single pancake, nor even upset the plate.

At two o'clock we start the meal. It lasts till six. We drink coffee until half past six—officer's coffee from the supply dump—and smoke officer's cigars and cigarettes—also from the supply dump. Punctually at half past six we begin supper. At ten o'clock we throw the bones of the sucking pigs outside the door. Then there is cognac and rum—also from the blessed supply dump—and once again long, fat cigars with belly-bands. Tjaden says that it lacks only one thing: Girls from an officer's brothel.

Late in the evening we hear mewing. A little gray cat sits in the entrance. We entice it in and give it something to eat. And that wakes up our own appetites once more. Still chewing, we lie down to sleep.

But the night is bad. We have eaten too much fat. Fresh baby pig is very griping to the bowels. There is an everlasting coming and going in the dugout. Two, three men with their pants down are always sitting about outside and cursing. I have been out nine times myself. About four o'clock in the morning we reach a record: all eleven men, guards and visitors, are squatting outside.

Burning houses stand out like torches against the night. Shells lumber across and crash down. Munition columns tear along the street. On one side the supply dump has been ripped open. In spite of all the flying fragments the drivers of the munition columns pour in like a swarm of bees and pounce on the bread. We let them have their own way. If we said anything it would only mean a good hiding for us. So we go differently about it. We explain that we are the guard and so know our way about, we get hold of the tinned stuff and exchange it for things we are short of. What does it matter anyhow—in a while it will all be blown to pieces. For ourselves we take some chocolate from the depot and eat it in slabs. Kat says it is good for loose bowels.

Almost a fortnight passes thus in eating, drinking and roaming about. No one disturbs us. The village gradually vanishes under the shells and we lead a charmed life. So long as any part of the supply dump still stands we don't worry, we desire nothing better than to stay here till the end of the war.

Tjaden has become so fastidious that he only half smokes his cigars. With his nose in the air he explains to us that he was brought up that way. And Kat is most cheerful. In the morning his first call is: "Emil, bring in the caviar and coffee." We put on extraordinary airs, every man treats the other as his valet, bounces him and gives him orders. "There is something itching under my foot; Kropp my man, catch that louse at once," says Leer, poking out his leg at him like a ballet girl, and Albert drags him up the stairs by the foot. "Tjaden!"—"What?"—"Stand at ease, Tjaden; and what's more, don't say 'What,' say 'Yes, Sir,'—now: Tjaden!" Tjaden retorts in the well-known phrase from Goethe's "Götz von Berlichingen," with which he is always free.

After eight more days we receive orders to go back. The palmy days are over. Two big motor lorries take us away. They are stacked high with planks. Nevertheless, Albert and I erect on top our four-poster bed complete with blue silk canopy, mattress, and two lace coverlets. And behind it at the head is stowed a bag full of choicest edibles. We often dip into it, and the tough ham sausages, the tins of liver sausages, the conserves, the boxes of cigarettes rejoice in our hearts. Each man has a bag to himself.

Kropp and I have rescued two big red armchairs as well. They stand inside the bed, and we sprawl back in them as in a theater box. Above us swells the silken cover like a baldaquin. Each man has a long cigar in his mouth. And thus from aloft we survey the scene.

Between us stands a parrot cage that we found for the cat. She is coming with us, and lies in the cage before her saucer of meat, and purrs.

Slowly the lorries roll down the road. We sing. Behind us shells are sending up fountains from the now utterly abandoned village.

A few days later we are sent to evacuate a village. On the way we meet the fleeing inhabitants trundling their goods and chattels along with them in wheelbarrows, in perambulators, and on their backs. Their figures are bent, their faces full of grief, despair, haste, and resignation. The children hold on to their mothers' hands, and often an older girl leads the little ones who stumble onward and are for ever looking back. A few carry miserable looking dolls. All are silent as they pass us by.

We are marching in column; the French certainly will not fire on a town in which there are still inhabitants. But a few minutes later the air screams, the earth heaves, cries ring out; a shell has landed among our rear squad. We scatter and fling ourselves down on the ground, but at that moment I feel the instinctive alertness leave me which hitherto has always made me do unconsciously the right thing under fire; the thought leaps up with a terrible throttling fear: "You are lost"—and the next moment a blow sweeps like a whip over my left leg. I hear Albert cry out; he is beside me.

"Quick, up, Albert!" I yell, for we are lying unsheltered in the open field.

He staggers up and runs. I keep beside him. We have to get over a hedge; it is higher than we are. Kropp seizes a branch, I heave him up by the leg, he cries out, I give him a swing and he flies over. With one bound I follow him and fall into a ditch that lies behind the hedge.

Our faces are smothered with duckweed and mud, but the cover is good. So we wade in up to our necks. Whenever a shell whistles we duck our heads under the water. After we have done this a dozen times, I am exhausted.

"Let's get away, or I'll fall in and drown," groans Albert.

"Where has it got you?" I ask him.

"In the knee I think."

"Can you run?"

"I think——"

"Then out!"

We make for the ditch beside the road, and stooping, run along it. The shelling follows us. The road leads toward the munition dump. If that goes up there won't be so much as a bootlace left of us. So we change our plan and run diagonally across country.

Albert begins to drag. "You go, I'll come on after," he says, and throws himself down.

I seize him by the arm and shake him. "Up, Albert, if once you lie down you'll never get any farther. Quick, I'll hold you up."

At last we reach a small dugout. Kropp pitches in and I bandage him up. The shot is just a little above his knee. Then I take a look at myself. My trousers are bloody and my arm, too. Albert binds up my wound with his field dressing. Already he is no longer able to move his leg, and we both wonder how we managed to get this far. Fear alone made it possible; we should have run even if our feet had been shot off;—we would have run on the stumps.

I can still crawl a little. I call out to a passing ambulance wagon which picks us up. It is full of wounded. There is an army medical lance corporal with it who sticks an anti-tetanus needle into our chests.

At the dressing station we arrange matters so that we lie side by side. They give us a thin soup which we spoon down greedily and scornfully, because we are accustomed to better times but are hungry all the same.

"Now for home, Albert," I say.

"Let's hope so," he replies, "I only wish I knew what I've got."

The pain increases. The bandages burn like fire. We drink and drink, one glass of water after another.

"How far above the knee am I hit?" asks Kropp.

"At least four inches, Albert," I answer. Actually it is perhaps one.

"I've made up my mind," he says after a while, "if they take off my leg, I'll put an end to it. I won't go through life as a cripple."

So we lie there with our thoughts and wait.

In the evening we are hauled on to the chopping block. I am frightened and think quickly what I ought to do; for everyone knows that the surgeons in the dressing stations amputate on the slightest provocation. Under the great business that is much simpler than complicated patching. I think of Kemmerich. Whatever happens I will not let them chloroform me, even if I have to crack a couple of their skulls.

It is all right. The surgeon pokes around in the wound and a blackness comes before my eyes. "Don't carry on so," he says gruffly, and hacks away. The instruments gleam in the bright light like marvelous animals. The pain is insufferable. Two orderlies hold my arms fast, but I break loose with one of them and try to crash into the surgeon's spectacles just as he notices and springs back. "Chloroform the scoundrel," he roars madly.

Then I become quiet. "Pardon me, Herr Doctor, I will keep still but do not chloroform me."

"Well now," he cackles and takes up his instrument again. He is a fair fellow, not more than thirty years old, with scars and disgusting gold spectacles. Now I see that he is tormenting me, he is merely raking about in the wound and looking up surreptitiously at me over his glasses. My hands squeeze around the grips, I'll kick the bucket before he will get a squeak out of me.

He has fished out a piece of shell and tosses it to me. Apparently he is pleased at my self-control, for he now sets my leg carefully in splints and says: "Tomorrow you'll be off home." Then I am put in plaster. When I am back again with Kropp I tell him apparently a hospital train comes in tomorrow morning.

"We must work the army medical sergeant major so that we can keep together, Albert."

I manage to slip the sergeant major two of my cigars with belly-bands, and then tip the word to him. He smells the cigars and says: "Have you got any more of them?"

"Another good handful," I say, "and my comrade," I point to Kropp, "he has some as well. We might possibly be glad to hand them to you out of the window of the hospital train in the morning."

He understands, of course, smells them once again and says: "Done."

We cannot get a minute's sleep all night. One of them sings hymns in a high cracked tenor before he begins to gurgle. Another has crept out of his bed to the window. He lies in front of it as though he wants to look out for the last time.

Our stretchers stand on the platform. We wait for the train. It rains and the station has no roof. Our blankets are thin. We have waited already two hours.

The sergeant major looks after us like a mother. Although I feel pretty bad I do not let our scheme out of my mind. Casually I let him see the packet and give him one cigar in advance. In exchange the sergeant major covers us over with a waterproof sheet.

"Albert, old man," I suddenly bethink myself, "our four-poster and the cat——"

"And the club chairs," he adds.

Yes, the club chairs with red plush. In the evening we used to sit in them like lords, and intended later on to let them out by the hour. One cigarette per hour. It might have turned into a regular business, a real good living.

"And our bags of grub, too, Albert."

We grow melancholy. We might have made some use of the things. If only the train left one day later Kat would be sure to find us and bring us the stuff.

What damned hard luck! In our bellies there is gruel, mean hospital stuff, and in our bags roast pork. But we are so weak that we cannot work up any more excitement about it.

The stretchers are sopping wet by the time the train arrives in the morning. The sergeant major sees to it that we are put in the same car. There is a crowd of Red Cross nurses. Kropp is stowed in below. I am lifted up and told to get into the bed above him.

"Good God!" I exclaim suddenly.

"What is it?" asks the sister.

I cast a glance at the bed. It is covered with clean snow-white linen, that even has got the marks of the iron still on it. And my shirt has gone six weeks without being washed and is terribly muddy.

"Can't you get in by yourself?" asks the sister gently.

"Why yes," I say in a sweat, "but take off the bed cover first."

"What for?"

I feel like a pig. Must I get in there?—"It will get——" I hesitate.

"A little bit dirty?" she suggests helpfully. "That doesn't matter, we will wash it again afterward."

"No, no, not that——" I say excitedly. I am not equal to such overwhelming refinement.

"When you have been lying out there in the trenches, surely we can wash a sheet," she goes on.

I look at her, she is young and crisp, spotless and neat, like everything here; a man cannot realize that it isn't for officers only, and feels himself strange and in some way even alarmed.

All the same the woman is a tormentor, she is going to force me to say it. "It is only——" I try again, surely she must know what I mean.

"What is it then?"

"Because of the lice," I bawl out at last.

She laughs. "Well, they must have a good day for once, too."

Now I don't care any more. I scramble into bed and pull up the covers.

A hand gropes over the bed cover. The sergeant major. He goes off with the cigars.

An hour later we notice we are moving.

I wake up during the night. Kropp is restless too. The train rides easily over the rails. I cannot realize it all yet; a bed, a train, home. "Albert!" I whisper.

"Yes——"

"Do you know where the latrine is?"

"The door is on the right, I think."

"I'm going to have a look." It is dark, I grope for the edge of the bed and cautiously try to slide down. But my foot finds no support, I begin to slip, the plaster leg is no help, and with a crash I lie on the floor.

"Damn!" I say.

"Have you bumped yourself?" asks Kropp.

"You could hear that well enough for yourself," I growl, "my head——"

A door opens at the rear of the car. The sister comes with a light and looks at me.

"He has fallen out of bed——"

She feels my pulse and smooths my forehead. "You haven't any fever, though."

"No," I agree.

"Have you been dreaming then?" she asks.

"Perhaps——" I evade. The interrogation starts again. She looks at me with her clear eyes, and the more wonderful and sweet she is the less am I able to tell her what I want.

I am lifted up into bed again. That will be all right. As soon as she goes I must try to climb down again. If she were an old woman, it might be easier to say what a man wants, but she is so very young, at the most twenty-five, it can't be done, I cannot possibly tell her.

Then Albert comes to my rescue, he is not bashful, it makes no difference to him who is upset. He calls to the sister. She turns round. "Sister, he wants——" but no more does Albert know how to express it modestly and decently. Out there we say it in a single word, but here, to such a lady—All at once he remembers his school days and finishes hastily: "He wants to leave the room, sister."

"Ah!" says the sister, "but he shouldn't climb out of his bed with plaster bandage. What do you want then?" she says turning to me.

I am in mortal terror at this turn, for I haven't any idea what the things are called professionally. She comes to my help.

"Little or big?"

Shocking business! I sweat like a pig and say shyly: "Well, only quite a little one——"

At any rate it produces the effect.

I get a bottle. After a few hours I am no longer the only one, and by morning we are quite accustomed to it and ask for what we want without any false modesty.

The train travels slowly. Sometimes it halts and the dead are unloaded. It halts often.

Albert is feverish. I don't feel too bad; I have some pain, but the worst of it is that apparently there are still lice under the plaster bandage. They itch terribly, and I cannot scratch myself.

We sleep through the days. The country glides quietly past the window. The third night we reach Herbesthal. I hear from the sister that Albert is to be put off at the next station because of his fever. "How far does the train go?" I ask.

"To Cologne."

"Albert," I say "we stick together; you see."

On the sister's next round I hold my breath and press it up into my head. My face swells and turns red. She stops. "Are you in pain?"

"Yes," I groan, "all of a sudden."

She gives me a thermometer and goes on. I would not have been under Kat's tuition if I did not know what to do now. These army thermometers are not made for old soldiers. All one has to do is to drive the quicksilver up and then it stays without falling again.

I stick the thermometer under my arm at a slant, and flip it steadily with my forefinger. Then I give it a shake. I send it up to 100.2 degrees. But that is not enough. A match held cautiously near to it brings it up to 101.6 degrees.

As the sister comes back, I blow myself out, breathe in short gasps, goggle at her with vacant eyes, toss about restlessly, and mutter in a whisper: "I can't bear it any longer——"

She notes me down on a slip of paper. I know perfectly well my plaster bandage will not be reopened if it can be avoided.

Albert and I are put off together.

We are in the same room in a Catholic Hospital. That is a piece of luck, the Catholic infirmaries are noted for their good treatment and good food. The hospital has been filled up from our train, there are a great many bed cases amongst them. We do not get examined today because there are too few surgeons. The flat trolleys with the rubber wheels pass continually along the corridor, and always with someone stretched at full length upon them. A damnable position, stretched out full length like that;—the only time it is good is when one is asleep.

The night is very disturbed. No one can sleep. Toward morning we doze a little. I wake up just as it grows light. The doors stand open and I hear voices from the corridor. The others wake up too. One fellow who has been there a couple of days already explains it to us: "Up here in the corridor every morning the sisters say prayers. They call it Morning Devotion. And so that you can get your share, they leave the door open."

No doubt it is well meant, but it gives us aches in our heads and bones.

"Such an absurdity!" I say, "just when a man dropped off to sleep."

"All the light cases are up here, that's why they do it here," he replies.

Albert groans. I get furious and call out: "Be quiet out there!"

A minute later a sister appears. In her black and white dress she looks like a beautiful tea-cozy. "Shut the door, will you, sister?" says someone.

"We are saying prayers, that is why the door is open," she responds.

"But we want to go on sleeping——"

"Prayer is better than sleeping," she stands there and smiles innocently. "And is is seven o'clock already."

Albert groans again. "Shut the door," I snort.

She is quite disconcerted. Apparently she cannot understand. "But we are saying prayers for you too."

"Shut the door, anyway."

She disappears, leaving the door open. The intoning of the litany proceeds.

I feel savage, and say: "I'm going to count up to three. If it doesn't stop before then I'll let something fly."

"Me too," says another.

I count up to five. Then I take hold of a bottle, aim, and heave it through the door into the corridor. It smashes into a thousand pieces. The praying stops. A swarm of sisters appear and reproach us in concert.

"Shut the door!" we yell.

They withdrew. The little one who came first is the last to go. "Heathen," she chirps but shuts the door all the same. We have won.

At noon the hospital inspector arrives and abuses us. He threatens us with clink and all the rest of it. But a hospital inspector is just the same as a commissariat inspector, or any one else who wears a long sword and shoulder straps, but is really a clerk, and is never considered even by a recruit as a real officer. So we let him talk. What could they do to us anyway——

"Who threw the bottle?" he asks.

Before I can think whether I should report myself, someone says: "I did."

A man with a bristling beard sits up. Everyone is excited; why should he report himself?

"You?"

"Yes. I was annoyed because we were waked up unnecessarily and lost my senses so that I did not know what I was doing."

He talks like a book.

"What is your name?"

"Reinforcement Reservist Josef Hamacher."

The inspector departs.

We are all curious. "But why did you say you did it? It wasn't you at all."

He grins. "That doesn't matter. I have a shooting license."

Then of course, we all understood. Whoever has a shooting license can do just whatever he pleases.

"Yes," he explains. "I got a crack in the head and they presented me with a certificate to say that I was periodically not responsible for my actions. Ever since then I've had a grand time. No one dares to annoy me. And nobody does anything to me.

"I reported myself because the shot amused me. If they open the door again tomorrow we will pitch another."

We are overjoyed. With Josef Hamacher in our midst we can now risk anything.

Then come the soundless, flat trollies to take us away.

The bandages are stuck fast. We bellow like steers.

There are eight men in our room. Peter, a curly black-haired fellow, has the worst injury;—a severe lung wound. Franz Wächter, alongside him, has a shot in the arm which didn't look too bad at first. But the third night he calls out to us, telling us to ring, he thinks he has a haemorrhage.

I ring loudly. The night sister does not come. We have been making rather heavy demands on her during the night, because we have all been freshly bandaged, and so have a good deal of pain. One wants his leg placed so, another so, a third wants water, a fourth wants her to shake his pillow;—in the end the buxom old body grumbled bad-temperedly and slammed the doors. Now no doubt she thinks it is something of the same sort and so she is not coming.

We wait. Then Franz says: "Ring again."

I do so. Still she does not put in an appearance. In our wing there is only one night sister, perhaps she has something to do in one of the other rooms. "Franz, are you quite sure you are bleeding?" I ask. "Otherwise we shall be getting cursed again."

"The bandage is wet. Can't anybody make a light?"

That cannot be done either. The switch is by the door and none of us can stand up. I hold my thumb against the button of the bell till it becomes numb. Perhaps the sister has fallen asleep. They certainly have a great deal to do and are all overworked day after day. And added to that is the everlasting praying.

"Should we smash a bottle?" asks Josef Hamacher of the shooting license.

"She wouldn't hear that any more than the bell."

At last the door opens. The old lady appears, mumbling. When she perceives Franz's trouble she begins to bustle, and says: "Why did not someone say I was wanted?"

"We did ring. And none of us here can walk."

He has been bleeding badly and she binds him up. In the morning we look at his face, it has become sharp and yellow, whereas the evening before he looked almost healthy. Now a sister comes oftener.

Sometimes there are Red Cross voluntary aid sisters. They are pleasant, but often rather unskilled. They frequently give us pain when remaking our beds, and then are so frightened that they hurt us still more.

The nuns are more reliable. They know how they must take hold of us, but we would be better pleased if they were somewhat more cheerful. A few of them have real spirit, they are superb. There is no one but would do anything for Sister Libertine, this marvelous sister, who spreads good cheer through the whole wing even when she can only be seen in the distance. And there are others like her. We would go through fire for her. A man cannot really complain, here he is treated by the nuns exactly like a civilian. And just to think of a garrison hospital gives one the creeps.

Franz Wächter does not regain his strength. One day he is taken away and does not come back. Josef Hamacher knows all about it: "We shan't see him again. They have put him in the Dead Room."

"What do you mean, Dead Room?" asks Kropp.

"Well, Dying Room——"

"What is that, then?"

"A little room at the corner of the building. Whoever is about to kick the bucket is put in there. There are two beds in it. It is generally called the Dying Room."

"But what do they do that for?"

"They don't have so much work to do afterward. It is more convenient, too, because it lies right beside the lift to the mortuary. Perhaps they do it for the sake of the others also, so that no one in the ward dies in sympathy. And they can look after him better, too, if he is by himself."

"But what about him?"

Josef shrugs his shoulders. "Usually he doesn't take much notice any more."

"Does everybody know about it then?"

"Anyone who has been here long enough knows, of course."

In the afternoon Franz Wächter's bed has a fresh occupant. A couple of days later they take the new man away, too. Josef makes a significant glance. We see many come and go.

Often relatives sit by the beds and weep or talk softly and awkwardly. One old woman will not go away, but she cannot stay there the whole night through. The next morning she comes very early, but not early enough; for when she goes up to the bed, someone else is in it already. She has to go to the mortuary. The apples that she has brought with her she gives to us.

And then little Peter begins to get worse. His temperature chart looks bad, and one day the flat trolley stands beside his bed. "Where to?" he asks.

"To the bandaging ward."

He is lifted out. But the sister makes the mistake of removing his tunic from the hook and putting it on the trolley, too, so that she should not have to make two journeys. Peter understands immediately and tries to roll off the trolley. "I'm stopping here!"

They push him back. He cries out feebly with his shattered lung: "I won't go to the Dying Room."

"But we are going to the bandaging ward."

"Then what do you want my tunic for?" He can speak no more. Hoarse, agitated, he whispers: "Stopping here!"

They do not answer but wheel him out. At the door he tries to raise himself up. His black curly head sways, his eyes are full of tears. "I will come back again! I will come back again!" he cries.

The door shuts. We are all excited; but we say nothing. At last Josef says: "Many a man has said that. Once a man is in there, he never comes through."

I am operated on and vomit for two days. My bones will not grow together, so the surgeons' secretary says. Another fellow's have grown crooked; his are broken again. It is damnable.

Among our new arrivals there are two young soldiers with flat feet. The chief surgeon discovers them on his rounds, and is overjoyed. "We'll soon put that right," he tells them, "we will just do a small operation, and then you will have perfectly sound feet. Enter them down, sister."

As soon as he is gone, Josef, who knows everything, warns them: "Don't you let him operate on you! That is a scientific stunt of the old boy's. He goes absolutely crazy whenever he can get hold of anyone to do it on. He operates on you for flat feet, and there's no mistake, you don't have them anymore; you have club feet instead, and have to walk all the rest of your life on sticks."

"What should a man do, then?" asks one of them.

"Say No. You are here to be cured of your wound, not your flat feet. Did you have any trouble with them in the field? No, well, there you are! At present you can still walk, but if once the old boy gets you under the knife you'll be cripples. What he wants is little dogs to experiment with, so the war is a glorious time for him, as it is for all the surgeons. You take a look down below at the staff; there are a dozen fellows hobbling around that he has operated on. A lot of them have been here all the time since 'fourteen and 'fifteen. Not a single one of them can walk better than he could before, almost all of them worse, and most only with plaster legs. Every six months he catches them again and breaks their bones afresh, and every time is going to be the successful one. You take my word, he won't dare to do it if you say No."

"Ach, man," says one of the two wearily, "better your feet than your brain-box. There's no telling what you'll get if you go back out there again. They can do with me just as they please, so long as I get back home. Better to have a club foot than be dead."

The other, a young fellow like ourselves, won't have it done. The next morning the old man has the two hauled up and lectures and jaws at them so long that in the end they consent. What else could they do?—They are mere privates, and he is a big bug. They are brought back chloroformed and plastered.

It is going badly with Albert. They have taken him and amputated his leg. The whole leg has been taken off from the thigh. Now he will hardly speak any more. Once he says he will shoot himself the first time he can get hold of his revolver again.

A new convoy arrives. Our room gets two blind men. One of them is a very youthful musician. The sisters never have a knife with them when they feed him; he has already snatched one from a sister. But in spite of this caution there is an incident. In the evening, while he is being fed, the sister is called away, and leaves the plate with the fork on his table. He gropes for the fork, seizes it and drives it with all his force against his heart, then he snatches up a shoe and strikes with it against the handle as hard as he can. We call for help and three men are necessary to take the fork away from him. The blunt prongs had already penetrated deep. He abuses us all night so that no one can go to sleep. In the morning he has lockjaw.

Again beds are empty. Day after day goes by with pain and fear, groans and death gurgles. Even the Death Room is no use any more, it is too small; fellows die during the night in our room. They go even faster than the sisters can cope with them.

But one day the door flies open, the flat trolley rolls in, and there on the stretcher, pale, thin, upright and triumphant, with his shaggy head of curls sits Peter. Sister Libertine with beaming looks pushes him over to his former bed. He is back from the Dying Room. We have long supposed him dead.

He looks round: "What do you say now?"

And Josef has to admit that it is the first time he has ever known of such a thing.

Gradually a few of us are allowed to get up. And I am given crutches to hobble around on. But I do not make much use of them; I cannot bear Albert's gaze as I move about the room. His eyes always follow me with such a strange look. So I sometimes escape to the corridor;—there I can move about more freely.

On the next floor below are the abdominal and spine cases, head wounds and double amputations. On the right side of the wing are the jaw wounds, wounds in the joints, wounds in the kidneys, wounds in the testicles, wounds in the intestines. Here a man realizes for the first time in how many places a man can get hit.

Two fellows die of tetanus. Their skin turns pale, their limbs stiffen, at last only their eyes live—stubbornly. Many of the wounded have their shattered limbs hanging free in the air from a gallows; underneath the wound a basin is placed into which drips the pus. Every two or three hours the vessel is emptied. Other men lie in stretching bandages with heavy weights hanging from the end of the bed. I see intestine wounds that are constantly full of excreta. The surgeon's clerk shows me X-ray photographs of completely smashed hipbones, knees and shoulders.

A man cannot realize that above such shattered bodies there are still human faces in which life goes its daily round. And this is only one hospital, one single station; there are hundreds of thousands in Germany, hundreds of thousands in France, hundreds of thousands in Russia. How senseless is everything that can ever be written, done, or thought, when such things are possible. It must be all lies and of no account when the culture of a thousand years could not prevent this stream of blood being poured out, these torture chambers in their hundreds of thousands. A hospital alone shows what war is.

I am young, I am twenty years old; yet I know nothing of life but despair, death, fear, and fatuous superficiality cast over an abyss of sorrow. I see how peoples are set against one another, and in silence, unknowingly, foolishly, obediently, innocently slay one another. I see that the keenest brains of the world invent weapons and words to make it yet more refined and enduring. And all men of my age, here and over there, throughout the whole world see these things; all my generation is experiencing these things with me. What would our fathers do if we suddenly stood up and came before them and proffered our account? What do they expect of us if a time ever comes when the war is over? Through the years our business has been killing;—it was our first calling in life. Our knowledge of life is limited to death. What will happen afterward? And what shall come out of us?

The oldest man in our room is Lewandowski. He is forty, and he has already lain ten months in the hospital with a severe abdominal wound. Just in the last few weeks he has improved sufficiently to be able to hobble about doubled up.

For some days past he has been in great excitement. His wife has written to him from the little home in Poland where she lives, telling him that she has saved up enough money to pay for the fare and is coming to see him.

She is already on the way and may arrive any day. Lewandowski has lost his appetite, he even gives away red cabbage and sausage after he has had a couple of mouthfuls. He goes round the room perpetually with the letter. Everyone has already read it a dozen times, the postmarks have been examined heaven knows how often, the address is hardly legible any longer for spots of grease and thumbmarks, and in the end what is sure to happen, happens. Lewandowski develops a fever, and has to go back to bed.

He has not seen his wife for two years. In the meantime she has given birth to a child, whom she is bringing with her. But something else occupies Lewandowski's thoughts. He had hoped to get permission to go out when his old woman came; for obviously seeing is all very well, but when a man gets his wife again after such a long time, if at all possible, a man wants something else besides.

Lewandowski has discussed it all with us at great length; in the army there are no secrets about such things. And what's more, nobody finds anything objectionable in it. Those of us who are already able to go out have told him of a couple of very good spots in the town, parks and squares, where he would not be disturbed; one of us even knows of a little room.

But what is the use, there Lewandowski lies in bed with his troubles. Life holds no more joy for him if he has to forgo this affair. We console him and promise to get over the difficulty somehow or other.

The next afternoon his wife appears, a tousled little woman with anxious, quick eyes like a bird, in a sort of black crinkly mantilla with ribbons; heaven knows where she inherited the thing.

She murmurs something softly and stands shyly in the doorway. It terrifies her that there are six of us men present.

"Well, Marja," says Lewnadowski, and gulps dangerously with his Adam's apple "you can come in all right, they won't hurt you."

She goes round and proffers each of us her hand. Then she produces the child, which in the intervals has done something in its napkin. From a large handbag embroidered with beads she takes out a clean one and makes the child fresh and presentable. This dispels her first embarrassment, and the two begin to talk.

Lewandowski is very fidgety, every now and then he squints across at us most unhappily with his round goggle eyes.

The time is favorable, the doctor's visit is over, at the most one of the sisters might come in. So one of us goes out to prospect. He comes back and nods. "Not a soul to be seen. Now's your chance, Johann, set to."

The two speak together in an undertone. The woman turns a little red and looks embarrassed. We grin good-naturedly and make pooh-poohing gestures, what does it matter! The devil take all conventions, they were made for other times; here lies the carpenter Johann Lewandowski, a soldier shot to a cripple, and there is his wife;

who knows when he will see her again? He wants to have her, and he should have her, good.

Two men stand at the door to forestall the sisters and keep them occupied if they chance to come along. They agree to stand guard for a quarter of an hour or thereabouts.

Lewandowski can only lie on his side, so one of us props a couple of pillows against his side. Albert gets the child to hold, we all turn round a bit, the black mantilla disappears under the bedclothes, we make a great clatter and play skat noisily.

All goes well. I hold a club solo with four jacks which nearly goes the round. In the process we almost forget Lewandowski. After a while the child begins to squall, although Albert, in desperation, rocks it to and fro. There is a bit of creaking and rustling, and as we look up casually we see that the child has the bottle in its mouth and is back again with its mother. The business is over.

We now feel ourselves like one big family, the woman is happy, and Lewandowski lies there sweating and beaming.

He unpacks the embroidered handbag, and some good sausages come to light; Lewandowski takes up the knife with a flourish and saws the meat into slices.

With a handsome gesture he waves toward us—and the little woman goes from one to another and smiles at us and hands round the sausage; she now looks quite handsome. We call her Mother, she is pleased and shakes up our pillows for us.

After a few weeks I have to go each morning to the massage department. There my leg is harnessed up and made to move. The arm has healed long since.

New convoys arrive from the line. The bandages are no longer made of cloth, but of white crêpe paper. Rag bandages have become scarce at the front.

Albert's stump heals well. The wound is almost closed. In a few weeks he should go off to an institute for artificial limbs. He continues not to talk much, and is much more solemn than formerly. He often breaks off in his speech and stares in front of him. If he were not here with us he would have shot himself long ago. But now he is over the worst of it, and he often looks on while we play skat.

I get convalescent leave.

My mother does not want to let me go away. She is feeble. It is all much worse than it was last time.

Then I am recalled to my regiment and return once more to the line.

Parting from my friend Albert Kropp was very hard. But a man gets used to that sort of thing in the army.

11

We count the weeks no more. It was winter when I came up, and when the shells exploded the frozen clods of earth were just as dangerous as the fragments. Now the trees are green again. Our life alternates between billets and the front. We have almost grown accustomed to it; war is the cause of death like cancer and tuberculosis, like influenza and dysentery. The deaths are merely more frequent, more varied and terrible.

Our thoughts are clay, they are moulded with the changes of the days;—when we are resting they are good; under fire, they are dead. Fields of craters within and without.

Everyone is so, not only ourselves here—the things that existed before are no longer valid, and one practically knows them no more. Distinctions, breeding, education are changed, are almost blotted out and hardly recognizable any longer.

Sometimes they give an advantage for profiting by a situation;—but they also bring consequences along with them, in that they arouse prejudices which have to be overcome. It is as though formerly we were coins of different provinces; and now we are melted down, and all bear the same stamp. To rediscover the old distinctions, the metal itself must be tested. First we are soldiers and afterward, in a strange and shamefaced fashion, individual men as well.

It is a great brotherhood, which adds something of the goodfellowship of the folk song, of the feeling of solidarity of convicts, and of the desperate loyalty to one another of men condemned to death, to a condition of life arising out of the midst of danger, out of the tension and forlornness of death—seeking in a wholly unpathetic way a fleeting enjoyment of the hours as they come. If one wants to appraise it, it is at once heroic and banal—but who wants to do that?

It is this, for example, that makes Tjaden spoon down his ham-and-pea soup in such tearing haste when an enemy attack is reported, simply because he cannot be sure that in an hour's time he will be alive. We have discussed it at length, whether it is right or not to do so. Kat condemns it, because, he says, a man has to reckon with the possibility of an abdominal wound, and that is more dangerous on a full stomach than on an empty one.

Such things are real problems, they are serious matters to us, they cannot be otherwise. Here, on the borders of death, life follows an amazingly simple course, it is limited to what is most necessary, all else lies buried in gloomy sleep;—in that besides our primitiveness and our survival. Were we more subtly differentiated we must long since have gone mad, have deserted, or have fallen. As in a polar expedition, every expression of life must serve only the preservation of existence, and is absolutely focused on that. All else is banished because it would consume energies unnecessarily. That is the only way to save ourselves. In the quiet hours when the puzzling reflection of former days like a blurred mirror, projects beyond me the figure of my present existence, I often sit over against myself, as before a stranger, and wonder how the unnameable active principle that calls itself to life has adapted itself even to this form. All other expressions lie in a winter sleep, life is simply one continual watch against the menace of death;—it has transformed us into unthinking animals in order to give us the weapon of instinct—it has reinforced us with dullness, so that we do not go to pieces before the horror, which would overwhelm us if we had clear, conscious thought—it has awakened in us the sense of comradeship, so that we escape the abyss of solitude—it has lent us the indifference of wild creatures, so that in spite of all, we perceive the positive in every moment, and store it up as a reserve against the onslaught of nothingness. Thus we live a closed, hard existence of the utmost superficiality, and rarely does an incident strike out a spark. But then unexpectedly a flame of grievous and terrible yearning flares up.

Those are the dangerous moments. They show us that the adjustment is only artificial, that it is not simple rest, but sharpest struggle for rest. In the outward form of our life we are hardly distinguishable from Bushmen; but whereas the latter can be so always, because they are so truly, and at best may develop further by exertion of their spiritual forces, with us it is the reverse;—our inner forces are not exerted toward regeneration, but toward degeneration. The Bushmen are primitive and naturally so, but we are primitive in an artificial sense, and by virtue of the utmost effort.

And at night, waking out of a dream, overwhelmed and bewitched by the crowding apparitions, a man perceives with alarm how slight is the support, how thin the boundary that divides him from the darkness. We are little flames poorly sheltered by frail walls against the storm of dissolution and madness, in which we flicker and sometimes almost go out. Then the muffled roar of the battle becomes a ring that encircles us, we creep in upon ourselves, and with big eyes stare into the night. Our only comfort is the steady breathing of our comrades asleep, and thus we wait for the morning.

Every day and every hour, every shell and every death cuts into this thin support, and the years waste it rapidly. I see how it is already gradually breaking down around me.

There is the mad story of Detering.

He was one of those who kept himself to himself. His misfortune was that he saw a cherry tree in a garden. We were just coming back from the front line, and at a turning of the road near our billets, marvelous in the morning twilight, stood this cherry tree before us. It had no leaves, but was one white mass of blossom.

In the evening Detering was not to be seen. Then at last he came back and had a couple of branches of cherry blossom in his hand. We made fun of him, and asked whether he was going to a wedding. He made no answer, but lay down on his bed. During the night I heard him making a noise, he seemed to be packing. I sensed something amiss and went over to him. He made out it was nothing, and I said to him, "Don't do anything silly, Detering."

"Ach, why—it's merely that I can't sleep——"

"What did you pick the cherry branches for?"

"Surely I can pick cherry blossom if I want to!" he replied evasively—and after a while: "I have a big orchard with cherry trees at home. When they are in blossom, from the hay loft they look like one single sheet, so white. It is just the time."

"Perhaps you will get leave soon. You may even be sent back as a farmer."

He nodded but he was far away. When these peasants are excited they have a curious expression, a mixture of cow and yearning god, half stupid and half rapt. In order to turn him away from his thoughts I asked him for a piece of bread. He gave it to me without a murmur. That was suspicious, for he is usually tightfisted. So I stayed awake. Nothing happened; in the morning he was as usual.

Apparently he had noticed that I had been watching him;—but the second morning he was gone. I noticed it, but said nothing, in order to give him time; he might perhaps get through. Various fellows have already got into Holland.

But at roll call he was missed. A week after we heard that he had been caught by the field gendarmes, those despicable military police. He had headed toward Germany, that was hopeless, of course—and, of course, he did everything else just as idiotically. Anyone might have known that his flight was only homesickness and a momentary aberration. But what does a court-martial a hundred miles behind the front line know about it? We have heard nothing more of Detering.

But sometimes it broke out in other ways, this danger, these pent-up things, as from an overheated boiler. It will be enough to tell how Berger met his end.

Our trenches have now for some time been shot to pieces, and we have an elastic line, so that there is practically no longer any proper trench warfare. When attack and counterattack have waged backwards and forwards there remains a broken line and a bitter struggle from crater to crater. The front line has been penetrated, and everywhere small groups have established themselves, the fight is carried on from clusters of shell-holes.

We are in a crater, the English are coming down obliquely, they are turning our flank and working in behind us. We are surrounded. It is not easy to surrender, fog and smoke hang over us, no one would recognize that we wanted to give ourselves up, and perhaps we don't want to, a man doesn't even know himself at such moments. We hear the explosions of the hand grenades coming toward us. Our machine gun sweeps over the semicircle in front of us. The cooling water evaporates, we hastily pass round the case, every man pisses in it, and thus we again have water, and are able to continue firing. But behind us the attack crashes ever nearer.

A few minutes and we are lost.

Then, at closest range, a second machine gun bursts out. It is set up in a crater alongside us; Berger has fetched it, and now the counterattack comes over from behind; we are set free and make contact with the rear.

Afterward, as we lie in comparatively good cover, one of the food carriers reports that a couple of hundred yards distant there lies a wounded messenger dog.

"Where?" asks Berger.

The other describes the place to him. Berger goes off either to fetch the beast in or to shoot it. Six months ago he would not have cared, he would have been reasonable. We try to prevent him. Then, as he goes off grimly, all we can say is: "You're mad," and let him go. For these cases of front line madness become dangerous if one is not able to fling the man to the ground and hold him fast. And Berger is six feet and the most powerful man in the company.

He is absolutely mad for he has to pass through the barrage; but this lightning that lowers somewhere above us has struck him and made him demented. It affects others so that they begin to rave, to run away—there was one man who even tried to dig himself into the ground with hands, feet, and teeth.

It is true, such things are often simulated, but the pretence itself is a symptom. Berger, who means to finish off the dog, is carried away with a wound in the pelvis, and one of the fellows who carry him gets a bullet in the leg while doing it.

Müller is dead. Someone shot him point-blank in the stomach with a Verey light. He lived for half an hour, quite conscious, and in terrible pain.

Before he died he handed over his pocketbook to me, and bequeathed me his boots—the same that he once inherited from Kemmerich. I wear them, for they fit me quite well. After me Tjaden will get them, I have promised them to him.

We have been able to bury Müller, but he is not likely to remain long undisturbed. Our lines are falling back. There are too many fresh English and American regiments over there. There's too much corned beef and white wheaten bread. Too many new guns. Too many airplanes.

But we are emaciated and starved. Our food is bad and mixed up with so much substitute stuff that it makes us ill. The factory owners in Germany have grown wealthy;—dysentery dissolves our bowels. The latrine poles are always densely crowded; the people at home ought to be shown these gray, yellow, miserable, wasted faces here, these bent figures from whose bodies the colic wrings out the blood, and who with lips trembling and distorted with pain, grin at one another and say:

"It is not much sense pulling up one's trousers again——"

Our artillery is fired out, it has too few shells and the barrels are so worn that they shoot uncertainly, and scatter so widely as even to fall on ourselves. We have too few horses. Our fresh troops are anaemic boys in need of rest, who cannot carry a pack, but merely know how to die. By thousands. They understand nothing about warfare, they simply go on and let themselves be shot down. A single flyer routed two companies of them for a joke, just as they came fresh from the train—before they had ever heard of such a thing as cover.

"Germany ought to be empty soon," says Kat.

We have given up hope that some day an end may come. We never think so far. A man can stop a bullet and be killed; he can get wounded, and then the hospital is his next stop. There, if they do not amputate him, he sooner or later falls into the hands of one of those staff surgeons who, with the War Service Cross in his button-hole, says to him: "What, one leg a bit short? If you have any pluck you don't need to run at the front. The man is A1. Dismiss!"

Kat tells a story that has traveled the whole length of the front from the Vosges to Flanders;—of the staff surgeon who reads the names on the list, and when a man comes before him, without looking up, says: "A1. We need soldiers up there." A fellow with a wooden leg comes up before him, the staff surgeon again says A1——"And then," Kat raises his voice, "the fellow says to him: 'I already have a wooden leg, but when I go back again and they shoot off my head, then I will get a wooden head made and become a staff surgeon.'" This answer tickles us all immensely.

There may be good doctors, and there are, lots of them; all the same, every soldier some time during his hundreds of inspections falls into the clutches of one of these countless hero-grabbers who pride themselves on changing as many C3's and B3's as possible into A1's.

There are many such stories, they are mostly far more bitter. All the same, they have nothing to do with mutiny or lead-swinging. They are merely honest and call a thing by its name; for there is a very great deal of fraud, injustice, and baseness in the army. It is nothing that regiment after regiment returns again and again to the ever more hopeless struggle, that attack follows attack along the weakening, retreating, crumbling line.

From a mockery the tanks have become a terrible weapon. Armored they come rolling on in long lines, more than anything else embody for us the horror of war.

We do not see the guns that bombard us; the attacking lines of the enemy infantry are men like ourselves; but these tanks are machines, their caterpillars run on as endless as the war, they are annihilation, they roll without feeling into the craters, and climb up again without stopping, a fleet of roaring, smoke-belching armorclads, invulnerable steel beasts squashing the dead and the wounded—we shrivel up in our thin skin before them, against their colossal weight our arms are sticks of straw, and our hand grenades matches.

Shells, gas clouds, and flotillas of tanks—shattering, corroding, death.

Dysentery, influenza, typhus—scalding, choking, death.

Trenches, hospitals, the common grave—there are no other possibilities.

In one attack our Company Commander, Bertinck, falls. He was one of those superb front line officers who are foremost in every hot place. He was with us for two years without being wounded, so that something had to happen in the end.

We occupy a crater and get surrounded. The stink of petroleum or oil blows across with the fumes of powder. Two fellows with a flame-thrower are seen, one carries the tin on his back, the other has the hose in his hands from which the fire spouts. If they get so near that they can reach us we are done for, we cannot retreat yet.

We open fire on them. But they work nearer and things begin to look bad. Bertinck is lying in the hole with us. When he sees that we cannot hit them because under the sharp fire we have to think too much about keeping under cover, he takes a rifle, crawls out of the hole, and lying down propped on his elbows, he takes aim. He fires—the same moment a bullet smacks into him, they have got him. Still he lies and aims again;—once he shifts and again takes aim; at last the rifle cracks. Bertinck lets the gun drop and says: "Good," and slips back into the hole. The hindermost of the two flame-throwers is hit, he falls, the hose slips away from the other fellow, the fire squirts about on all sides and the man burns.

Bertinck has a chest wound. After a while a fragment smashes away his chin, and the same fragment has sufficient force to tear open Leer's hip. Leer groans as he supports himself on his arm, he bleeds quickly, no one can help him. Like an emptying tube, after a couple of minutes he collapses.

What use is it to him now that he was such a good mathematician at school.

The months pass by. The summer of 1918 is the most bloody and the most terrible. The days stand like angels in blue and gold, incomprehensible, above the ring of annihilation. Every man here knows that we are losing the war. Not much is said about it, we are falling back, we will not be able to attack again after this big offensive, we have no more men and no more ammunition.

Still the campaign goes on—the dying goes on——

Summer of 1918—Never has life in its niggardliness seemed to us so desirable as now;—the red poppies in the meadows round our billets, the smooth beetles on the blades of grass, the warm evenings in the cool, dim rooms, the black mysterious trees of the twilight, the stars and the flowing waters, dreams and long sleep——O Life, life, life!

Summer of 1918—Never was so much silently suffered as in the moment when we depart once again for the front line. Wild, tormenting rumors of an armistice and peace are in the air, they lay hold on our hearts and make the return to the front harder than ever.

Summer of 1918—Never was life in the line more bitter and full of horror than in the hours of the bombardment, when the blanched faces lie in the dirt and the hands clutch at the one thought: No! No! Not now! Not now at the last moment!

Summer of 1918—Breath of hope that sweeps over the scorched fields, raging fever of impatience, of disappointment, of the most agonizing terror of death, insensate question: Why? Why do they make an end? And why do these rumors of an end fly about?

There are so many airmen here, and they are so sure of themselves that they give chase to single individuals, just as though they were hares. For every one German plane there come at least five English and American. For one hungry, wretched German soldier come five of the enemy, fresh and fit. For one German army loaf there are fifty tins of canned beef over there. We are not beaten, for as soldiers we are better and more experienced; we are simply crushed and driven back by overwhelming superior forces.

Behind us lay rainy weeks—gray sky, gray fluid earth, gray dying. If we go out, the rain at once soaks through our overcoat and clothing;—and we remain wet all the time we are in the line. We never get dry. Those who will wear high boots tie sand bags round the tops so that the mud does not pour in so fast. The rifles are caked, the uniforms caked, everything is fluid and dissolved, the earth one dripping, soaked, oily mass in which lie yellow pools with red spiral streams of blood and into which the dead, wounded, and survivors slowly sink down.

The storm lashes us, out of the confusion of gray and yellow the hail of splinters whips forth the childlike cries of the wounded, and in the night shattered life groans painfully into silence.

Our hands are earth, our bodies clay and our eyes pools of rain. We do not know whether we still live.

Then the heat sinks heavily into our shell-holes like a jellyfish, moist and oppressive and on one of these late summer days, while bringing food, Kat falls. We two are alone. I bind up his wound; his shin seems to be smashed. It has got the bone, and Kat groans desperately: "At last—just at the last——"

I comfort him. "Who knows how long this mess will go on yet! Now you are saved——"

The wound begins to bleed fast. Kat cannot be left by himself while I try to find a stretcher. Anyway, I don't know of a stretcher-bearer's post in the neighborhood.

Kat is not very heavy; so I take him up on my back and start off to the dressing station with him.

Twice we rest. He suffers acutely on the way. We do not speak much. I have opened the collar of my tunic and breathe heavily, I sweat and my face is swollen with the strain of carrying. All the same I urge him to let us go on, for the place is dangerous.

"Shall we go on again Kat?"

"Must, Paul."

"Then come."

I raise him up, he stands on the uninjured leg and supports himself against a tree. I take up the wounded leg carefully, then he gives a jump and I take the knee of the sound leg also under my arm.

The going is more difficult. Often a shell whistles across. I go as quickly as I can, for the blood from Kat's wound drips to the ground. We cannot shelter ourselves properly for the explosions; before we can take cover the danger is all over.

We lie down in a small hole to wait till the shelling is over. I give Kat some tea from my water bottle. We smoke a cigarette. "Well, Kat," I say gloomily, "We are going to be separated at last."

He is silent and looks at me.

"Do you remember, Kat, how we commandeered the goose? And how you brought me out of the barrage when I was still a young recruit and was wounded for the first time? I cried then. Kat, that is almost three years ago."

He nods.

The anguish of solitude rises up in me. When Kat is taken away I will not have one friend left.

"Kat, in any case we must see one another again, if it is peacetime before you come back."

"Do you think that I will be marked A1 again with this leg?" he asks bitterly.

"With rest it will get better. The joint is quite sound. It may get all right again."

"Give me another cigarette," he says.

"Perhaps we could do something together later on, Kat." I am very miserable, it is impossible that Kat—Kat my friend, Kat with the drooping shoulders and the poor, thin mustache, Kat, whom I know as I know no other man, Kat with whom I have shared these years—it is impossible that perhaps I shall not see Kat again.

"In any case give me your address at home, Kat. And here is mine, I will write it down for you."

I write his address in my pocket book. How forlorn I am already, though he still sits here beside me. Couldn't I shoot myself quickly in the foot so as to be able to go with him.

Suddenly Kat gurgles and turns green and yellow, "Let us go on," he stammers.

I jump up, eager to help him, I take him up and start off at a run, a slow, steady pace, so as not to jolt his leg too much.

My throat is parched; everything dances red and black before my eyes, I stagger on doggedly and pitilessly and at last reach the dressing station.

There I drop down on my knees, but have still enough strength to fall on to the side where Kat's sound leg is. After a few minutes I straighten myself up again. My legs and my hands tremble. I have trouble in finding my water bottle, to take a pull. My lips tremble as I try to think. But I smile—Kat is saved.

After a while I begin to sort out the confusion of voices that falls on my ears.

"You might have spared yourself that," says an orderly.

I look at him without comprehending.

He points to Kat. "He is stone dead."

I do not understand him. "He has been hit in the shin," I say.

The orderly stands still. "That as well."

I turn round. My eyes are still dulled, the sweat breaks out on me again, it runs over my eyelids. I wipe it away and peer at Kat. He lies still. "Fainted," I say quickly.

The orderly whistles softly. "I know better than that. He is dead. I'll lay any moment on that."

I shake my head: "Not possible. Only ten minutes ago I was talking to him. He has fainted."

Kat's hands are warm, I pass my hand under his shoulders in order to rub his temples with some tea. I feel my fingers become moist. As I draw them away from behind his head, they are bloody. "You see——" The orderly whistles once more through his teeth.

On the way without my having noticed it, Kat has caught a splinter in the head. There is just one little hole, it must have been a very tiny, stray splinter. But it has sufficed. Kat is dead.

Slowly I get up.

"Would you like to take his paybook and his things?" the lance corporal asks me.

I nod and he gives them to me.

The orderly is mystified. "You are not related, are you?"

No, we are not related. No, we are not related.

Do I walk? Have I feet still? I raise my eyes, I let them move round, and turn myself with them, one circle, one circle, and I stand in the midst. All is as usual. Only the Militiaman Stanislaus Katczinsky has died.

Then I know nothing more.

12

It is autumn. There are not many of the old hands left. I am the last of the seven fellows from our class.

Everyone talks of peace and armistice. All wait. If it again proves an illusion, then they will break up; hope is high, it cannot be taken away again without an upheaval. If there is not peace, then there will be revolution.

I have fourteen days rest, because I have swallowed a bit of gas; in the little garden I sit the whole day long in the sun. The armistice is coming soon, I believe it now too. Then we will go home.

Here my thoughts stop and will not go any farther. All that meets me, all that floods over me are but feelings—greed of life, love of home, yearning for the blood, intoxication of deliverance. But no aims.

Had we returned home in 1916, out of the suffering and the strength of our experience we might have unleashed a storm. Now if we go back we will be weary, broken, burned out, rootless, and without hope. We will not be able to find our way any more.

And men will not understand us—for the generation that grew up before us, though it has passed these years with us already had a home and a calling; now it will return to its old occupations, and the war will be forgotten—and the generation that has grown up after us will be strange to us and push us aside. We will be superfluous even to ourselves, we will grow older, a few will adapt themselves, some others will merely submit, and most will be bewildered;—the years will pass by and in the end we shall fall into ruin.

But perhaps all this that I think is mere melancholy and dismay, which will fly away as the dust, when I stand once again beneath the poplars and listen to the rustling of their leaves. It cannot be that it has gone, the yearning that made our blood unquiet, the unknown, the perplexing, the oncoming things, the thousand faces of the future, the melodies from dreams and from books, the whispers and divinations of women; it cannot be that this has vanished in bombardment, in despair, in brothels.

Here the trees show gay and golden, the berries of the rowan stand red among the leaves, country roads run white out to the sky line, and the canteens hum like beehives with rumors of peace.

I stand up.

I am very quiet. Let the months and years come, they can take nothing from me, they can take nothing more. I am so alone, and so without hope that I can confront them without fear. The life that has borne me through these years is still in my hands and my eyes. Whether I have subdued it, I know not. But so long as it is there it will seek its own way out, heedless of the will that is within me.

*   *   *

He fell in October 1918, on a day that was so quiet and still on the whole front, that the army report confined itself to the single sentence: All quiet on the Western Front.

He had fallen forward and lay on the earth as though sleeping. Turning him over one saw that he could not have suffered long; his face had an expression of calm, as though almost glad the end had come.

Translated by A. W. Wheen

Joseph Roth

Job: The Story of a Simple Man (abridged)

Part 1

1

Many years ago there lived in Zuchnow in Russia, a man named Mendel Singer. He was pious, God-fearing, and ordinary, an entirely commonplace Jew. He practiced the simple profession of a teacher. In his house, which was merely a roomy kitchen, he instructed children in the knowledge of the Bible. He taught with honorable zeal and without notable success. Hundreds of thousands before him had lived and taught as he did.

As insignificant as his nature was his pale face. A full beard of ordinary black framed it. The mouth was hidden by the beard. The eyes were large, black, dull, and half veiled by heavy lids. On the head sat a cap of black silk rep, a stuff out of which unfashionable and cheap cravats are sometimes made. His body was stuck into the customary half-long Jewish caftan of the country, the skirts of which flapped when Mendel Singer hurried through the street and struck with a hard regular tact like the beat of wings against the shafts of his high leather boots.

Singer seemed to have little time and a lot of pressing engagements. True, his life was always hard and at times even a torment to him. A wife and three children had to be clothed and fed. (She was carrying a fourth.) God had given fertility to his loins, equanimity to his heart, and poverty to his hands. They had no gold to weigh and no bank notes to count. Nevertheless his life flowed along like a poor little brook between bare banks. Every morning

Mendel thanked God for his sleeping, for his awakening, and for the dawning day. When the sun went down he said his prayers once again. When the first stars began to sparkle, he prayed for the third time, and before he laid himself down to sleep he whispered a hurried prayer, with tired but zealous lips. His sleep was dreamless, his conscience was pure, his soul was chaste.

He had nothing to regret, and he coveted nothing. He loved the woman, his wife, and took delight in her flesh. His two small sons, Jonas and Shemariah, he beat when they were disobedient, but the youngest, his daughter Miriam, he was constantly caressing. She had his black hair and his black, soft, and indolent eyes. Her limbs were tender and fragile. A young gazelle.

He instructed twelve six-year-old scholars in the reading and memorizing of the Bible. Each of the twelve brought him twenty kopecks every Friday. This was Mendel Singer's only income. He was just thirty years old but his chances of earning more were small, perhaps non-existent. When the students grew older they would go to other, wiser teachers. Living became dearer from year to year. The crops were always poorer and poorer. The carrots diminished, the eggs were hollow, the potatoes froze, the soup was watery, the carp thin, the pike short, the ducks lean, the geese tough, and the chickens amounted to nothing.

Thus sounded the complaints of Deborah, the wife of Mendel Singer. She was a woman; sometimes she seemed possessed. She looked askance at the possessions of the well-to-do and envied merchants their profits. In her eyes Mendel Singer was inconsiderable. She blamed him for the children, for her pregnancy, for the high prices, for his poor fees, and sometimes, even, for the bad weather. On Friday she scrubbed the floor until it was yellow as saffron. Her broad shoulders bobbed up and down in an even rhythm; her strong hands rubbed the length and breadth of each single board; and her fingernails sought in the cracks between the boards, scratched out the black dirt, and destroyed it with splashes of water from her pail. She crept through the bare blue-whitewashed room like a broad, mighty, and movable mountain. Outside, before the door, she aired the furniture, the brown wooden bed, the sacks of straw, the scrubbed deal table, two long, narrow benches, each a horizontal board nailed on two vertical ones. As soon as the first twilight misted the windows, Deborah lighted the candles in the plated candlesticks, threw her hands over her face, and prayed.

Her husband came home, in silky black; the floor shone up at him, yellow as melted sunshine; his countenance shimmered whiter than usual, and blacker than on weekdays gleamed his beard. He sat down, sang a little song, and then parents and children sipped their soup, smiled at the plates, and spoke no word. Warmth rose in the room. It exuded from the pots, from the platters, and from their bodies. The cheap candles in the plated candlesticks could not stand it, they began to bend. Tallow dropped upon the red-and-blue checked tablecloth, and became encrusted immediately. The window was thrown open; the candles manfully took hold of themselves and burned peacefully to the end. The children laid themselves upon the straw sacks, near the stove, but the parents sat awhile and gazed with troubled solemnity into the last blue flames which rose up out of the sockets of the candlesticks and wavered back, a fountain-play of fire. The tallow smouldered, thin blue threads of smoke drew upward toward the ceiling from the embers of wick. "Ah!" sighed the woman. "Do not sigh," warned Mendel Singer. They were silent. "Let us sleep, Deborah," he commanded. And they began to murmur the nightly prayer.

At the end of each week the Sabbath dawned thus, with silence, candles, and song. Twenty-four hours later the Sabbath sank into night; the gray procession of weekdays began, a weary cycle.

On a hot midsummer day, Deborah was confined. Her first cries pierced the sing-song of the twelve studying children. They all went home for a week's vacation. Mendel got a new child, a fourth, a boy. Eight days later he was circumcised and named Menuchim.

Menuchim had no cradle. He swung in a basket of braided reeds, secured to a hook in the middle of the ceiling, like a chandelier. From time to time Mendel Singer pushed the hanging basket with a gentle, not unloving finger, and immediately it began to swing back and forth. But sometimes nothing would still the infant's desire to whimper and cry. His voice croaked over the voices of the twelve studying children, an ugly and profane noise above the Bible's holy verses. Deborah stood on a footstool and lifted the infant down. White, swollen, and colossal, her breast flowed from her open blouse and drew the glances of the boys irresistibly. All present seemed to suckle at Deborah. Her own three older children stood about her, jealous and greedy; the room became still. One heard the smacking of the infant.

Days drew themselves out into weeks, weeks grew into months, twelve months made a year. Menuchim still drank his mother's thin clear milk. She could not wean him. In the thirteenth month of his life he began to make faces and to groan like an animal, to breathe hastily and to gasp in an extraordinary fashion. His great skull hung heavy as a pumpkin on his thin neck. His broad brow was criss-crossed with folds and wrinkles like a crumpled parchment. His legs were crooked and lifeless, like two wooden bows. His meager little arms twitched and fidgeted. His mouth stammered ridiculous noises. When he got an attack he was taken from his cradle and given a good shaking until his face was blue and his breath almost failed. Then he slowly recovered. Little sacks of tea-leaves were laid upon his poor breast and a poultice of herbs was bound about his thin neck. "It's nothing," said his father. "Just growing-pains." "Sons take after the brothers of their mother. My brother had it five years!" said the mother. "He'll grow out of it!" said the others.

Then one day smallpox broke out in the town; the authorities ordered vaccination, and the doctors forced their way into the houses of the Jews. Many hid themselves, but Mendel Singer, the righteous, fled before no punishment of God. Resigned, he even accepted the vaccination.

It was a warmy sunny morning when the commission came through Mendel's street. In the row of Jewish houses Mendel's was the last. Accompanied by a policeman, who carried a big book under his arm, Dr. Soltysiuk went to perform the vaccination, a fluttering, blond mustache in his brown face, a gold-rimmed pince-nez on his reddened nose, taking long steps, creaking in his yellow leather leggings. Because of the heat his coat hung on his shoulders over his blue smock so that its sleeves looked like an extra pair of arms, also prepared to do vaccinations. Thus came Dr. Soltysiuk into the streets of the Jews. About him resounded the lamentations of women and the howls of children who had not been able to hide themselves. The policeman pulled women and children out of deep cellars and down from high attics, out of narrow closets and great straw baskets. The sun brooded, the doctor sweated. He had to vaccinate no less than one hundred and seventy-six Jews; for each who escaped and could not be reached, he thanked God in his heart. When he reached the fourth of the little blue-whitewashed houses, he winked at the policeman not to search too zealously. The farther the doctor went, the louder swelled the screaming. It floated before his steps. The howling of those who were still afraid united with the curses of those who were already inoculated. Weary and distrait, he sank with a heavy groan upon the bench in Mendel's kitchen and asked for a glass of water. His glance fell upon little Menuchim. He lifted the cripple and said: "He will be an epileptic." He planted anxiety in the father's heart. "All children have their periods," put in the mother. "It's not that," insisted the doctor. "But perhaps I could cure him. There is life in his eyes."

He wanted to take the little one to the hospital immediately. Deborah was ready. "They will cure him free," she said. But Mendel replied: "Be still, Deborah! No doctor can cure him, if God does not will it. Should he grow up among Russian children? Never hear a holy word? Eat milk with meat and chickens roasted in butter, the way people get them in the hospital? We are poor, but I will not sell Menuchim's soul just because he can be cured free. One is not healed in strange hospitals."

Like a hero Mendel held out his scraggy white arm to be vaccinated. But he would not give Menuchim away. He decided to beseech God's help for his youngest and to fast twice in the week, Mondays and Thursdays. Deborah undertook pilgrimages to the cemetery; she called upon the bones of her ancestors to plead her cause before the Almighty. Thus would Menuchim become well and no epileptic.

Nevertheless, after the hour of the vaccination, fear hung over the house of Mendel Singer like a monster, and care blew steadily through their hearts like a hot, piercing wind. Deborah would sigh and her husband did not reprove her. When she prayed, she held her face buried longer than usual in her hands, as though she created her own night in which to bury her fears, and her own darkness in which to find peace. For she believed, as it stands written, that God's light shines in the darkness and His goodness illumines the black night.[. . .][1]

One day, a week before the holy days (the summer had turned into rain and the rain sought to turn into snow), Deborah packed her

son in a basket, laid a blanket over him, put him on the cart of the
driver Sameshkin, and journeyed to Kluczýsk, where the Rabbi
lived. [. . .][2]

Someone opened the door. The Rabbi stood at the window, his
back turned to her, a narrow black line. Suddenly he turned to face
her. She stopped on the threshold, holding out her son upon both
arms, as one offers a sacrifice. She caught a gleam from the man's
white countenance, which seemed one with his white beard. She
had intended to gaze into the eyes of the Holy One, to convince
herself that a powerful goodness really lived in them. But now that
she stood there, a sea of tears blurred her vision, and she saw the
man behind a white wave of water and salt. He lifted his hand; she
thought she recognized two thin fingers, the instrument of blessing.
But very near her she heard the voice of the Rabbi although he only
whispered:

"Menuchim, Mendel's son, will be healed. There will not be
many like him in Israel. Pain will make him wise, ugliness good,
bitterness mild, and sickness strong. His eyes will see far and deep.
His ears will be clear and full of echoes. His mouth will be silent,
but when he opens his lips they will announce good tidings. Have
no fear, and go home!"

"When, when, when will he be well?" Deborah whispered.

"After many years," said the Rabbi, "but ask me no more. I have
no time and this is all I know. Do not leave your son even if he is a
great burden to you. Do not send him away from your side; he is
yours even as a healthy child is. And now go! . . ."

Outside they cleared a way for her. Her cheeks were pale, her
eyes dry, her lips were lightly opened as though she breathed in
hope. With grace in her heart she turned homeward.[. . .][3]

2

From this day on all desire between Mendel Singer and his wife
ceased. Like two people of the same sex they went to sleep, slept
through the night, awoke in the morning. They became shy with
each other and were silent, as in the first days of their marriage. At

the beginning of their desire there had been shame, and at the end of their desire there was shame.

Then it also was overcome. They spoke to each other again. Their eyes no longer avoided each other, and their faces and bodies aged in the same rhythm, like the faces and bodies of twins.

The summer was sultry and poor in rain. Doors and windows stood open. The children were seldom at home. Outside they grew quickly, vitalized by the sun.

Even Menuchim grew. His legs, to be sure, remained crooked, but unquestionably they became longer. So did the rest of his body. Suddenly, one morning, he let out a strange, shrill cry. Then he was silent. A little while later he said quite clearly and understandably: "Mama."

Deborah threw herself upon him, and from her eyes, which had long remained dry, tears flowed, hot, strong, big, salty, painful, and sweet. "Say Mama!"

"Mama," echoed the little one.

A dozen times he repeated the word. A hundred times Deborah repeated it. Not in vain had been her prayers. Menuchim spoke. And this one word of the deformed child was sublime as a revelation, mighty as thunder, warm as love, gracious as Heaven, wide as the earth, fertile as a field, sweet as a sweet fruit. It was more than the health of the healthy children. It meant that Menuchim would be strong and big, wise and good, as the words of the blessing had promised.

To be sure no other understandable sounds issued from Menuchim's throat. For a long time this one word, which he had brought out after such a terrible silence, meant food and drink, sleep and love, pleasure and pain, heaven and earth. Although he used this word for every situation, he seemed to his mother as loquacious as a pracher and as rich in expression as a poet. She understood all the words which were buried in this single one. She neglected the older children. She turned away from them. She had but one son, an only son: Menuchim.

3

Perhaps blessings need a longer time for their fulfillment than curses. Ten years had passed since Menuchim had spoken his first and only word. He could still say nothing else.

Sometimes when Deborah is alone in the house with her sick son, she bolts the door, sits down beside Menuchim on the floor, and stares into the little one's face. Then she remembers the dreadful day in summer when the Countess drove before the church. She sees the open door of the church. A golden gleam from a thousand candles, from colored pictures wreathed in light, from three priests in robes who stand far back near the altar, with black beards and white, hovering hands, shines out into the sunny, dusty square. Deborah is in the third month; Menuchim stirs in her body; she holds delicate little Miriam fast by the hand. Suddenly there is shouting. It drowns out the chant of the prayerful in the church. There is heard the clacking trample of horses; a cloud of dust whirls up; the dark-blue equipage of the Countess stops before the church. The peasant children hurrah. The beggars on the steps hobble toward the carriage to kiss the hand of the Countess. Suddenly Miriam breaks loose. In no time she has disappeared. Deborah trembles; she freezes, in the midst of the heat. Where is Miriam? she asks one peasant child after another. The Countess descends. Deborah approaches the carriage. The coachman with the silver buttons on his dark-blue livery sits so high that he can overlook everything. "Did you see where the little black-haired girl ran to?" asks Deborah, her head stretched backward, her eyes blinded by the sun and by the coachman's bright buttons. The coachman points with his white-gloved left hand toward the church. Miriam had gone in there.

Deborah considers a moment, then dashes into the church, into the midst of the golden shining, the full-voiced music, the organ's roar. In the entrance stands Miriam. Deborah grabs the child, drags her toward the square, rushes down the hot, white steps, flees as before a conflagration. She wants to beat the child but she is afraid.

She runs, dragging the child behind her, into a narrow street. Now she is quieter. "Tell your father nothing of this," she pants. "Do you hear, Miriam?"

From this day on, Deborah knew that a misfortune was under way. She carried a misfortune in her womb. She knew it and was silent.

Now she pushes the bolt back, there is a knock on the door. Mendel is home.

His beard is prematurely gray. Prematurely withered were also the face, the body, and the hands of Deborah. Strong and slow as a bear was the oldest son, Jonas; sly and nimble as a fox was the younger son, Shemariah; thoughtless and coquettish as a gazelle, the sister Miriam.

When Miriam hurried through the streets on errands, slender and small, a shimmering shadow, a brown face, a wide red mouth, a golden-yellow shawl knotted in two flying wings under her chin, and with two old eyes in the midst of the brown youth of her countenance, she attracted the attention of the officers of the garrison, and remained in their careless, pleasure-seeking minds. Occasionally one would lie in wait for her. She noticed nothing about her pursuers except the impression they made upon her outer senses: a silver clinking and rustling of spurs and arms, a pervasive smell of pomade and shaving soap, a fulminating gleam of gold buttons, silver braid, and bright-red reins of Russia leather. It was little, it was enough. Just behind the outer portal of her senses curiosity lurked in Miriam, curiosity which is the sister of youth and the awakener of desire. The girl fled before her pursuers in sweet and hot anxiety, only, in order to drag out the painfully exciting pleasure, she fled through many by-ways, prolonging her flight many minutes. She fled in a roundabout fashion. Only, in order to flee again, Miriam would leave home oftener than was necessary. At the street corner she would stop and cast a glance backward, baiting her huntsmen. It was Miriam's only pleasure. Even if there had been anyone at hand who could understand her, she would have kept her mouth closed. For delights are stronger the longer they remain secret.

Miriam did not yet know how threatening would be her relationship to the strange and terrible world of the military and how heavy were the destinies which had begun to collect over the heads of Mendel Singer, his wife, and his children. For Jonas and Shemariah were already at the age when, according to the law, they should become soldiers and, according to the tradition of their fathers, they must rescue themselves from military service.

A gracious and provident God had bestowed upon other youngsters some physical disability which caused them little inconvenience and protected them from this evil. Some had only one eye, some limped, this one had a rupture, that one twitched uncontrollably with his arms and legs, a few had weak lungs, others weak hearts, one heard badly and another stuttered and a third just suffered from general debility.

But it seemed as though the family of Mendel Singer little Menuchim had taken upon himself the whole catalogue of human suffering which a kind nature might otherwise have divided among all the members. Mendel's older sons were healthy. No defect could be found on their bodies, and they had to begin to torture themselves, to fast and drink black coffee and to hope for at least some temporary heart disease, although the war against Japan was already over. [. . .][4]

Finally, on the twenty-sixth of March, both brothers journeyed to Targi. Both drew service numbers in the lots. Both were perfectly healthy. Both were accepted. They were allowed to pass one more summer at home. They had to report in the autumn. On a Wednesday they became soldiers; on a Sunday they returned home. [. . .][5]

"We have been taken," said Jonas, without any other greeting.

A dreadful silence suddenly filled the room in which a moment before the voices of the children had sounded, an infinite silence much vaster than the space which contained it, and nevertheless born out of the one little word "taken" that Jonas had just spoken. In the middle of a word that they had memorized, the children stopped their lesson. Mendel who had been walking up and down in the room stopped in his tracks, stared before him, lifted his arms and let them fall. The mother, Deborah, sank upon one of the two stools which always stood near the stove as though she had long been waiting to take up the role of a mourning mother. Miriam, the daughter, groped her way to the corner; her heart beat loudly; she thouht that everyone must hear it. The children sat as though nailed to their places. Their legs in gaily striped woollen stockings, which had swung continually through the lesson, hung lifeless under the table. Outside, it snowed uninterruptedly, and the soft white of the flakes sent a dull stream of light through the window into the room and upon the faces of the silent people. Sometimes one heard an ember crackle in the stove, and the gentle rattle of the doorposts as the wind shook them. With their sticks still over their shoulders, the white bundles still on the sticks, the brothers stood in the doorway, heralds of misfortune and misfortune's children.

Suddenly Deborah cried: "Mendel, run, go and ask people for advice!"

Mendel Singer stroked his beard. The silence was broken, the children's legs began to swing, the brothers dropped their bundles and sticks and approached the table.

"What nonsense are you talking?" said Mendel Singer. "Where shall I go? And whom shall I ask for advice? Who will help a poor teacher and how can anyone help me? What sort of help do you await from mankind when God has so punished us?"

Deborah did not answer. She sat still for a little while upon the stool. Then she arose; kicked the stool as though it had been a dog, so that it spun away with a great din; grabbed her brown shawl, which had been lying on the floor like a little hill of wool; bound up her head and throat; tied the fringes in a hard knot at the nape of her neck with a furious gesture as though she wanted to strangle herself; became red in the face; stood there hissing as though she were filled with boiling water, and suddenly spat. She fired the white spittle like a poison shot before Mendel Singer's feet. And as though with this gesture alone she had not sufficiently expressed her contempt, she sent a cry after the spittle, which sounded very like a *pfui!*, but which could not be clearly understood. Before the astonished onlookers had really comprehended, she threw open the door. A strong wind scattered white flakes into the room, blew into Mendel Singer's face, grasped the children by their hanging legs. Then the door banged shut. Deborah had gone. [. . .][6]

4

Not far from the Kluczýsk relatives of Mendel Singer lived Kapturak, a man of no particular age, without a family, without friends, brisk and busy, and in right with the authorities. Deborah set about to obtain his help. Of the seventy rubles which Kapturak demanded before he would even discuss things with his clients, she had a bare twenty-five, saved secretly during the long years of toil and laid away in a durable leather bag under a floor-board in a place which she alone knew. Every Friday she took it up stealthily when she scoured the floor. To her maternal faith the difference of forty-five rubles seemed smaller than the sum which she already possessed. For to the latter she added the years in which she had piled up her money, the sacrifices to which every half-ruble owed its existence and the many quiet, warm joys she had felt in counting it.

Mendel Singer sought in vain to describe to her the inaccessibility of Kapturak, his hard heart, and his greedy pocket. "What are you thinking of, Deborah?" said Mendel Singer. "The poor are powerless, God does not throw them golden stones from Heaven, they never win in the lottery, and they have to bear their fate with humility. To one He gives and from the other He takes away. I do not know why He punishes us, first with the illness of Menuchim, and now with the health of the other children. Ah, the poor man has it hard; when he has sinned and when he is ill, he has it hard. Let each suffer his lot! Let the sons serve, they won't go to the bad; against the will of Heaven there is no power. 'He is the thunder and the lightning. He arches Himself over the whole world, no man can escape Him,' thus is it written."

But Deborah answered with her hands braced against her hips above the bundle of rusty keys: "God helps those who help themselves. That's also written, Mendel! You always know the false verses by heart. Thousands of verses are written, but you notice all of the unnecessary ones! You've become silly from teaching children! You give them what little sense you have, and they give you all their stupidity. You're a teacher, Mendel, a teacher!"

Mendel Singer was not vain either of his wits or of his profession. But the taunts of Deborah ate into him; her reproaches slowly broke down his good nature; and in his heart the white flames of indignation were already kindling. He turned away in order no longer to see his wife's face. It was as though he had already known it such a long time, far longer than the time since their wedding, perhaps since his childhood. For many years, it had looked to him exactly as on the day of his marriage. He had not seen how the flesh had withered on the cheeks like prettily painted plaster dropping from a wall, how the skin stretched itself across the nose, in order to flap the more loosely under the chin, how the eyelids wrinkled into a network above the eyes, and how the blackness of the eyes themselves faded to a cool and sober brown, cool, sensible, and hopeless.

One day—he did not remember when it could have been (perhaps it was that very morning when he himself had slept and only his eye had surprised Deborah before the mirror)—one day, anyhow, recognition had dawned on him. It was like a second marriage, this time with the ugliness, the bitterness, the advancing age of his wife. He found her closer to him than ever; almost physically joined to him, inseparable and for Eternity, but unendurable, painful, and even a little hateful. From a woman with whom he had only coupled himself in the darkness, she had become a disease that was bound to him by day and by night, belonging entirely to him, no longer something he shared with the world, whose faithful enmity was to mean his own destruction. Of course he was only a teacher! So had his father been and his grandfather before him. He himself could not be otherwise. Thus one attacked his very existence when one criticized his profession, one sought to erase him from the lists of the living. And against this Mendel Singer defended himself. [. . .][7]

Meanwhile, Deborah went to the driver Sameshkin and asked him whether he would take her to Kluczýsk sometime in the next few days for nothing.

"Yes," said the driver Sameshkin. He sat on the bare bench around the stove, without moving, his feet in great yellow bags tied round with string, and he stank of home-brewed spirits.

Deborah smelled out the brandy as though it were an enemy. It was the dangerous smell of the peasants, the forerunner of incomprehensible passions, the accompaniment of pogroms.

"Yes," said Sameshkin, "if the roads were better!"

"You took me once in the autumn, when the roads were still worse."

"You're wrong. It was a dry summer day."

"Not at all," answered Deborah, "it was autumn, and it rained, and I went to the Rabbi."

"You see," said Sameshkin, and his two feet in their rags began to swing softly, because the bench was rather high, and Sameshkin was rather short. "You see," he said, "that time when you went to the Rabbi was just before your Jewish holidays, and so I took you with me. But this time you aren't going to the Rabbi!"

"I am going on important business," said Deborah. "Jonas and Shemariah will never be soldiers!"

"I was a soldier, too," Sameshkin commented. "Seven years, though I sat in prison for two of them because I stole. That's nothing!"

Deborah became desperate. All his talk only showed her how foreign he was to her, to her and to her sons, who did not steal and who would never go to jail. She determined to drive her bargain quickly. "How much must I pay you?"

"Nothing at all. I'm not looking for money. I just don't want to go! The white horse is old, the brown one has lost two shoes. And he eats oats the whole day long, when he's run only two versts. I can't keep him any longer, I'm going to sell him. Anyhow, being a driver is no life!"

"Jonas will drive the brown horse to the blacksmith," said Deborah insistently. "He will pay for the shoeing himself."

"Maybe," answered Sameshkin. "If Jonas wants to do that himself he'll have to have a new wheel made, too."

"That, too," promised Deborah. "So then, we can start next week!"

Thus she journeyed to Kluczýsk, to the uncanny Kapturak. Of course she would much rather have gone to the Rabbi, for certainly one word from his thin, holy lips would have been more valuable than the patronage of Kapturak. But the Rabbi received no one between Passover and Pentecost, except in the most urgent cases, where it was a matter of life and death. She met Kapturak in the taproom, where he sat in a corner, at the window, surrounded by peasants and Jews, writing. His cap, with the lining turned upward, lay on the table, next to the papers, like an outstretched hand, and many silver pieces rested in it already, and drew the eyes of all those who stood around him. From time to time, Kapturak counted them, although he knew that no would dare to take even a kopeck. He wrote petitions, love letters, and postal checks for the illiterate. (He could also cut hair and extract teeth.)

"I have a very important matter to discuss with you," said Deborah, talking over the heads of the bystanders.

Kapturak shoved back all the papers with a single gesture. The people scattered. He reached for his cap, shook out the money into his hallowed hand, and tied it up in a handkerchief. Then he invited Deborah to sit down.

She looked into his hard little eyes, which were like light, staring buttons of horn. "My sons have been conscripted," she said.

"You are a poor woman," said Kapturak, in an absent, singing voice, as though he were reading a fortune from cards. "You have not been able to save any money, and no one can help you."

"But I have saved."

"How much?"

"Twenty-four rubles and seventy kopecks. But I've spent one ruble of that already, in order to get here to see you."

"So you've got twenty-three rubles left?"

"Twenty-three rubles and seventy kopecks."

Kapturak lifted his right hand, the index and middle fingers spread apart. "And two sons?"

"Yes," whispered Deborah.

"But a single one costs twenty-five rubles!"

"For me, too?"

"For you, too!"

For half an hour she bargained. At the end of it, Kapturak was satisfied with twenty-three rubles—for one. "At least one of them!" thought Deborah.

But under way, while she sat on Sameshkin's wagon, and the wheels rattled in her insides, and in her head, the situation seemed to her more miserable than ever. Who could choose between her two sons? Jonas or Shemariah? She asked herself this question tirelessly. Better one than both, said her reason, while her heart complained.

When she came home and began to report Kapturak's judgment to her sons, Jonas, the older, interrupted her to say: "I'm willing to join up."

Deborah, the daughter Miriam, Shemariah, and Mendel Singer waited as though turned to wood. Finally, when Jonas said nothing more, Shemariah spoke:

"That's a brother! You're a good brother!"

"No," said Jonas. "I'd like to be a soldier."

"Perhaps they will let you off in half a year," his father comforted him.

"No," answered Jonas. "I don't want to get off. I'll stay with the soldiers."

All murmured the evening prayer. Silently they undressed. Then Miriam, in her chemise, walked coquettishly on her toes to the lamp, and blew it out. They went to sleep.

The next day, Jonas had disappeared. They looked for him all morning. Finally, late in the evening, Miriam caught sight of him. He was riding a white horse, wore a brown blouse, and a soldier's cap.

"Are you a soldier already?" cried Miriam.

"Not yet," said Jonas, and stopped the horse. "Give my love to Father and Mother. I've got a job with Sameshkin, for the time being, until I join up. Tell them that I couldn't stand it at home any longer, though I like you all."

With this, he let his willow switch whistle, pulled on the reins, and rode on.

From now on, he was Sameshkin's stable boy. He currycombed the white horse and the brown, slept beside them in the stall, breathed in enjoyably the acrid smell of urine and sour sweat through distended nostrils. He got their oats and pails of water, hung new bells on the harnesses, filled the troughs, changed the dirty hay in the two wagons for clean straw, drank *samogonka* with Sameshkin, got drunk, and got the girls in a family way.

At home they mourned him as one lost, but they did not forget him. The summer came, hot and dry. The evening sank late and golden over the land. Before Sameshkin's hut, Jonas sat and played the accordion. He was very drunk, and did not recognize his own father, who sometimes slunk by, a shadow afraid of itself, a father who never ceased to wonder that this, his son, had sprung from his own loins.

5

On the twentieth of August a messenger appeared at Mendel Singer's house, to fetch Shemariah. [. . .][8]

Just behind the marketplace they found the horses, as the man had said. They needed no less than three days to reach the border, for they must avoid the railway. Under way it became clear that Shemariah's guide was thoroughly familiar with the country. He made it evident without Shemariah's asking him. He pointed to distant church steeples, and named the villages they belonged to. He named the farms and the estates, and he knew the names of the owners. He often departed from the highroad, and found his way quickly along narrow paths. It was as though he wanted to make Shemariah acquainted with his own country, before the young man departed to visit another.

An hour before midnight they came to the border tavern. It was a quiet night. The tavern stood alone, the only house in the night's stillness, silent, dark, with muffled windows behind which there was no sign of life. About it a thousand crickets chirped unintermittently, the whispering chorus of the night. Otherwise no voice disturbed it. The land was flat; the starry horizon drew a complete circle about it, dark-blue, broken only in the north-east by a light streak, like a blue ring with a setting of silver. One smelled the distant dampness of the swamp, which spread out in the west, and the slow wind which carried the smell over.

"A fine, real summer night," said Kapturak's courier. And for the first time since they came together he spoke of his business. "On quiet summer nights like this you can't always pass the border without trouble. For business like ours, rain is better."

He awakened a little anxiety in Shemariah. Since the tavern before which they stood was closed and silent, he had not thought of its significance until the words of his companion reminded him of their project.

"Let's go in," he said, speaking as one who will not postpone danger any longer.

"Don't be in a hurry; we will have to wait long enough."

Nevertheless, he went to the window and knocked lightly on the wooden shutters. The door opened and let a broad stream of yellow light fall over the darkened earth. They entered. Behind the bar, in the midst of the circle of light cast by a hanging lamp, stood the innkeeper, and nodded at them. On the floor squatted a few men, playing dice. Kapturak sat at a table, with a man in the uniform of a sergeant major. No one looked up. One heard the rattle of the dice and the tick of the clock on the wall. Shemariah sat down. His companion ordered drinks. Shemariah drank some spirits, he became warm, but quieted. He felt more secure than usual; he knew that he was living through one of those rare moments when a man has as much power over his own destiny as has the great power which conferred it upon him.

Shortly after the clock had struck midnight, a shot resounded, sharp and hard, with a slowly expiring echo. This was the sign which they had decided upon, with which the outpost let it be known that the nightly visit of the border officials was over. The watchman disappeared. Kapturak made a sign to the people to disperse. All rose wearily and shouldered their bundles and luggage. The door opened; one by one they dropped out into the night, and trod their way toward the border. They tried to sing, someone hushed them—it was Kapturak's voice. One did not know from whence it came, from the first rows, from the middle, or from the rear. Thus they walked silently, through the thick chirping of the crickets and the deep blueness of the night. After half an hour, Kapturak's voice commanded them: Lie down!

They fell upon the dew-dampened earth, lay motionless, pressed their pounding hearts against the wet soil, their hearts bidding their homeland farewell. Then someone commanded them to rise. They came to a wide shallow trench; to their left a light was blinking, the light of the sentry hut. Dutifully, but without aiming, the sentry fired a shot after them.

"We are over!" cried a voice.

In this moment, the heavens toward the east lighted up. The men looked backward, toward their homes, over which night seemed to lie, then turned again toward the day, and toward the unknown.

One began to sing; all the others fell in with him. Singing they continued the march. Only Shemariah did not sing with them. He thought about the immediate future (he possessed but two rubles). He thought what the morning at home would be like. In an hour his father would rise, murmur a prayer, clear his throat, gargle, go to the washbowl, and scatter water about. Mother would blow in the samovar. Menuchim would babble something or other into the morning; Miriam would comb the white feathers out of her black hair. Shemariah saw all this more clearly than he had ever seen it when he was still at home and himself a participant in the morning rites. He hardly heard the singing of the others, only his feet took up the rhythm and marched with it.

An hour later he glimpsed the first foreign town, the blue smoke from the first busy smokestacks, a man with a yellow armband who received the arrivals. A tower clock struck six.

The wall clock of the Singers who struck six. Mendel arose, gargled, cleared his throat, murmured a morning prayer. Deborah already stood at the stove and blew into the samovar. Menuchim babbled something incoherent in his corner. Miriam combed her hair before the blinded mirror. Then Deborah, still standing at the stove, swallowed her hot tea.

"Where is Shemariah?" she said suddenly. They had all been thinking of him.

"God will help him!" said Mendel Singer. And thus the day began.

And thus began the days which followed, empty days, wretched days. "A house without children—" thought Deborah. "I bore them all, I suckled them all, a wind has blown them away." She looked about for Miriam; she seldom found her daughter at home. Menuchim alone remained for his mother. Whenever she passed his corner he stretched out his arms. And when she kissed him, he sought for her breast, like an infant. She thought reproachfully of the blessing whose fulfilment was so long postponed, and she doubted whether she would live to see the healing of Menuchim.

The house was silent when the sing-song of the studying children ceased. It was silent and gloomy. Winter returned. One had to save oil. One went to bed early. One sank thankfully into the kindly night. From time to time Jonas sent a greeting. He served in Pskov, enjoyed his usual excellent health, and had no trouble with his superiors. Thus the years passed.

6

On a late summer afternoon a stranger entered the house of Mendel Singer. The door and windows stood open. Black and satiated, the flies stuck motionless to the hot sunny walls, and the sing-song of the scholars streamed out of the open house into the white street. Suddenly they observed the strange man framed in the doorway and became dumb. Deborah got up from her stool. Miriam hurried across from the other side of the street holding the wobbling Menuchim firmly by the hand. Mendel Singer stood before the stranger and measured him with his glance.

He was an extraordinary man. He wore a wide black hat, light-colored flapping trousers, good yellow boots, and over his bright green shirt a shrill red cravat floated like a flag. Without moving he said something, obviously a greeting, in an unintelligible language. It sounded as though he spoke with a cherry in his mouth. And furthermore green stems were sticking out of his coat pocket. His smooth long upper lip raised itself slowly like a curtain and revealed strong yellow teeth reminiscent of a horse. The children laughed, and even Mendel Singer grinned. The stranger pulled out a letter folded lengthwise and read the address and the names of the Singers in his peculiar fashion, so that everybody laughed again.

"America!" cried the man finally and handed Mendel Singer a letter. Happy anticipation awoke in Mendel and shone in his face.

"Shemariah," he said. With a gesture of his hand he dismissed the scholars, as one shoos away flies. They ran out. The stranger seated himself. Deborah set tea, preserves, lemonade upon the table. Mendel opened the letter. Deborah and Miriam also sat down. And Singer began to read the following:

Dear Father, beloved Mother, dear Miriam, and my good Menuchim! I don't address Jonas because he is with the soldiers. Also I beg you not to send this letter to him directly, because he might have unpleasant difficulties if he is found corresponding with a brother who is a deserter. That's why I've waited so long and have not written you through the post, until I finally had an opportunity to send you this letter with my good friend Mac. He knows all about you through the tales I have told him, but he won't be able to speak a word with you, because he's not only an American but his parents were born in America, and also he's not a Jew. But he's better than ten Jews.

Well, I must begin to tell you all about everything from the beginning until now: First, when I got over the border, I had nothing to eat, only two rubles in my pocket, but I thought to myself, God will provide. A man came along from a Trieste shipping company, he had on an official cap and he had to bring us from the border. There were twelve men of us, the other eleven all had some money; they bought themselves forged papers and steamship tickets, and the agent of the shipping company took them to the train. I went along. I thought to myself, it can't do any harm. I'll go along and in any case I'll see how one gets to go to America. So when I stayed back with the agent, he was surprised that I didn't travel with the others. 'I haven't got a kopeck,' I said to the agent. He asked whether I could read or write. 'A little,' I said, 'but perhaps not enough.' Well, to make a long story short, the man had a job for me. Every day when the deserters arrived, I had to go to the border, fetch them, buy everything for them, and talk to them into believing that America was a land flowing with milk and honey. Well, I began to work, and fifty per cent of everything I earned I had to give to the agent because I was only a subagent. He wore a cap with the firm's name on it in gold embroidery, but I just had an arm-band. After two months I told him I had to get sixty per cent or I'd throw up the job. He gave sixty. To make a long story short, I got acquainted with a pretty girl where I lived; Vega was her name, and now she's your daughter-in-law. Her father gave us some money so that I could go into business, but I never could forget how the other eleven went to America and how I alone remained behind. So I said goodbye to Vega. I knew all about ships— after all it was my trade—and so I went to America. And here I am. Vega came two months ago; we've gotten married and we're very happy. Mac has the pictures in his pocket. First I sewed buttons on pants, then I ironed pants, then I sewed the lining in the sleeves, and pretty soon I was almost a tailor, like all Jews in America. But then I met Mac on a ferry boat to Staten Island, going to Fort Lafayette. When you get here I'll show you the place. From then on I began to work with him at all sorts of businesses. Finally we took up insurance. I insure the Jews and he the Irish. I've even insured a few Christians. Mac will give you ten dollars from me. You buy something with it for the journey. Because soon, with God's help, I'll send you steamship tickets.

I embrace and kiss you all.

    Your son,
      Shemariah
      (here I'm called Sam)

When Mendel Singer had finished the letter there was a vibrant silence in the room that seemed to melt into the stillness of the late summer afternoon, and out of which all the members of the family seemed to hear the voice of the emigrant son. Yes, Shemariah himself spoke over there in faraway America, where in this hour it was perhaps night or morning. For a moment they all forgot Mac's pres ence. It was a though he had become invisible behind the distant Shemariah. He was like a messenger who delivers a letter, goes on, and disappears. He himself had to remind them of his presence.

He got up and reached into his trousers pockets like a magician who begins to conjure something. He brought out a pocketbook, and took out of it ten dollars and two photographs. One depicted Shemariah with his wife Vega on a bench in a park, and in the other he was along in a bathing suit on a beach, one body and one face among a dozen bodies and faces, no longer Shemariah but a Sam.

The stranger handed the money and the pictures to Deborah, after he had looked them all over as if to assure himself that each one of them belived in his trustworthiness. She held the note folded in one hand; with the other she put the pictures on the table beside the letter. All this lasted a few moments, in which everybody remained silent.

Finally, Mendel Singer laid his index finger upon the photographs and said: "That is Shemariah!"

"Shemariah!" repeated the others. And even Menuchim who now reached above the table gave a clear whinny, and cast one of his shy glances upon the pictures, with cross-eyed cautiousness.

Suddenly it seemed to Mendel Singer as though the stranger was no longer a stranger and as though he understood the same speech.

"Tell me something!" he said to Mac.

And the American as though he had understood Mendel's words, began to move his great mouth and to recount something unintelligible with gay energy, and spoke the words as though he were chewing something good with relish. He told the Singers that he had come to Russia to do some business with hops because he was thinking of starting a brewery in Chicago, but the Singers did not understand. Now that he was here he certainly didn't want to miss visiting the Caucasus and he especially wanted to climb Mount Ararat because he had read about it in the Bible. The audience strained themselves to listen to Mac's account, hoping that they would catch a single tiny intelligible syllable out of the storm of words, and their hearts leaped at the word Ararat which sounded strangely familiar to them although he had changed it dismayingly and rolled it out with a dangerous and terrible rumble.

Mendel Singer along could not stop smiling. He liked to hear the language which had now become that of his son Shemariah, and while Mac talked Mendel tried to imagine how the son looked when he also spoke such words. Presently it seemed to him as though the voice of his own son spoke out of the gaily grinding mill of the stranger's mouth.

The American ended his talk, went around the table, and pressed everybody heartily by the hand. He lifted Menuchim swiftly in the air; observed the distorted head, the thin neck, the blue, lifeless hands, and the crooked legs; and set him upon the ground with a tender and considerate contempt, as though he wished to express the idea that strange creatures like this should cower on the earth and not stand at tables. Then he went out through the open door, tall, broad, swaying a little as he walked, his hands in his trousers pockets, with the whole family crowding after him. They all shaded their eyes with their hands, looking into the sunny street through the midst of which strode Mac, and at the end of which he stopped again for a moment to wave back.

For a long time they stayed outside, even after Mac had disappeared. They held their hands above their eyes and gazed into the dust-laden rays of the sun on the empty street.

Finally Deborah said, "Well, he's gone!" And as though the stranger had just then disappeared, they all turned and stood each with his arm about another's shoulder before the photographs on the table.

"How much are ten dollars?" asked Miriam and began to count up.

"It doesn't matter," said Deborah, "how much ten dollars are. We certainly won't buy ourselves anything with it."

"Why not?" asked Miriam. "Shall we travel in these rags?"

"Who's traveling and where?" cried the mother.

"To America," said Miriam and smiled. "Sam wrote it himself."

For the first time a member of the family had called Shemariah Sam, and it was as though Miriam had intentionally used the American name of her brother in order to lend emphasis to his demand that the family should come to America.

"Sam!" cried Mendel Singer. "Who is Sam?"

"Yes," echoed Deborah. "Who is Sam?"

"Sam," said Miriam, still smiling, "is my brother in America and your son!"

The parents were silent. Suddenly Menuchim's voice sounded clearly out of the corner into which he had crept.

"Menuchim can't go!" said Deborah gently, as though she feared that the sick child might understand.

"Menuchim can't go!" repeated Mendel Singer just as softly.

The sun seemed to sink rapidly. The all started through the open window at the wall of the house across the way, upon which the black shadows rose visibly as a lake rises over its boundaries with the beginning of a flood. A faint wind stirred and the shutters rattled in their hinges.

"Close the door, there's a draught!" said Deborah.

Miriam went to the door. Before she touched the latch she stood still a second and looked through the door in the direction in which Mac had disappeared. Then Miriam banged the door and said, "That's the wind."

Mendel stood at the window. He saw how the evening shadows crept up the wall. He lifted his head and observed how the sun gilded the ridge-pole of the house across the street. He stood for a long time thus, the room, his wife, his daughter Miriam, and the sick Menuchim at his back. He felt all of them and was conscious of every move. He knew that Deborah laid her head on the table in order to weep, that Miriam turned her face toward the stove, and that her shoulders shook now and then, although she did not weep at all. He knew that his wife was only waiting for the moment when he would seize his prayer book, in order to go into the house of prayer for the evening service, and Miriam would take up her shawl to hurry across to the neighbors. [. . .][9]

The narrow street darkened completely, and came to life at the same time. The fat wife of Chaim, the glazier, and the ninety-year-old grandmother of the long dead locksmith, Yossel Kopp, fetched chairs out of their houses, in order to sit before their doorsteps and enjoy the fresh evening air. Black and hurrying, the Jews hastened to the synagogue, with curt murmured greetings. Then Mendel Singer turned around; it was also time for him to go. He passed Deborah, whose head still rested on the hard table. Her face, that Mendel Singer had been unable, for years, to stand the sight of, was buried now, as though planted in the hard wood, and the darkness which began to fill the room also covered the hardness and the shyness of Mendel Singer. His hand caressed the broad back of his wife. Once this flesh had been familiar to him; it was strange to him now.

She raised herself and said, "You are going to your prayers!" And because she was thinking of something else, she turned the phrase around, and said in an absent-minded voice, "To your prayers, you are going!"

Miriam in her yellow shawl left the house at the same time as her father, and went to the neighbors.

It was the first week in the month of Ab. The Jews assembled after evening prayers to greet the new moon, and, because the night was pleasant and refreshing after the hot day, they followed more willingly and believingly than usual the commandment of God to welcome the rebirth of the moon in an open place, over which the heavens could arch more widely than over the narrow streets of the little town. They hurried on, silent and black, in irregular groups, behind the houses; saw in the distance the forest, dark and silent as themselves but eternal in its deep-rootedness; saw the veils of night above the broad fields. Finally they stopped. They gazed at the heavens and sought for the silver curve of the new satellite that today should be born again as on the day of its creation. They closed their ranks, opened their prayer books—the pages shimmered white, the angular letters stood out black in the blue night light—and began to murmur the greeting to the moon, rocking their bodies to and fro, so that they looked as though shaken by an invisible wind. They swayed ever more rapidly; their prayers came louder and louder; they flung the native, primeval words aggressively at the distant skies. The earth on which they stood was alien to them; the forest stared back at them with enmity; the barking of the dogs, whose suspicious ears they had awakened, was full of malice. Only in the moon did they feel confidence, the moon, born today in this world as it had been in the land of their fathers, and in the Lord, who watched over all, at home and in exile.

With a loud *Amen* they closed the blessing, extended their hands to each other, and wished each other a happy month, prosperity in business, and health for the sickly. They parted; one by one they walked home, disappearing behind the little doors of their crooked houses. Only one Jew remained behind, Mendel Singer.

His companions had taken leave of him only a few minutes before, but it seemed to him that he had stood there for an hour. He breathed in the undisturbed peace of the open, took a few steps forward, felt tired, had the desire to lay himself upon the ground, but felt nervous about the unknown earth and the dangerous snakes which probably were hidden about. He thought of his lost son Jonas. Jonas slept in a barracks now, on the hay, in a stall, probably next to horses. His son Shemariah lived on the other side of the water. Who was farther way, Jonas or Shemariah? There at home Deborah had the dollars hidden, and Miriam was telling the neighbors, now, about the visit of the American.

The young sickle moon was already spreading a strong silver light. Faithfully accompanied by the brightest star of the heavens she sailed through the night. Sometimes the dogs howled and frightened Mendel. They tore at the peace of the earth and increased Mendel Singer's unrest. Although he was only five minutes away from the houses of the town, he seemed to himself infinitely distant from the inhabited world of the Jews, indescribably alone, threatened by dangers, and yet incapable of going back.

He turned northward. There breathed the dark forest. To the right of the swamp, with a few isolated, silvery willows, stretched away for many versts. To the left lay fields, under opal veils.

Sometimes Mendel thought he heard human sounds coming from an uncertain direction. He heard familiar voices, and it almost seemed to him as though he understood what they said. Then he remembered that he had heard them long ago, that he was listening to an echo which had long been waiting in his memory.

Suddenly there was a rustling to the left, in the wheat, although no wind stirred. The rustling seemed closer. Now Mendel could also see how the man-high ears of wheat moved. Something must be slinking amongst them, a human being, a huge animal, perhaps a monster. It would have been well to run away, but Mendel waited and prepared for death. A peasant or a soldier would now emerge from the grain, accuse Mendel of theft, and beat him then and there—stone him, perhaps. Or it might be a tramp, a murderer, a criminal, who would not wish to be seen or heard. "Almighty God!" whispered Mendel.

Then he heard voices. There were two of them, who passed through the grain, and that it was not one quieted the Jew, although he said to himself that there might well be two murderers. No, they were not murderers, but lovers. A girl's voice spoke. A man laughed. Even lovers could be dangerous. There were many cases where a man had become furious when he caught a witness of his love affair. Soon they must emerge from the field. Mendel Singer overcame his terrified disgust of snakes, and softly lay down, his eyes turned toward the wheat. Then the ears parted; the man emerged first, a man in uniform, a soldier in a dark-blue cap, booted and spurred, the metal shining and clinking softly. Behind him a yellow shawl gleamed, a yellow shawl, a yellow shawl. A voice arose, the voice of the girl. The soldier turned, laid his arm about her shoulders; now the shawl parted, the soldier went behind the girl, his hands held her breasts, she sank back against him.

Mendel Singer closed his eyes, and let the catastrophe pass by him in darkness. If he had not feared to reveal himself, he would have stopped his ears also, in order not to hear. But as it was he had to hear: dreadful words, the silver clink of spurs, suppressed, senseless giggles, and a deep laugh from the man. Now, with longing, he awaited the yapping of the dogs. If only they would howl loudly, very loudly. If only murderers would come out of the wheat, to attack him! The voices became more distant. Everything was gone. Nothing had been.

Mendel Singer stood up hurriedly, looked round about him, lifted with both hands the skirts of his long coat, and fled in the direction of the town. The shutters were closed, but many women sat before the doors and gossiped or called to each other stridently. He slowed his walk. in order not to attract attention; but he took long strides, his coat skirts still in his hands. He stopped before his own house. He knocked on the window. Deborah opened it.

"Where is Miriam?" asked Mendel.

"She has gone for a walk," said Deborah. "You can't hold her any longer. Day and night she goes walking. She is hardly in the house for half an hour. God has punished me with these children. Did anyone ever in this world—"

"Be quiet," Mendel Singer interrupted her. "When Miriam comes home, say that I was asking for her. I shall not come home tonight, only tomorrow morning. Today is the anniversary of the death of my grandfather Zallel. I go to pray."

And he departed without waiting for an answer from his wife.

It could hardly have been three hours since he had left the synagogue. Now that he entered it again, it seemed to him as though he had returned there after many weeks, and he stroked with a tender hand the lid of his old prayer desk and celebrated the homecoming with it. He lifted the lid and reached for his old, black, heavy book, which felt so at home in his hands that he would have recognized it instantly, without hesitation, among a thousand similar books. So familiar to him was the leathern smoothness of the binding, with the round, raised little islands of tallow, the encrusted remains of innumerable candles burned long ago; so familiar the under corners of the pages, yellowish, porous, greasy, thrice curled by a decade of turning them with moistened fingers. Any prayer that he needed at the moment he could turn to immediately. It was buried in his memory with the smallest feature of that physiognomy which it carried in this book, the number of the line, the character and size of the print, and the exact color tone of the page.

It was twilight in the synagogue. The yellow light of the candles on the eastern wall, next to the cabinet with the Torah rolls, did not dismiss the darkness, but seemed rather to bury itself in it. Through the window one saw the heavens, and a few stars. One could recognize all the objects in the room, the desks, pews, the table, the benches, the paper shavings on the floor, the candelabra on the walls, a few covers with golden fringes. Mendel Singer lighted two candles, stuck them fast to the naked wood of his desk, shut his eyes, and began to pray. With closed eyes he knew where a page came to an end, and mechanically turned to the next. Gradually his torso slipped into the old, customary swaying, his whole body prayed with him, the feet scraped the floor, the hands closed to fists and pounded like hammers on the desk, on his breast, on the book, and in the air. On the stove bench slept a homeless Jew. His breathing accompanied and supported Mendel Singer's monotonous song, which was like a hot chant in the yellow desert, lost, and familiar with death.

His own voice and the breathing of the sleeper numbed Mendel, drove every thought out of his heart; he was nothing more than a man praying; the words passed through him to Heaven; he was a hollow vessel, a funnel for prayer. So his prayers went out to meet the morning.

Day breathed on the windows. The lights faltered and dimmed. Behind the low huts one saw the sun rise, filling with red flames the two eastern windows of the room. Mendel extinguished the candles, put away the book, opened his eyes, and turned to go. He walked into the open air. It smelled of summer, dry swamps, and awakened green. The shutters were still closed. People slept.

Mendel knocked three times with his hand upon his door. He was strong and fresh, as though he had slept dreamlessly and long. He knew exactly what he must do. Deborah opened the door.

"Make me some tea," said Mendel. "Then I have something to say to you. Is Miriam at home?"

"Of course," said Deborah, "where else should she be? Do you think she is already in America?"

The samovar hummed; Deborah breathed into a drinking glass and polished it brightly. Then Mendel and Deborah drank together, with pursed, sipping lips. Suddenly Mendel set down his glass and said:

"We will go to America. Menuchim must remain behind. We must take Miriam with us. Misfortune hangs over us if we stay."

He was quiet for a moment and then said softly:

"She is going with a Cossack."

The glass fell ringing from Deborah's hand.

Miriam awoke in the corner, and Menuchim moved in his heavy sleep. Then all was still. Above the house, under the skies, a million larks were trilling.

With a bright flash the rising sun struck the window, lit the polished tin of the samovar, and transformed it into a curved mirror.

Thus the day began.

7

One traveled to Dubno with Sameshkin's wagon; one traveled to Moscow by railway; but in order to get to America one traveled not only with a ship, but with documents. And in order to get these one had to go to Dubno. [. . .][10]

"I have talked with Sameshkin," began Deborah. "I start for Dubno Monday at five in the morning to get the documents. He wants thirty-five kopecks." And because she was ridden by the devil of vanity she added: "He takes only me so cheaply!"

"You can't go alone, anyway," said Mendel Singer with weariness in his voice and dread in his heart. "I have talked with many Jews who know all about it. They say that I must appear in person before the *uriadnik*."

"You before the *uriadnik*?"

It was really not simple to imagine Mendel Singer in an office. Never in his life had he spoken with a *uriadnik*. He had never met a policeman without trembling. He carefully avoided uniformed men, horses, and dogs. Mendel should speak with the *uriadnik*?

"Don't mix in with things that you can only mess up, Mendel," said Deborah. "I'll fix everything myself."

"All Jews," insisted Mendel, "have told me that I must appear personally."

"Then we will go together on Monday!"

"And where will Menuchim be?"

"Miriam will stay with him!"

Mendel looked at his wife. He sought, with his glance, to catch her eyes, which hid themselves fearfully under her lids. Miriam, who watched the table from her corner, caught her father's glance, and her heart beat faster. Monday she had a rendezvous. She had a rendezvous on Monday. She had a rendezvous for the whole hot midsummer. Her love blossomed late, among the high ears of the wheat. Miriam feared the harvest. Already she sometimes heard the peasants preparing for it, whetting their scythes on the blue grindstones. Where could they go when the fields were bare? She must go to America. She had a vague picture of freer love in America, among the tall houses that hid one better than the ears of corn in the field, and this comforted her about the approach of the harvest. It would be here soon. Miriam had no time to lose. She loved Stepan. He would stay behind. She loved all men; storms broke from them, their violent hands kindled flames in the heart which only they could quiet. The men were called Stepan—Ivan—Vsevolod. But in America there were many more men.

"I don't want to stay alone in the house," said Miriam. "I'm afraid."

"We ought to put a Cossack in the house for her, to guard her," Mendel could not keep from saying.

Miriam reddened. She thought that her father saw her blushes, although she stood in the corner, in the shadow. Her blushes must shine through the darkness; Miriam's face glowed like a red lamp. She covered it with her hands, and broke into tears.

"Go on out," said Deborah. "Close the shutters. It is late."

She felt her way out, cautiously, her hands still before her eyes. Outside she stopped a moment. All the stars of heaven stood there, near, and alive, as though they had awaited Miriam before the house. Their clear golden splendor contained all the glory of the great free world; they were tiny mirrors, in which the wonder of America was reflected.

She went to the window, looked in, trying to discover from the mien of her parents what they spoke about. She released the shutters from the iron hooks that held them back, and closed both wings, as one closes a cupboard. She thought of a coffin. She buried her parents in the little house. She felt no sorrow. Mendel and Deborah Singer were buried. The world was wide and full of life. Stepan, Ivan, and Vsevolod were alive. America was alive, on the other side of the great water, with all its tall houses and its millions of men. [. . .]¹¹

At five o'clock on Monday morning, Mendel Singer arose. He drank tea, prayed, then laid the phylacteries away quickly and went to Sameshkin.

"Good morning," he called, while he was still a long way off. It was as though Mendel Singer already began to negotiate with the authorities, before he even entered Sameshkin's wagon, and as though he must treat Sameshkin like an *uriadnik*.

"I'd rather go with your wife!" said Sameshkin. "She's still good looking for her years, and has a decent bosom."

"Let us start," said Mendel.

The horses whinnied, and switched their hind parts with their tails. "Hai! Vyo!" cried Sameshkin, and cracked his whip.

At eleven o'clock in the morning they came to Dubno.

Mendel had to wait. He stepped, his cap in his hand, through the great door. The porter carried a sabre.

"Where do you want to go?" he asked.

"I want to go to America. What must I do?"

"What is your name?"

"Mendel Mechelovich Singer."

"Why do you want to go to America."

"To earn money; I am badly off."

"You go to number eighty-four," said the porter. "There are many waiting there already."

They sat in a great, vaulted corridor, tinted a mustard color. Men in blue uniforms were on guard before the door. All along the walls stood brown benches—all the benches were occupied. But as soon as a newcomer arrived, the men in blue uniforms made a motion of the hand, and the occupants crowded together, and each time made a new place. They smoked, spat, cracked squash seeds, and snored. The day here was no day. Through the opaque glass of a high, very distant skylight, one got a pale apprehension of day. Clocks ticked somewhere but they seemed to go along independently of time, which in these high corridors stood still.

Sometimes a man in a blue uniform called out a name. All the sleepers awakened. The one called rose, scrambled toward the door, pulled his clothes into order, and walked through one of the high double doors which had a round white button in the place of a latch.

Mendel considered how he would handle this button in order to open the door. He stood up. His limbs ached from long sitting crowded in amongst the others. Hardly had he risen, when one of the blue uniforms approached him.

"*Sidai!*" called the blue man. "Sit down, you!"

Mendel Singer no longer found a place on the bench. He stood beside it, pressed himself against the wall, and wished he could become as flat as the wall.

"Are you waiting for number eighty-four?" asked the blue man.

"Yes," said Mendel. He was convinced now that they intended to throw him out. Deborah would have to come. Fifty kopecks plus fifty make a ruble.

But the blue man had no intention of throwing Mendel out. The blue man set great store by having all the waiting crowd in their places where he could observe them. If one stood up, he might be preparing to throw a bomb. Anarchists sometimes disguised themselves, thought the man at the door. And he beckoned Mendel to come to him, felt him over, asked for his papers. When he found everything in order and saw that Mendel had no place to sit, the blue man said: "Listen. You see that glass door? Open that. There is number eighty-four."

"What are you after here?" yelled a broad-shouldered man who was sitting behind a desk. The official sat directly under the picture of the Tsar. He consisted of a mustache, a bald head, epaulets, and buttons. He was like a fine bust, behind his marble ink-stand.

"Who let you come in here like that? Why didn't you have yourself announced?" rumbled a voice out of the bust.

Mendel Singer bowed himself to the ground. He was not prepared for such a reception. He bowed and let the thunder roll over his back; he wished he could become infinitesimal, one with the earth. It was as though a storm had overtaken him in an open field. The folds of his long coat parted, and the official saw a bit of Mendel Singer's threadbare trousers, and the scuffed leather of his boot shafts. The sight made the official milder.

"Come here," he commanded, and Mendel drew nearer, his head pushed forward, as though he would beat it against the writing desk. Only when he saw that he was reaching the hem of the carpet, did Mendel lift his head a little. The official smiled.

"Let me see your papers," he said.

Then it was quiet. One heard the ticking of the clock. Through Venetian blinds the golden light of late afternoon shone. The papers rustled. Once the official meditated, gazed into the air, and suddenly swatted a fly with his hand. He held the tiny animal in his huge fist, opened his hand cautiously, pulled off a wing, then another, and watched for a second how the crippled insect crept about the desk.

"The petition?" he asked suddenly. "Where is the petition?"

"I cannot write Russian, your Excellency," Mendel excused himself.

"I know that, you idiot. Sure you can't write! I didn't ask for testimonials of your writing ability, but for the petition. And why do we keep a writer? Eh? On the parterre floor? In number three? Eh? For you, you ass, just because you can't write. So go to number three. Write the petition. Say I sent you, so you won't have to wait, and will be taken care of immediately. Then come back to me. But tomorrow. And tomorrow afternoon, as far as I am concerned, you can leave."

Once again Mendel bowed low. He walked out backward, he dared not turn his back on the official, and the way to the door seemed to him infinitely long. He thought he had walked for an hour. At last he felt the door. He turned hastily, grasped the knob, turned it first left, then right. Then he bowed once more. At last he stood again in the corridor.

In number three sat an ordinary official, without epaulets. It was a low, stuffy room. Many people stood about the table. The clerk wrote and wrote, jabbing the pen each time impatiently into the bottom of the inkwell. He wrote briskly, but he was never finished. New people came all the time. And yet he found time to notice Mendel.

"His Excellency, the gentleman in number eighty-four, sent me," said Mendel.

"Come here," said the clerk.

They made room for Mendel Singer.

"One ruble for the stamp!" said the clerk. Mendel fished a ruble out of his blue handkerchief. It was a hard, shiny ruble. The clerk did not take the trouble. He expected another fifty kopecks, at least. Mendel did not understand the rather apparent wish of the clerk.

Then the clerk was angry.

"Are those papers!" he cried. "They're rags! They fall to pieces in one's hands!" And he tore one of the documents, as though by accident. It fell into two parts, and the official reached for the paste-pot to stick it together again. Mendel Singer trembled.

The paste was dry. The official spat into the bottle, then he breathed on it. But it stayed dry. Suddenly he had an idea. One saw in his face that he had an idea. He opened a drawer, shoved Mendel Singer's papers into it, closed it again, tore a little green slip from a pad of paper, stamped it, gave it to Mendel, and said:

"I'll tell you what. You come back tomorrow morning at ten o'clock! Then we will be alone. Then we can talk with each other in peace. Leave your papers with me. You can get them tomorrow morning. Just show the slip."

Mendel left. Sameshkin was waiting outside. He sat beside his horses, on a stone. The sun was setting. Evening had come.

"We don't go until tomorrow," said Mendel. "I've got to come back at ten in the morning."

He sought for a synagogue, where he might spend the night. He bought some bread and two onions, stuck everything in his pocket, stopped a Jew and asked him where the synagogue was.

"We'll go together," said the Jew.

On the way Mendel told him his story.

"Among us, in the synagogue," said the Jew, "you will find a man who will take care of the whole matter for you. He has already sent lots of Jews to America. Do you know Kapturak?"

"Kapturak? Of course! He got my son over!"

"Old clients!" said Kapturak. In the late summer he stayed in Dubno; he served in the synagogue. "That time before, your wife came to see me. I still remember your son. He's had good luck, eh? Kapturak has a lucky hand."

It came out that Kapturak was prepared to take over the arrangements. For the time being, his price was ten rubles per head. Mendel could not pay an advance of ten rubles. Kapturak knew a way. He got the address of young Singer. In four weeks he would have an answer and money, if the son really intended to bring his parents over.

"Give me your green slip, the letter from America, and depend on me!" said Kapturak. And the bystanders nodded. "You go on home today. In a few days I'll be coming your way. Depend upon Kapturak!"

A few bystanders repeated, "Depend upon Kapturak!"

"It's great luck that I met you here," said Mendel.

All of them shook hands with him and wished him a good journey. He returned to the marketplace where Sameshkin was waiting. Sameshkin was just about to go to sleep in his wagon.

"Only the Devil can make sure arrangements with a Jew," he said. "Well, let's start."

"They started. [. . .]¹²

8

Two weeks later a small two-wheeled wagon rolled before Mendel Singer's house in a great cloud of dust, and brought a guest: it was Kapturak.

He announced that the papers were ready. Should an answer come within four weeks from Shemariah, called Sam, the journey of the Singer family would be certain. That was all Kapturak had to say, and that an advance of twenty rubles would be more satisfactory to him than having to deduct the sum later, from what Shemariah would send.

Deborah went into the storeroom, built of decayed wooden boards in the courtyard, pulled her blouse over her head, drew a knotted handkerchief from her bosom, and counted eight hard rubles into her hand. Then she turned down her blouse again, went into the house, and said to Kapturak:

"This is all that I have been able to raise among the neighbors. You'll have to be content with it."

"One makes allowances for an old customer," said Kapturak, swung himself up on his little yellow featherweight wagon, and disappeared as quickly as he had come, in a cloud of dust.

"Kapturak was at Mendel Singer's," cried the people in the little town. "Mendel is going to America."

Actually, Mendel Singer's journey to America had already begun. Everybody gave him advice against seasickness. A few buyers came to look at Mendel's house. They were prepared to pay a thousand rubles for it, a sum for which Deborah would have given five years of her life.

But Mendel Singer said, "Do you realize, Deborah, that Menuchim must stay behind? With whom will he stay? Next month Billes marries his daughter to Fogl, the musician. Until they have a child of their own, they can keep Menuchim. And for that we will give them the house and take no money."

"Is it settled as far as you are concerned that Menuchim stays behind? There are still a few weeks, at least, before we leave, and in this time God might make a miracle."

"If God makes a miracle, He won't announce it in advance," answered Mendel. "One must hope. If we don't go to America, there will be a misfortune with Miriam. If we go to America, we must leave Menuchim behind. Shall we send Miriam to America by herself? Who knows what she would do, alone on the joruney, and alone in America! Menuchim is so sick that only a miracle can help him. If a miracle helps him, he can follow us. Because although America is a long way off, it is still in this world."

Deborah was silent. She heard the words of the Rabbi of Klucz-ýsk: "Do not leave him, stay with him, as though he were a healthy child." She was not staying with him. For long years, day and night, hour after hour, she had waited for the promised miracle. The dead, beyond, did not help; the Rabbi did not help; God did not want to help. She had wept an ocean of tears. Night had been in her heart, misery in every pleasure, since the day of Menuchim's birth. All festivals had been tortures, and all holidays had been days of mourning. There was no spring and no summer. All seasons were winter. The sun rose, but it did not warm. Hope alone refused to die. "He will always be a cripple," said the neighbors. For they had not been visited with misfortune, and he who has had no misfortunes does not believe in miracles.

Yes, and those who have misfortunes do not believe in miracles. Miracles happened long, long ago, when the Jews still lived in Palestine. Since then there have been no more. And yet—hadn't people told of many miraculous deeds of the Rabbi of Kluczýsk? The Rabbi had looked at her, had said his say, had spat three times. And Piczenik's daughter had gone away whole, light-hearted and clear-headed.

Other folk have luck, thought Deborah. For miracles to happen one has to have luck. But Mendel Singer's children had no luck! They were just a teacher's children!

"If you were clever," she said to Mendel, "you would go to Klucz-ýsk tomorrow, and ask the Rabbi's advice."

"I?" asked Mendel. "I should go to the Rabbi? You were there once. Go again. You believe in him; he would give you advice. You know that I don't believe in that sort of thing. No Jew needs a mediator between himself and God. He hears our prayers if we are righteous. When we sin, though, He can punish us."

"Why does He punish us now? Have we sinned? Why is He so cruel?"

"You blaspheme Him, Deborah. Leave me in peace—I cannot talk with you any longer." And Mendel Singer buried himself in a pious book.

Deborah caught up her shawl and went out. Outside stood Miriam. She stood there, rosy from the setting sun, with her smooth, shining black hair, wearing a white dress that now shimmered an orange color. She was gazing straight into the sunset with her great black eyes, which she held wide open, although it seemed the sun would blind them.

"She is beautiful," thought Deborah. "I was as beautiful as that once—as beautiful as my daughter. And what has become of me? I have become Mendel Singer's wife. Miriam goes with a Cossack; she is beautiful—perhaps she is right."

Miriam seemed not to see her mother. She observed with passionate intensity the glowing sun, which was now settling behind a violet wall of cloud. For several days this dark mass had appeared every evening, had prophesied storm and rain, and had disappeared next day. Miriam had noticed that, at the moment when the sun finally sank, over there in the cavalry barracks the soldiers would begin to sing; the whole company would sing, and always the same song: *polubyl ya tibia za tvoyu krasatu.* The day's work was finished; the Cossacks greeted the evening.

Miriam hummed the text of the song, of which she only knew the first two verses: I have fallen in love with you, because of your beauty. A whole company sang this song to her! A hundred men sang to her! In an hour she would meet one of them, or maybe two. Simetimes, even, three came.

She caught sight of her mother and remained standing quiet. She knew that Deborah would come over to her. For weeks the mother had not dared to call Miriam to her. It was as though Miriam exhaled the terror which surrounded the Cossacks, as though she was already under the protection of the strange, wild barracks.

No, Deborah no longer called Miriam. Deborah came to Miriam. Deborah, in an old shawl, stood there, old, ugly, nervous, before the gilded Miriam, holding the rail of the wooden pavement, as though she followed an old law which commanded an ugly mother to stand below a beautiful daughter.

"Your father is angry, Miriam," said Deborah.

"Let him be angry," said Miriam. "Your Mendel Singer!"

For the first time Deborah heard the father's name from the mouth of one of her children. For a moment it seemed to her that a stranger spoke, not Mendel's child. A stranger—why should she say "Father." Deborah wanted to turn away; she had made a mistake; she had spoken to a stranger. She did half-turn.

"Wait!" said Miriam, and Deborah felt, for the first time, how hard her daughter's voice was. "A copper voice," thought Deborah. It sounded like one of the church bells which she hated and feared.

"Stay here, Mother," repeated Miriam. "Let him alone, that man! Go with me to America! Leave Mendel Singer and Menuchim, the idiot, here!"

"I begged him to go to the Rabbi, and he won't. I won't go alone again to Kluczýsk. I'm afraid. He has forbidden me once to leave Menuchim, even if his illness should last for years. What could I say to him, Miriam? Shall I tell him that we go to America because you—because you—"

"Because I run around with Cossacks," finished Miriam, without moving. And she contined: "Tell him what you will; it's none of my business. In America, I'll be even better able to do as I please. Because you married a Mendel Singer, do I have to marry one? Maybe you have a better husband for me? Have you a dowry for your daughter?"

Miriam did not raise her voice, and her questions did not sound like questions; it was as though she spoke of everyday things, as though she gave information about the price of greens and eggs. "She's right," thought Deborah. "God help us, she's right!"

Deborah called upon all the good spirits to help her. For she felt that her daughter was right; she herself spoke out of the mouth of her daughter. And she began to fear herself, as a moment before she had feared Miriam. Threatening things were happening. The song of the soldiers drifted over, continually. The little strip of red sun still shone over the violet.

"I must go," said Miriam, and drew away from the wall against which she had been leaning, fluttered light as a white butterfly from the pavement, walked with quick, coquettish feet, in the middle of the street, out in the direction of the barracks, toward the beckoning song of the Cossacks.

Fifty paces from the barracks, in the middle of a little path between the great forest and Sameshkin's fields, she waited for Ivan.

"We are going to America," said Miriam.

"You won't forget me," begged Ivan. "Always, at this time, when the sun goes down, think of me and not of the others. And perhaps, with God's help, I'll come after you. You must write. Pavel will read me your letters; don't write about our secrets, or I'll be ashamed."

He kissed Miriam, warmly, and many times. His kisses resounded like shots through the evening. A devil of a girl, he thought; now she goes off to America, and I shall have to find me another. There isn't another one about here as beautiful as she, and I have four years still to serve. He was huge, strong as a bear, and shy. His great hands trembled when he went to touch a girl. And he had not been at home in love. Miriam had taught him all he knew. And what ideas she had had!

They embraced, as they had done yesterday, and the day before, in the middle of the field, bedded amidst the fruits of the earth, surrounded and shaded by the vaulted arch of the wheat. The ears of grain lay down willingly when Miriam and Ivan sank upon them; before the two sank on them, the ears seemed to lay themselves down. Today their love was shorter, more passionate, and at the same time anxious. It was as though Miriam must go to America tomorrow. The farewell already trembled in their love making. Even while they grew into each other, they were far apart, separated by an ocean.

"How good," thought Miriam, "that I am going away and not he; that it's not I who'll be left behind!"

They lay for a long time, exhausted, helpless, speechless, as though sorely wounded. A thousand thoughts went to and fro in their brains. They did not notice the rain, which had come at last. It began softly and craftily; it was a long time before the drops were heavy enough to break through the thick golden enclosure of the ears. Suddenly they were at the mercy of the streaming water. They awakened, and began to run. The rain confused them, changed the world completely, took away their sense of time. They thought it must already be late; they listened for the sound of the bells in the tower, but only the rain roared, louder, faster, stilling mysteriously all the other sounds of the night. They kissed each other on their wet faces, pressed each other's hands. Water was between them; neither could feel the body of the other. They took leave of each other hastily; their ways parted; already Ivan was enveloped and invisible in the rain.

"I shall never see him again," thought Miriam, as she ran home. "The harvest is here. Tomorrow the peasants will be scared, because one rain brings others."

She reached home, and waited awhile under the shelter of the eaves, as though it were possible to become dry in a moment. She resolved to enter the room. It was dark. They were all asleep. She lay down quietly, wet as she was, let her clothes dry on her body, and did not stir again. Outside, the rain poured down.

Everybody knew now that Mendel was going to America. One pupil after another absented himself from instruction. There were only five boys left, and they came irregularly. Kapturak had not yet brought their papers; Sam had not yet sent the steamship tickets. But the house of Mendel Singer began to collapse.

"How rotten it must have been," thought Mendel Singer. "It was rotten, and we had not noticed it. He who does not give heed is like a deaf man, but is worse off than a deaf man—so it is written somewhere or other. My father was teacher here, and my grandfather; and here I, too, was a teacher. Now I am going to America. The Cossacks have taken my son Jonas, and they want to take Miriam from me also. Menuchim—what will become of Menuchim?"

On the evening of this same day he paid a visit to the Billes family. [...][13]

It was fixed that Mendel Singer should turn the use of his house over to the Billes family before simple witnesses, and avoid all official measures, which would cost money. Three or four respectable Jews would be sufficient as witnesses. In the meantime, Mendel received an advance of thirty rubles, because his students had ceased to come, and money was still going out.

A week later Kapturak rolled up again in his light yellow wagon. Everything had come: money, steamship tickets, passports, visas, the head tax for each, and even the fee for Kapturak.

"A punctual payer," said Kapturak. "Your son Shemariah, called Sam, is a punctual payer. A gentleman, as they say over there."

Kapturak intended to accompany the Singer family to the border. In four weeks the steamship *Neptune* was sailing from Bremen to New York.

The Billes family came to take an inventory. Deborah was taking with her the bedding, six pillows, six sheets, and six red-and-blue checked quilts. The straw matresses and Menuchim's poor bedding would remain.

Although Deborah had little to pack, and although every stick and stitch of her possessions was listed in her head, she was eternally busy. She packed; she unpacked. She counted the dishes, and then counted them once again. Menuchim broke two plates. He seemed all of a sudden to abandon his stupid inactivity. He called his mother oftener than usual. The single word that he had been able to speak all these years was repeated a dozen times even when his mother was nowhere around.

He was an idiot, this Menuchim. An idiot! How easily one said that! But who could say what storms of terror and misery Menuchim's soul had to bear in these days—Menuchim's soul, which God had buried in the impenetrable fastnesses of his feeble mind! Yes, he was frightened, the cripple, Menuchim! He sometimes crept by himself out of his corner to the door, where he squatted on the sill in the sun like a sick dog, and blinked at the passersby, seeming to see only their boots, their trousers, their stockings, and their coats. Sometimes he would pull suddenly at his mother's apron, and whimper. Deborah would take him in her arms, although he was heavy.

Nevertheless, she held him in her arms, and sang two or three broken snatches of a lullaby that she herself had already forgotten, but that began to awaken in her memory whenever she held her unfortunate son in her arms. Then she set him down again, and went back to her work, which for days had consisted of packing and counting.

She stood still for a moment with meditative eyes. They were not unlike Menuchim's; so without life were they, so helplessly seeking in the unknown distance for the thoughts which her brain refused to deliver. Her distrait glance fell upon the sack into which she was going to sew the pillows, and it occurred to her: "Couldn't we sew Menuchim into a sack?" Immediately she trembled, imagining that the customs officials might stick spears through the passengers' sacks. And she began to unpack, resolved to stay, and to follow the words of the Rabbi of Kluczýsk: "Do not leave your son; he is yours even as a healthy child is." But the strength which belongs with faith was no longer hers, and gradually she was also losing the strength which is needed to endure despair.

It was as though they—Deborah and Mendel—had not voluntarily made the decision to go to America, but as though America had overcome them, had beset them, with Shemariah, Mac, and Kapturak. They could no longer save themselves from America. The documents came to them, the steamship tickets, the head taxes.

"How would it be," asked Deborah, "if Menuchim should suddenly become well—today, or tomorrow?"

Mendel shook his head. Then he said: "If Menuchim becomes well, we take him with us!" And both of them indulged silently in the hope that Menuchim would rise from his bed tomorrow or the day after, strong and well, with sound limbs and a complete vocabulary.

They were to start on Sunday. It was Thursday. For the last time Deborah stood before her stove to prepare the Sabbath meal, the white poppy-seed bread, the briaded hard rolls. The fire burned, hissed, and crackled, and smoke filled the room, as it had on every Thursday for thirty years. Outside it was raining. The rain in the chimney drove the smoke back into the room; the old, familiar jagged dent in the ceiling plaster displayed itself again in its fresh dampness. For ten years the hole in the roof's shingles should have been repaired; the Billes family would do it. The great iron-bound brown trunks stood ready packed, with strong iron rods across the openings, and with two brand new gleaming iron locks.

Sometimes Menuchim crept about them and pounded them with his fists. Then there was an unholy rattling; the locks smote against the iron bands, and trembled, and would not stop. And the fire crackled, and smoke filled the room. [. . .][14]

On Sunday at eight o'clock in the morning, a messenger came from Kapturak. It was the man with the blue cap, the same fellow who had taken Shemariah over the frontier. Today, also, the man with the blue cap stood outside the door, refused the tea which was offered him, silently helped to roll out the trunks and put them on the wagon. A comfortable wagon. Place for four persons. Their feet rested in soft hay; the wagon smelled like the whole land in late summer. The backs of the horses gleamed, brushed and shining, convex brown mirrors. A wide yoke, with many little silver bells, was across their proud and slender necks. Although it was bright daylight, one saw the shower of sparks which their hoofs beat from the stones of the road.

Once again Deborah held Menuchim in her arms. The Billes family were already there; they surrounded the wagon and talked continually. Mendel Singer sat next to the driver, and Miriam leaned her back against her father's. Only Deborah still stood before the door, with the cripple Menuchim in her arms.

Suddenly she left him. She laid him gently down upon the doorsill as one lays a corpse in a coffin, stood up, stretched herself erect, and let her tears flow. Naked tears over her naked face. She had made up her mind. Her son was to stay. She would go to America. There had been no miracle.

Weeping, she climbed into the wagon. She did not see the faces of the people whose hands she pressed. Her two eyes were two great oceans of tears. She heard the clatter of the horses' hoofs. She was off.

She cried aloud; she did not know that she cried aloud; something cried in her; her heart had a mouth and cried. The wagon stopped; she leapt out of it, as light-footed as a boy. Menuchim still sat on the doorsill. She fell on her knees before him. Mama! Mama! babbled Menuchim. She could not rise.

The Billes family lifted Deborah. She screamed; she thrust them off; finally she was quiet. They helped her to the wagon and laid her in the hay. The wagon rolled quickly toward Dubno.

Six hours later they sat in the railway carriage in the slow train, together with many unknown people. The train journeyed gently through the land; the fields and meadows where the harvest was being gathered, the peasants and the peasant women, the herds and the huts seemed to be greeting the train. The sleepy song of the wheels lulled the passengers. Deborah had not spoken a word. She slumbered. The wheels of the train repeated endlessly, endlessly: Do not leave him! Do not leave him!

Mendel Singer prayed. He knew his prayers by heart; he prayed mechanically. He did not think of the meaning of the words; their sound alone was sufficient; God understood what they meant. Thus Mendel Singer deadened his great fear of the water, on which he soon would be. Sometimes he cast an absentminded glance at Miriam. She sat opposite him, beside the man with the blue cap. Mendel did not see how she snuggled close to the man. The man did not speak to her; he waited for the short quarter of an hour between the time when twilight would descend and when the conductor would light the gas lamps. The man with the cap was promising himself all sorts of delights in this quarter of an hour—and later, in the night, when the gas flame would be put out.

Next morning he took leave of the older Singers indifferently. But he pressed Miriam's hand with silent warmth. They had reached the border. The border control took their passports. When they called Mendel's name he trembled. Without any reason. Everything was in order. They were passed.

They climbed into the next train, saw more stations, heard new signals, saw new uniforms. They traveled for three days, and changed once. On the afternoon of the third day they arrived in Bremen. A man from the steamship company bellowed: Mendel Singer! The Singer family revealed themselves. The official awaited no less than nine families. He stood them in a row, counted them three times, called out their names, and gave each a number. Now they stood there, with no idea what to do with the lead checks. He had promised to come back soon. But the nine families—twenty-five persons—did not move. They stood in a row on the railway platform, the checks in their hands, their bundles at their feet. At the farthest corner, to the left, because he had announced himself so late, stood Mendel Singer.

During the entire journey he had hardly exchanged a word with his wife and daughter. Both women had been dumb. But now Deborah seemed unable to endure her silence any longer.

"Why don't you move?" asked Deborah.

"No one is moving," answered Mendel.

"Why don't you ask the people around what we should do?"

"No one is asking."

"What are we waiting for?"

"I don't know why we are waiting."

"Do you think I might sit on my bag?"

"Sit on your bag."

In the very moment, however, when Deborah had spread her skirts to sit down, the official from the steamship company appeared and announced in Russian, Polish, German, and Yiddish that he now planned to accompany all nine families to the harbor; that he would settle them in a barracks there for the night; and that the next day, at seven in the morning, the *Neptune* would lift anchor.

They slept in the barracks, in Bremerhaven, the checks clasped tightly in their fists, even while they slumbered. The balcony trembled and the little yellow electric bulbs swung softly to and fro from the snoring of the twenty-five, and from their constant turning on the hard pallets. It was forbidden to make tea. They had gone to sleep with dry mouths. But a Polish barber had offered Miriam red bon-bons. Miriam went to sleep with a great sticky candy-drop in her mouth.

Mendel awoke at five o'clock in the morning. He climbed out of his wooden bunk with difficulty, looked for the water faucet, went out to see in which direction lay the east. Then he returned, stood in a corner, and prayed. He whispered his prayer, but while he whispered, such intense pain attacked him, clawing and tearing violently at his heart, that he groaned aloud. A few sleepers awakened, looked down, and grinned at the Jew, who hopped and swayed in the corner, rocking his body backward and forward, in a miserable dance to the glory of God.

Mendel had not yet finished when the official pulled open the door. A sea wind seemed to have blown him into the barracks.

"Everybody up!" he cried several times, in all the languages of the world.

It was still early when they reached the ship. They were allowed to peep a few times into the dining rooms of the first and second class, before they were pushed between decks. Mendel Singer did not move. He stood on the top step of a narrow iron ladder. At his back was the harbor, the land, the continent, his home, the past. At his left beamed the sun. The sky was blue. The ship was white. The water was green. A sailor came and ordered Mendel Singer to leave the stairs. He dismissed the sailor with a gesture. He was entirely calm, and without fear. He cast a fleeting glance at the ocean, and drank solace from the infinitude of the moving waters. The ocean was eternal. Mendel knew that God Himself had created it. He had poured it out from His inexhaustible fountains. Now it rocked to and fro between the lands of the earth. Deep down, at the bottom of the sea, Leviathan lay curled, the holy fish, whom the pious and the righteous would eat on the Day of Judgment. The ship on which Mendel stood was called *Neptune*. It was a great ship. But compared with Leviathan, with the ocean, with the heavens, and with the wisdom of the Eternal, it was a tiny ship. No, Mendel felt no anxiety. He quieted the sailor, he, a little black Jew on an enormous ship, before the eternal ocean. He turned again, describing a semi-circle, and murmuring the blessing which is to be said at the first sight of the sea. He turned, in a half-circle, and strewed the isolated words of the blessing over the green surging: "Praised art thou, eternal One, our God, who hast created the ocean and with it hast divided the continents!"

At this moment the siren sounded. The engines began to rumble. And air, and ship, and men all trembled. Only the sky remained blue and silent, silent and blue.

9

The fourteenth night of the journey was lighted by great round fiery spheres discharged by the lightships.

"Now," said a Jew who had made the trip twice to Mendel Singer, "we shall see the Statue of Liberty. She is a hundred and fifty feet high, is hollow in the center, and you can climb up in her. Around her head she wears a crown of light. In her right hand she holds a torch. And the best of all is that this torch burns in the night, and yet is never burned up. Because it's only electric light. That's the kind of trick that they can do in America!"

They disembarked on the fifteenth day. Deborah, Miriam, and Mendel stood close together, because they were afraid of losing each other. Men in uniform appeared. They seemed a little dangerous to Mendel, although they carried no sabres. A few wore clothes as white as blossoms, and looked somewhat like gendarmes and somewhat like angels. Those must be the American Cossacks, thought Mendel, and watched his daughter Miriam.

They were called according to the alphabet. Each arrived at his luggage; no one pierced it with sharp spears. Perhaps we could have brought Menuchim along, thought Deborah.

Suddenly Shemariah stood before them.

All three of them started, in the same fashion.

All three of them saw, simultaneously, their little old house, the old Shemariah, and the new Shemariah, called Sam.

They saw Shemariah and Sam at the same time; as though Sam were superimposed on Shemariah, a transparent Sam.

To be sure it was Shemariah, but it was also Sam.

There were two of them. The one wore a black cap, a black robe, and high boots, and the first downy black hairs sprouted from the pores of his cheeks.

The second wore a light gray coat, a snow-white cap, like that of the captain, wide yellow trousers, a brilliant shirt of green silk, and his countenance was as smooth as an elegant gravestone.

The second was almost Mac.

The first spoke with his old voice; they heard the voice, not the words.

The second slapped his father on the shoulder with a heavy hand, and said—and now they heard the words: "Hello, old man!" But they understood nothing.

The first was Shemariah. The second, though, was Sam.

First, Sam kissed his father, then his mother, then Miriam. All three sniffed Sam's shaving soap, which smelled a little like the lilies-of-the-valley from the woods at home, and a little like carbolic acid. Sam reminded them at once of a garden and a hospital.

Silently, they repeated to themselves that Sam was Shemariah. Then, at length, they were glad.

"All the others," said Sam, "have to go through quarantine. Not you! Mac fixed it. He has two cousins working here."

Half an hour later Mac appeared.

He looked exactly as he had before, when he appeared in the little town; broad-shouldered, loud-voiced, rumbling forth an unintelligible language, his pockets swollen with cookies which he immediately distributed and which he himself began to munch. A screaming red tie flapped over his breast like a flag.

"You've got to go through quarantine after all," said Mac. For, it came out, Mac had exaggerated. To be sure he had two cousins in the service, but they were only in the customs department. "But I'll go with you. Don't worry."

They really had no need to worry. Mac yelled at all the officials that Miriam was his betrothed, and Mendel and Deborah his parents-in-law.

Every afternoon at three o'clock, Mac came to visit them. He stuck a hand through the wire, although this was prohibited, and greeted everyone. After four days he succeeded in freeing the Singer family. How he managed it, he did not divulge. For it was characteristic of Mac that he would brag with enthusiasm of things which were total fabrications, and remain entirely silent about things which he really accomplished.

He insisted that they must see America thoroughly—from an open wagon belonging to his firm—before they went home. He invited Mendel Singer, Deborah, and Miriam, and showed them the sights.

It was a clear, hot day. Mendel and Deborah sat facing the front. Miriam sat opposite them. The heavy wagon rattled through the streets with angry momentum. It seemed to Mendel Singer as though the wagon intended to crush the stone and asphalt of the street for ever, and shake the houses to their foundations. The leather seats burned under Mendel Singer's body like a hot oven. Although they kept in the dark shadows of the high buildings, the heat burned like melted lead through the old cap of black silk rep which Mendel wore on his skull, penetrated into his brain, and soldered it up, with a damp, sticky, painful glow. Since his arrival he had not slept, had hardly eaten, and had drunk almost nothing. He wore his native galoshes of rubber over his heavy shoes, and his feet burned as in an open fire. He held his umbrella cramped between his knees. Its wooden handle was as hot as red iron. Before Mendel's eyes floated a thick veil of soot, dust, and heat. He thought of the desert through which his ancestors had wandered forty years. But they, at least, went on foot, he said to himself. The mad haste in which they now traveled created, to be sure, a wind, but it was a hot wind, the fiery breath of hell. Instead of being cool, it glowed. The wind was no wind; it was shouting and alarm; it was a floating noise. In it were the shrill ringing of hundreds of invisible bells; the dangerous metallic thunder of trains; the tooting of countless horns; the beseeching scream of the tracks at the curves of the streets; the roaring of Mac; the murmur of people around Mendel; the raucous laughter of someone sitting at his back; the unintermittent talk which Sam hurled into his father's face, which Mendel did not understand, but which he answered constantly by a nod, a fearful and yet friendly smile fixed on his lips as though clamped there with iron.

Even if he had had the courage to maintain an earnest mien, as befitted his station, he could not have stopped smiling. He did not have the strength to change his expression. The muscles of his face were paralyzed. He could rather have wept, like a small child. He smelled the sharp tar odor of the melting asphalt; the dry, parched dust in the air; the rancid and greasy stink of the river and the cheese shops; the mordant smell of onions; the sweetish gasoline fumes of automobiles; the foul, swampy smell of fish markets; and the carbolic acid and lilies-of-the-valley on the cheeks of his son.

All the smells united in a hot vapor, together with the noise which filled his ears and threatened to split his skull. Soon he no longer knew whether he was hearing, seeing, smelling. He went on smiling and nodding. America pressed down on him; America broke him; America shattered him. After a few minutes he became unconscious.

He awakened in a lunchroom, where they had brought him in haste, to bathe his face. In a round mirror, wreathed with a hundred little glowing electric bulbs, he glimpsed his white beard and his bony nose, and believed, for a moment, that nose and beard belonged to someone else. He recognized himself only when he saw his family standing about him. He was embarrassed. With difficulty he opened his lips and begged his son's pardon. Mac grasped his hand and shook it, as though he congratulated Mendel on a successful trick or on a bet he had won. The iron clamp of the smile again settled around Mendel's lips, and the unknown power again moved his head so that it seemed as though Mendel nodded. He saw Miriam. Her black hair was disarranged under her yellow shawl, and there was soot on her pale cheeks. Deborah crouched, broad and silent, with distended nostrils and a bosom which rose and fell, on a round stool without a back, and looked as though she would fall any moment.

"What are these people to me!" thought Mendel Singer. "What is all of America to me? My son, my daughter, my wife, this Mac? Am I still Mendel Singer? Is this still my family? Where is my son, Menuchim?"

It was a though he had been cast out of himself, separated from himself, and doomed to live on. It was as though he had left himself behind, in Zuchnow, near Menuchim. And while his lips smiled, and his head nodded, his heart began slowly to freeze. It pounded like a metal drumstick against cold glass. Already he was alone, was Mendel Singer. Already he was in America. . . .

Part 2

10

A few hundred years earlier, an ancestor of Mendel Singer had probably gone from Spain to Volhynia. He had a luckier, more ordinary fate than that of his descendant; in any case, no one recorded it, and therefore we do not know whether it took him many years or few to become naturalized in a strange land. But of Mendel Singer we know that in a few months he was quite at home in New York.

Yes, he was almost a native of America! He already knew that "old man" meant father and "old lady" mother, or vice versa. He knew a few tradesmen from the Bowery who came to see his son; he knew Essex Street, where he lived, and Houston Street, where was his son's place of business—his son Sam. He knew that Sam was already an "American fellow"; that, if one was a refined gentleman, one said "Good bye," "How do you do," and "Please"; that a Grand Street merchant could command respect and might even live on Riverside Drive; and that Sam himself was beginning to think of that address, for himself.

They had told him that America was "God's own country," as Palestine had once been; that New York was veritably a "wonder city," a town of miracles, as Jerusalem had once been. Praying, however, was called "service," and so were good deeds. Sam's small son, born barely a week after the arrival of his grandfather, was called nothing less than Mac Lincoln, and—for time passes quickly in America—would be a "college boy" soon. The daughter-in-law already called the little one "my dear boy."

Incredible to believe, she herself was still called Vega! She was blonde and gentle, with blue eyes which seemed to Mendel Singer to reflect more goodness than cleverness. Let her be stupid! Women need no brains. God bless her. Amen.

Between twelve and two, one eats "lunch"; between six and eight, "dinner." But Mendel did not observe these hours. He ate at three in the afternoon, and at ten at night, as at home, although, to be sure, it must still be daylight at home when he sat down to his evening meal, or even, perhaps, early morning. Who knows! "All right" meant "I agree"; and instead of "Ja" one said "Yes." If one wished another well, one did not wish him health and happiness, but prosperity. In the immediate future Sam contemplated an apartment on the Drive, with a parlor. He already possessed a phonograph; Miriam borrowed it occasionally and carried it tenderly through the streets, as though it were a sick child. The phonograph could play many waltzes, but it also could play Kol-Nidre.

Sam washed twice a day, and the suit he often wore in the evening he called "dress." Deborah had already been ten times to the moving pictures and three times to the theater. She had a dark gray silk dress. Sam had given it to her. She wore a great golden chain around her neck; she reminded one of the Babylonish women, of whom the Scriptures told. Miriam was a saleslady in Sam's store. She came home at midnight, and left at seven in the morning. She said: "Good evening, Father," and "Good morning, Father." And apart from this, nothing at all.

Now and then Mendel Singer heard from the talk around him—it flowed past his ears as a river flows past the feet of an old man who stands on its banks—that Miriam went walking with Mac, that she danced with him, went swimming with him, went to the theater with him. Mendel Singer knew that Mac was no Jew. The Cossacks were also not Jews; this affair had not gone so far; God will help; we shall see. Deborah and Miriam were getting on well together. There was peace in the house. The mother and daughter whispered together, late, after midnight. Mendel pretended to sleep.

He could pretend easily. He slept in the kitchen; mother and daughter slept in the single living room. One did not dwell in palaces, even in America! But at least they lived on the first floor. What luck! How easily they might have had to live on the second, third, or fourth! The stairs were steep and dirty, and always dark. Even during the day one had to strike matches to see the way. It smelled warm, damp, and clammy, and it smelled of cats. And yet one had to mix rat poison and ground glass with dough, and put it in the corners every night. Deborah scrubbed the floor every week, but it was never so saffron yellow as it had been at home. What was the reason? Had Deborah become weak? Was she lazy? Was she old?

All the boards squeaked when Mendel walked through the room. Now it was impossible to guess where Deborah hid her money. Sam gave ten dollars a week. Nevertheless Deborah was indignant. She was a woman; sometimes she seemed possessed. She had a kind, gentle daughter-in-law. But Deborah maintained that

Vega indulged in luxuries. When Mendel heard this sort of talk he said:

> Keep still, Deborah! Be satisfied with the children! Aren't you old enough yet to have learned to hold your tongue! Is it that you can't complain any more that I don't earn enough; does it make you miserable that you can't quarrel with me any more? Shemariah has brought us here, so that we can grow old and die near to him. His wife honors us both, as she should. What more do you want, Deborah?

She did not really know what she wanted. [. . .]¹⁵

No, she did not really know what was lacking. Menuchim was lacking. She missed Menuchim. Sometimes in sleep, or awake, or as she shopped, or in the moving pictures, or as she cleaned the rooms, or baked the bread, she heard him call. "Mama! Mama!" he called. The only word which he had learned to speak he must, by now, have forgotten. She heard strange children cry Mama and the mothers replied. No mother on earth would willingly leave her child. They ought not to have come to America. But they could always go back!

"Mendel," she said, sometimes. "Shan't we go back, and see Menuchim?"

"And the money, and the journey, and how shall we live? Do you think Shemariah has so much? He is a good son, but he is no Vanderbilt. Probably it had to be. Wait, for the time being. We shall see Menuchim here yet, when he is well."

And nevertheless the thought of returning stuck fast in Mendel Singer's mind, and never left him. Once, when he went to visit his son in his store (he sat in the office behind a glass door, and saw every customer come and go, and in silence blessed everyone who entered), Mendel said to Shemariah: "What would you think if I went over to see him?"

Shemariah, called Sam, was an American fellow. He said, "Father, that's impractical. If only we could bring Menuchim here, he'd get well, right off. American medicine is the best in the world. I just read it in the newspaper. They cure such diseases with injections, simply with injections! But since we can't bring him over here, poor Menuchim, why spend the money? I won't say that it's out of the question. But just now, when Mac and I are making big business plans and are short of money, we can't even discuss it. Wait a few weeks. Confidentially, Mac and I are speculating in real estate. We've had an old house in Delancy Street torn down. I tell you, Father, it costs almost as much to tear down as to build! But one can't complain. We're getting on. When I think how we started with insurance! Ups and downs! And now we have this business, you can almost say, this department store! Now the insurance agents come to me! I look at them, think to myself, I know that business, and throw them out! I throw them all out!"

Mendel Singer was not quite sure why Sam threw out all the agents and why he was so pleased about it. Sam felt this, and said, "Will you have lunch with me, Father?" He acted as though he had forgotten that his father only ate at home; he gladly created the opportunity to emphasize how far removed he was from his native customs; he struck his brow, as though he were Mac, and said, "But of course! I had forgotten! But you will eat a banana, Father." And he ordered a banana brought for his father.

"About Miriam now," he continued, in the midst of his meal. "She is getting on. She's the prettiest girl in the shop. If she were working for strangers they would have offered her a job as model, long ago. But I don't want to see my sister showing off her figure in clothes that aren't her own. And Mac doesn't want it, either."

He waited to see whether his father would say anything about Mac. But Mendel Singer was silent. He was not suspicious. He had hardly heard the last sentence. He was filled with admiration for his children, especially for Shemariah. How clever he was, how quickly he thought, how fluently he spoke English, how he could press buttons, and call messenger boys! He was a "boss."

He went into the department for shirts and cravats, to see his daughter.

"Good morning, Father!" she called, in the midst of serving a customer. She respected him. It had been otherwise at home. Probably she didn't care for him. But it is not written: Love thy father and thy mother, but: Honor thy father and thy mother. He nodded to her, and went on. He went home.

He was comforted. He walked slowly, in the middle of the street, greeted neighbors, was pleased by the children. He still wore his cap of black silk rep, the half-length caftan, and the high boots. But the skirts of his coat no longer beat with the tact of hasty wings against his boot shafts. For in America, where everybody hurried, Mendel Singer had first learned to walk slowly.

Thus he wandered toward old age, from morning prayer to evening prayer, from breakfast to supper, from awakening to sleep. In the afternoon, at the hour when his pupils had been accustomed to come, he laid himself on the horsehair sofa, slept an hour, and dreamed of Menuchim. Then he read a little in the Yiddish newspaper. Afterward he went into the shop of the Skovronnek family where phonographs, records, sheet music, and song texts were sold, played, and sung. All the older folk of the neighborhood foregathered there. They talked politics, and told anecdotes about home. Sometimes, when it grew late, they would go into the living room of the Skovronneks and rush through the evening prayer.

On the way back, which Mendel usually tried to prolong, he would imagine that at home a letter would be awaiting him. The letter would set forth clearly and positively, first, that Menuchim had become quite well and intelligent; second, that Jonas, because of some minor offence, had left the service and was coming to America.

Mendel Singer knew that this letter had not come. But at the same time he encouraged himself to believe in it, so that he would have a pleasure in entering his house. He would turn the knob with a lightly palpitating heart. But the moment that he caught sight of Deborah, all was over. The letter was not yet there. This would be an evening like every other. [. . .]¹⁶

It was not Deborah whom he saw first when he entered, but his son Sam. Mendel hesitated a moment on the doorsill. Although he was prepared for nothing except a pleasurable surprise, he suddenly was frightened; a misfortune might have occurred. Yes, his heart was so accustomed to misfortune that he always started with a shock, even after long preparation for good luck. What joyful surprise, he thought, can a man like me experience? Everything sudden is evil; the good creeps slowly.

But Shemariah's voice quieted him.

"Come in!" said Sam.

He drew his father by the hand into the room. Deborah had lighted two lamps. His daughter-in-law Vega, Miriam, and Mac were sitting at the table. The whole house seemed to Mendel to have changed. The two lamps—they were exactly the same—looked like twins, and they lighted the house less than they did each other. It was a though they laughed at each other, and the thought made Mendel gay.

"Sit down, Father," said Sam.

He was not curious, Mendel. Already he was afraid that one of those American stories was coming, which all the world seemed to find funny, and which Mendel could find no pleasure in at all.

"What's going to happen?" he thought. "They will have given me a phonograph. Or they have decided to get married."

He sat down carefully. Everyone was silent. Then Sam said—and it was as though he lighted a third lamp in the room—"Father, we have earned fifteen thousand dollars at one stroke!"

Mendel arose, and shook hands with everyone. Finally he reached Mac. Mendel said to him: "I thank you." Sam immediately translated the three words into English. Mac arose and embraced Mendel. Then he began to speak. He did not cease thereafter. Apart from Mac no one spoke a word during the rest of the evening.

Deborah changed the sum into rubles, and it seemed that she never would be done with figuring. Vega thought about new furniture, and, in particular, about a piano. Her son ought to have piano lessons. Mendel thought of a trip home. Miriam only heard Mac talking, and did her best to understand him. Because she did not entirely understand what he said, she thought that Mac spoke too cleverly to be easily understood. Sam considered whether he ought to put the whole sum of money into his business. Only Mac thought little, if at all; he had no cares, built no plans. He said what came into his head.

The next day they went to Atlantic City. "Nature here is beautiful," said Deborah. Mendel saw only the water. And he remembered the wild night at home when he had lain with Sameshkin in the ditch by the side of the road. And he heard the chirp of the crickets and the croaking of the frogs.

"At home," he said suddenly, "the earth is as wide as the water is in America." He had not wanted to say that at all.

"Did you hear what your father said?" commented Deborah. "He's getting old."

Yes, yes, I am getting old, thought Mendel.

When they reached home a thick, swollen letter was sticking out of the letter box. The postman had not been able to get it in.

"Look," said Mendel. "This letter is a good letter. Our luck has begun. One luck brings another, praise God. May He help us further."

It was a letter from the Billes family. And it was indeed a good letter. It contained the news that Menuchim had suddenly begun to talk.

"Doctor Soltysiuk saw him," wrote the Billes family. "He couldn't believe it. They want to send Menuchim to Petersburg. The big doctors will rack their brains over him. One day, it was Thursday, he was home along and there was a fire in the stove, like every Thursday. A burning stick fell out and now the whole floor is scorched and the walls, we had to tint them over. It cost a pretty penny, too. Menuchim ran into the street, he can walk quite well now, and cried, 'It's burning.' And since then he can speak a few words.

"Too bad, though, that it all happened a week after Jonas left. Because your Jonas was here, on a vacation, and he is really already a great soldier, and he didn't even know you were in America. And he is writing to you, too, on the other side."

Mendel turned the page over and read:

Dear Father, dear Mother, dear Brother, and dear Sister!

So you are in America! It struck me like lightning. It's my own fault, of course, because I never, or I guess just once, wrote to you, just the same, as I say, it struck me like lightning. Don't worry though, I am fine. Everybody is good to me, and I get on with everyone. I am especially good with horses. I can ride like the best Cossack and pick a handkerchief off the ground with my teeth at full gallop. I like such things and I like the army too. I am going to stay here after my service term is up. They take care of you in the army, you get your food, the ones above tell you everything you have to do, you don't have to do any thinking yourself. I don't know whether I write it so that you can really understand what I mean. It's warm in the stalls, and I like the horses. If one of you should come over here you could see me. My captain said that if I stay such a good soldier I can petition the Tsar, I mean his noble and gracious Majesty, to pardon my brother's desertion. That would be my greatest joy, to see Shemariah again in this life; after all we grew up together.

Sameshkin sends best wishes. He's fine.

Here they say sometimes that there'll be a war. If it really should come you must be prepared for me to die, just as I'm prepared for it, because I'm a good soldier.

Just in case that should happen I embrace you all, once and for ever. But don't be sad. Perhaps I'll live.

Your son Jonas.

Mendel Singer laid aside his glasses, observed that Deborah wept, and for the first time in many long years, he grasped both her hands. He drew her hands away from her tear stained countenance and said, almost solemnly:

"Well, Deborah, God has helped us. Take your shawl, run down and bring a bottle of mead."

They sat at the table and drank the mead from tea glasses, gazed at each other, and thought the same thoughts.

"The Rabbi was right," said Deborah. Her memory clearly dictated to her the words which had slumbered in it, for so long: "Pain will make him wise, ugliness good, bitterness mild, and sickness strong."

"You never told me that," said Mendel.

"I had forgotten it."

"You ought to have taken Jonas to Kluczýsk, too. He loved his horses more than he does us."

"He's still young," comforted Deborah. "Perhaps it's well that he loves horses." And because she could never let an opportunity for malice pass, she added: "He certainly doesn't get his love of horses from you."

"No," said Mendel, and smiled peaceably.

He began to think of returning home. Now, perhaps, one could soon bring Menuchim to America. He lighted a candle, extinguished the lamp, and said, "Go to sleep, Deborah! When Miriam comes home I'll show her the letter. Tonight, I shall stay up."

From his trunk, he fetched his old prayerbook, so familiar to his hand. He opened immediately to the Psalms, and sang one after the other. He had experienced grace and joy.

God's broad, wide, kindly hand arched protectingly over him, too. Sheltered by it, and in honor of it, he sang the Psalms, one after the other. The candle flickered in the gentle but fervent breeze kindled by Mendel's swaying body. With his feet he kept time to the rhythm of the Psalms. His heart rejoiced, and his body had to dance.

11

Now care, for the first time, deserted the house of Mendel Singer. She had become familiar to him as a hated member of the family. He was now fifty-nine years old. And for fifty-eight years he had known care. Care left him; death approached. His beard was white; his eyes weak. His back was bent; his hands trembled. His sleep was light, and the nights were long. He wore contentment as a strange, borrowed garment.

His son moved into a wealthy neighborhood. Mendel stayed in his alley, in his old flat, with the blue gas lamp, in the neighborhood of the poor, the cats, and the mice. He was pious, God-fearing, and ordinary, an entirely commonplace Jew.

Few observed him; many people failed to notice him at all. By day he visited a few old friends: Menkes, who kept a fruit shop; Skovronnek, who had the music store; Rottenberg, the Bible copyist; Groschel, the shoemaker. Once a week his three children visited him, with his grandchild and Mac. He had nothing to say to them. They spoke of the theater, of society, of politics. He listened and dozed. When Deborah called him, he opened his eyes.

"I wasn't asleep," he assured them.

Mac laughed, Sam smiled. Miriam and Deborah whispered together. Mendel would stay awake awhile, and then nod again.

Immediately he would dream. He dreamed of events at home, and things which he had only heard about in America: theaters, acrobats and dancers in red and gold, the President of the United States, the White House, the millionaire Vanderbilt, and ever and ever again—Menuchim. The little cripple was mixed up with his dreams of prima donnas in red and gold; or he became a poor gray spot amidst the pale beams in which the White House stood. Mendel was too old to look at this or that with open eyes. He took his children's word for it, that America was God's country, New York a city of miracles, and English the most beautiful language in the world.

Americans were healthy, their women pretty, sport was important, time was money, poverty was a crime, riches a service, virtue was half of success, and belief in oneself the whole of it, dancing was hygienic, rollerskating a duty, charity was an investment, anarchism a crime, strikers were enemies of mankind, agitators instruments of the Devil, modern machinery a gift of God, Edison the world's greatest genius.

Soon men would fly like birds, swim like fishes, foresee the future like prophets, live in eternal peace and harmony, and build skyscrapers to touch the stars.

The world will be very beautiful, thought Mendel. How lucky my grandchild is! He will live through it all!

And, nevertheless, mixed with his admiration for the future was a nostalgia for Russia, and it calmed and comforted him to think that, before the living had their triumph, he would be dead. He did not know why he felt so. But it eased him. He was already too old for these new things, and too weak for triumph. But he had one hope left: to see Menuchim. Sam or Mac would go over and fetch him. Perhaps Deborah would go, too.

It was summer. The vermin in Mendel's flat reproduced themselves zealously, although the little metal wheels on the feet of the bed stood day and night in basins of kerosene, and although Deborah, with a feather dipped in turpentine, painted all the cracks in the furniture. The bedbugs marched down the walls in orderly ranks, went into formations on the ceiling, waited with bloodthirsty malice for the advent of darkness, and fell upon the camp of the sleepers. The cockroaches ran out of the cracks near the kitchen sink, among the dishes, into the food. The nights were hot and oppressive. Through the open window came, from time to time, the distant rumble of unknown trains, the short, regular thunder of miles of busy world, and the thick steam from neighbors' houses, from garbage cans and dirty gutters. Cats yowled, homeless dogs howled, infants shrieked through the night, and above Mendel Singer's head the footsteps of the sleepless creaked, the sneezes of those who had caught cold boomed, and he could hear, he thought, the meowing yawns of the weary.

Mendel Singer lighted the candle in the green bottle next to his bed, and went to the window. There he saw the red reflection of a night life which was going on somewhere afar, and the regularly recurrent, silver finger of a great searchlight which swept the sky as if desperately searching for God. Yes, and Mendel even saw a few stars, a few miserable stars, scattered from the main design of the heavens. Mendel remembered the clear, starry nights at home, the deep blue of the great spanning heavens, the softly curving sickle of the moon, the dark rustle of the forest firs, and the voices of the crickets and the frogs. It came to him that it would be easy now to leave the house, to wander out through the night, until he was again under the open sky and could hear the frogs and the crickets and the whimpering of Menuchim. Here, in America, he allied himself with the numerous voices in which the homeland sang and spoke to him—with the chirping of the crickets and the quacking of the frogs. But between them lay the ocean, thought Mendel. One must get into a ship, another ship again, and again travel twenty days and nights. Then he would be at home, with Menuchim.

His children begged him to leave this part of town, once and for all. But he was afraid. He did not want to be rash. Now, when everything was beginning to go well, one must not call down God's wrath. When had he seen better times? Why should he move to another neighborhood? The few years which he expected to live he could pass in the company of the vermin.

He turned about. There lay Deborah, asleep. Formerly she had slept here, in this room, with Miriam. Now Miriam lived with her brother. Or, perhaps, with Mac, thought Mendel, swiftly, furtively. Deborah slept peacefully, half covered, a broad smile on her broad face. What is she to me? thought Mendel. Why do we live together? Our desire for each other is past, our children are grown and cared for, why am I with her? For the meals which she has cooked? It is written, it is not good for man to be alone. Thus we live together.

For a long time they had lived together; now it was just a question which would die first. Probably I, thought Mendel. She is healthy and her cares are few. She still hides money under some floorboard or other. She does not know that it is a sin to do so. Let her hide it!

The candle in the bottle neck burned to its end.

The night was over. One heard the first noises of the morning even before one saw the sun. Somewhere or other people opened creaking doors, blundering steps could be heard on the hallway stairs, the sky was a dull gray, and from the earth yellowish fumes arose, dust and sulphur from the gutters.

Deborah awoke, sighed, and said: "It's going to rain! The gutter stinks; close the window."

Thus began the summer days. In the afternoons, Mendel did not come home to nap. He went to the children's playground. He found pleasure in the chirping of a few sparrows, sat for a long time on a bench, drew with his umbrella crazy designs in the sand. The noise of the water, sprinkled from a long rubber hose over the little lawn, cooled Mendel Singer's countenance. He thought he could feel the water, and he dozed. He dreamed of the theater, of acrobats in red and gold, of the White House, of the President of the United States, of Vanderbilt the millionaire, and of Menuchim.

One day Mac came. He said (Miriam accompanied him and translated) that at the end of July or in August he was going to Russia to fetch Menuchim.

Mendel guessed why Mac was going. Probably he wanted to marry Miriam. He was doing everything he could for the Singer family.

When I die, thought Mendel, Mac will marry Miriam. They are both waiting for my death. I have time. I am waiting for Menuchim.

It is June, a hot and especially long month. When will July finally come?

Toward the end of July Mac ordered his steamship ticket. They wrote to the Billes family. Mendel went into Skovronnek's shop, to tell his friends that his youngest son was also coming to America.

In the shop of the Skovronnek family many more people than usual had assembled. Each had a newspaper in his hand. The war had broken out in Europe.

Mac would not be able to go to Russia. Menuchim would not be able to come to America. The war had started. [. . .][17]

12

All the people who had wagered in political discussions at Skovronnek's that America would stay neutral lost their bets.

It was early winter. At seven in the morning, Mendel Singer awakened. At eight he already stood in the street before his house. The snow was still hard and white, as at home in Zuchnow. But here it would melt quickly. In America it seldom lasted more than one night. The hurrying feet of the newsboys had already been kneading it. Mendel Singer waited until one of them passed. He bought a newspaper and went back into the house. The blue gas lamp was still burning. It lighted the morning, which was gloomy as night itself.

Mendel Singer unfolded the newspaper, which was greasy, sticky, and wet. He read the war news twice, thrice, four times. He read that fifteen thousand Germans had been taken prisoner at one time, and that the Russians were resuming their offensive in Bukovina.

This alone did not satisfy him. He laid aside his glasses, polished them, and read the report from the front once again. His eyes seemed to sift the lines. Would not the names Sam Singer, Jonas, Menuchim, fall out of them?

"What's the news in the papers?" Deborah asked every morning.

"None at all," answered Mendel. "The Russians are winning, and the Germans are being taken prisoner."

It was still. Over an alcohol lamp the tea was brewing. It sang almost as it did in the samovar at home. But the tea tasted different; it was rancid, an American tea, although the little package came wrapped in Chinese paper.

"One can't even drink the tea!" said Mendel, and wondered at himself for mentioning such trivialities. Perhaps he wanted to say something else. There was so much of importance in the world, and Mendel complained of the tea. The Russians were conquering, the Germans were being taken prisoner. But one heard nothing from Sam, and nothing from Menuchim.

Mendel had written two weeks before. And the Red Cross had reported that Jonas was missing.

"He is probably dead," thought Deborah, in silence. Mendel thought the same. But they spoke for a long time over the exact meaning of the word "missing," and always as though this word definitely shut out any possibility of death. They spoke as though it could mean only "taken prisoner," or "deserted," or "wounded and in prison."

Why did Sam wait so long to write? Well, he was probably on a prolonged march, or was being "shifted." At Skovronnek's they talked very wisely about "shiftings" and "regroupings."

"One daren't say it aloud," thought Mendel, "but Sam oughtn't to have gone."

Nevertheless, he uttered the second part of the sentence out loud. Deborah heard.

"You don't understand, Mendel," said Deborah. All the arguments for Sam's participation in America's war, Deborah had gotten from Miriam. "America isn't Russia, America is a real fatherland. Every decent person is dutybound to go to war for his own fatherland. Anyhow, God be praised, he is with the regimental staff. They don't fall there. Because if they allowed all the high officers to die, they'd never win! And Sam, God be praised, is along with the high officers."

"I gave one son to the Tsar. That ought to be enough."

"The Tsar is different, and America is different!"

Mendel did not argue further. He had heard it all already. He still remembered the day when they departed, Mac and Sam. Both had sung an American song, marching in the middle of the street. In the evening, at Skovronnek's, the people had said: "Sam, may his luck hold, is a fine-looking soldier."

Perhaps America was a real fatherland, war a duty, cowardice shameful, and death—when one was attached to the regimental staff—out of the question. Just the same, thought Mendel, I am a father, I should have had a word to say. "Sam, stay," I should have said. "I have waited many years for just a morsel of good fortune. Now Jonas is a soldier, who knows what will happen to Menuchim, you have a wife, a child, a business. Stay, Sam!" Perhaps he might have stayed.

Mendel stood at the window, as was his custom, with his back to the room. He looked straight ahead of him, at the Lemmels' broken window across the way, on the first floor. The window had been mended with brown cardboard. Underneath was a Jewish delicatessen store. There was a sign on the door in Hebrew—white, dirty letters on a pale blue background. Lemmel's son had also gone to the war. The whole Lemmel family went to night school and learned English. Evenings they went, like little children, carrying their copybooks. Perhaps they were right. Probably Mendel and

Deborah should have gone to the school. America was a real fatherland.

It still snowed a little—slow, lazy, damp flakes. The Jews, with
open umbrellas waving over their heads, began their promenade up
and down. More and more came. They walked in the middle of the
street; the last white scraps of snow melted under their feet; it
looked as though they had to walk up and down by order of the
authorities, until the snow had entirely disappeared. From his window Mendel could not see the sky. But he knew that it was gloomy.
In all the windows opposite he saw the yellow reflection of gaslight.
Gloomy were the heavens; in every house was gloom.

Soon a window opened here, and another there. One saw the
busts of neighbor women. They hung red and white tickings, and
naked yellow-skinned pillows out of the windows. Suddenly the
whole street was colorful and gay. The neighbor women called loud
greetings to one another. From inside the rooms sounded the rattle
of plates and the cries of children. One might have believed it was
peacetime if martial music had not been booming through the
streets from Skovronnek's phonographs.

"When will it be Sunday?" thought Mendel. Once he had lived
from one Saturday to the next; now he lived from one Sunday to
the next. On Sunday visitors came—Miriam, Vega, the grandchild.
They brought letters from Sam, or at least news of a general nature.
They knew everything. They read the newspapers. They were running the business together, now. It was still going well; they were
all industrious; they put money by, and waited for Sam's return.

Sometimes Miriam brought Mr. Glueck, the general manager,
with her. She went dancing with Glueck; she went bathing with
Glueck. Another Cossack! thought Mendel. But he said nothing.

"I can't go to the war, unfortunately," sighed Mr. Glueck. "I
have a serious palpitation of the heart, the only thing which I inherited from my father of blessed memory."

Mendel regarded Glueck's rosy cheeks, his little brown eyes, and
his downy, coquettish mustache, which he wore in disregard of the
mode, and with which he was constantly playing. He sat between
Miriam and Vega. Once when Mendel suddenly stood up in the
midst of a conversation, he thought that he saw one of Mr. Glueck's
hands in Vega's lap, while the other rested on Miriam's thigh. Men-

del went out into the street; he walked up and down until the guests departed.

"You act like a Russian Jew," said Deborah, when he came back.

"I am a Russian Jew," answered Mendel.

One day, a weekday early in February, while Mendel and Deborah were sitting at table, Miriam entered.

"Good day, Mother," she said, and "Good day, Father," and stood there, still.

Deborah laid down her spoon and pushed back her plate. Mendel looked at both women. He knew that something extraordinary had happened. Miram had come on a weekday, at a time when she should have been at business. His heart beat loudly. But he was self-possessed. It seemed to him that he could recall this scene. It had been played somewhere, once before. There stood Miriam, in her raincoat, and was dumb. There sat Deborah, the plate pushed far away from her, almost to the center of the table, and outside it snowed, gently, flakily. The gas lamp burned with a feeble yellow light. It fought against the dark day, which was dank and weak, but nevertheless mighty enough to paint the whole room with its grayness. Mendel Singer remembered this light exactly. He had dreamed this scene. He knew, too, what was coming. Mendel knew everything, as though it had happened long ago, and as though the pain of it had turned, many years ago, into grief. Mendel was quite calm.

Silence reigned for a few seconds. Miriam did not speak. It was as though she hoped that her father or mother would free her, by a question, from announcing her news. She stood still, and was silent. None of the three moved.

Mendel stood up and said: "A misfortune has happened."

Miriam said: "Mac has come back. He has brought Sam's watch, and his last words."

Deborah sat quiet, silent upon her chair, as though nothing had happened. Her eyes were dry and empty, like two little pieces of glass. She sat opposite the window, and it seemed as though she were counting the snowflakes.

It was so still, one heard the sharp ticking of the clock.

Suddenly Deborah began, very slowly, with stroking fingers, to rumple her hair. She pulled one strand after another over her face, which was pale and immobile as plaster. One after another she rent the strands of hair, one after another, in the same tempo in which, outside, the flakes were falling. Two, then three, white islands appeared amidst her hair, a few spots the size of a dollar where the naked scalp showed, and a few tiny drops of red blood. No one moved. The clock ticked, the snow fell, and Deborah quietly tore out her hair.

Miriam sank to her knees, buried her head in Deborah's lap, and moved no more. In Deborah's countenance not a feature changed. Her two hands tore—now one, now the other—at her hair. Her hands were like pale, fleshy, five-footed animals, feeding themselves on hair.

Mendel stood, his arms folded over the back of the chair.

Deborah began to sing. She sang in a deep, male voice, which sounded as though there were an invisible singer in the room. The strange voice sang an old Jewish song without words, a dark lullaby, for dead children.

Miriam rose, pulled her hat straight, went to the door and let Mac in.

In uniform he looked larger than in his ordinary clothes. In his two hands, which he held before him like platters, he held Sam's watch, his pocketbook, his billfold.

These objects Mac laid slowly upon the table, directly in front of Deborah. He watched her for a while, tearing at her hair. Then he went to Mendel, laid both hands on the old man's shoulders, and wept, silently. His tears ran, a heavy rain, over his uniform.

It was still. Deborah's song had ceased. The clock ticked; evening sank suddenly over the world; the gas no longer shone with a yellow light, but was white. Outside the windowpanes, the world was black; one could see no more snowflakes.

All of a sudden a suppressed scream came from Deborah's breast. It sounded like the rest of the melody which she had been singing, a broken, bursted note.

Then she fell from her chair. Deborah lay, a soft, crumpled mass, upon the floor.

Mac threw open the door, left it standing wide. It was cold in the room.

He came back, bringing a doctor, a little, bustling, gray-haired man.

Miriam stood across from her father.

Mac and the doctor carried Deborah to the bed. The doctor sat on the edge of the bed and said, "She is dead."

"Menuchim, too, is dead. Alone, among strangers," thought Mendel Singer.

13

Seven days round Mendel Singer sat on a stool beside the clothes closet and looked at the windowpane where a scrap of white linen was hung as a symbol of mourning, and where day and night one of the blue lamps burned. Seven round days rolled one after the other, like great, slow black wheels, with no beginning and no end, round and endless as grief.

The neighbors came in turn: Menkes, Skovronnek, Rottenberg, and Groschel. They brought Mendel Singer hard-boiled eggs and the hard circular rolls called *beugels*, round things to eat, without beginning and without end, like the seven days of mourning.

Mendel spoke little with his visitors. He hardly noticed that they came and went. Day and night his door stood open, with the useless bolt thrust back. Who wished to come, came; who wished to go, went. This one or that tried to begin a conversation. But Mendel Singer avoided it. While the others spoke of living things, he talked with his dead wife.

"You are well off, Deborah," he said to her, "It is only sad that you have no son left to mourn you. I myself must say the prayer for the dead, but I will soon die, and no one will weep for us. Like two tiny specks of dust, we shall be scattered. Like two tiny tapers, we shall be extinguished. I have begotten children, your womb has borne them, death has taken them. Meaningless and full of poverty was your life.

"In my youth I took delight in your flesh; in later years I scorned it. Perhaps that was our sin. Because the warmth of love was not in us, but only the frost of familiarity, everything around us perished, or was ruined. You are well off, Deborah. God had pity on you. You are dead and buried. Toward me He shows no pity. For I am dead, and yet live. If you can, pray for me, that I shall be stricken from the book of the living.

"See, Deborah, the neighbors come to me, to comfort me. But although they are many, and they all think hard, they can find no comfort for my condition. My heart still beats, my eyes still see, my limbs still move, my feet still go. I eat and drink, pray and breathe. But my blood congeals, my hands are limp, my heart is empty. I am no longer Mendel Singer, I am but the remains of Mendel Singer. America has killed us.

"America is a real fatherland, indeed, but a death-dealing fatherland. What was life, with us, is death here. The son, who at home was called Shemariah, here was called Sam. You are buried in America, Deborah, and I, too, will be buried in America."

On the eighth day when Mendel Singer stood up from his mourning, his daughter-in-law came to him, with Mr. Glueck.

"Mr. Singer," said Mr. Glueck, "you must come with us immediately. The car is waiting below. Something has happened to Miriam."

"Very well," said Mendel Singer indifferently, as though one had announced to him that a room had to be papered. "Very well, give me my coat."

Mendel crept into his coat with his weak arms and went down the stairs. Mr. Glueck helped him into the car. They drove, and no word was spoken between them. Mendel did not ask what had happened to Miriam. Perhaps she too is dead, he thought calmly. Mac has killed her, out of jealousy.

For the first time he entered the dwelling of his dead son. Someone pushed him into a room. There lay Miriam, in a wide, white bed. Her hair was flowing loosely, in a sparkling blue-black wave over the white pillows. Her face glowed red, and her black eyes had wide, round red rims; circled with rings of flame were Miriam's eyes. A nurse sat near her. Mac stood in a corner, huge and motionless as a piece of furniture.

"There is Mendel Singer," cried Miriam. She stretched her hand toward her father, and began to laugh. Her laugh lasted a few minutes. It sounded like the ringing of the clear, continuous signals at railway stations, and as though someone beat with a thousand brass hammers upon a thousand thin crystal glasses. Suddenly the laugh broke. For a second there was silence. Then Miriam began to sob. She pushed back the coverlet, her naked legs beat a tattoo, her feet beat in a quick, regular rhythm upon the soft bed, ever faster, ever more evenly, while her balled fists struck at the air in the same rhythm.

The nurse held Miriam fast, by main force. She became quieter.

"Good day, Mendel Singer," said Miriam. "You are my father. I can tell you all. I love Mac—there he stands—but I have deceived him. I slept with Mr. Glueck. Yes, with Mr. Glueck. Mac is my Mac; I like Mendel Singer, too, and if you like—"

Then the nurse clapped her hand over Miriam's mouth, and Miriam was silent.

Mendel Singer still stood in the doorway; Mac still stood in the corner. Both men gazed intently at each other. Since they could not communicate with each other in words, they spoke with their eyes.

"She has gone mad," said Mendel Singer's eyes to the eyes of Mac. "She could not live without men. She has gone mad."

Vega entered and said, "We have called a specialist. He ought to be here any moment. Since yesterday Miriam has been speaking strangely. She went walking with Mac, and when she came back she began to act in this queer way. The doctor must be here any moment."

The doctor came. He was a German. He could talk with Mendel.

"We will have to take her to a sanatorium," said the doctor. "Your daughter, I am sorry to say, must go to a sanatorium. Wait just a moment. I will have to make it easier for her."

Mac still stood in the room.

"Will you hold her fast?" asked the doctor. Mac held Miriam with his two great hands. The doctor drove a hypodermic needle into her thigh. "She will soon be quiet," he said.

The ambulance came, two bearers entered the room with a stretcher. Miriam slept. They bound her to the stretcher, Mac, Mendel, and Vega rode behind the ambulance.

"That has been spared you," Mendel Singer addressed his wife Deborah, as they rode. "I must go through with it, but I have known it all the time. Ever since the evening when I saw Miriam with the Cossack in the field I have known it. The Devil entered her. Pray for us, Deborah, that he will leave her again. [. . .][18]

The doctor came in, drew Mendel into a corner, and said softly: "Pull yourself together. Your daughter is very ill. There are lots of such cases now; the war, you understand, and the misery in the world—it's a bad time. Medicine doesn't know yet how to heal this illness. One of your sons is an epileptic, I have heard. You will pardon me—something of the sort seems to run in the family. We physicians call it 'degenerative psychosis.' It can pass. But it can also appear as an illness which we physicians call dementia: dementia praecox—but even the name is uncertain. Anyhow, it is one of the rare cases that we can do little for. You are a pious man, Mendel Singer. The good God can help. Only pray zealously to the good God. By the way, would you like to see your daughter? Come with me!"

A bundle of keys rattled, a door slammed with a loud detonation, and Mendel walked through a long corridor past white doors with black numbers, like coffins set on end. Again the attendant's bundle of keys rattled, a coffin was opened, inside lay Miriam, asleep, with Mac and Vega standing beside her.

"We must go now," said the doctor.

"Drive me right home, to my street," commanded Mendel.

His voice sounded so hard, that all were shocked. They looked at him. His appearance did not seem to have changed. Nevertheless this was another Mendel. He was dressed exactly as he had been in Zuchnow, and during the whole time in America. In high boots, a half-length caftan, in his cap of black silk rep.

What had changed him so? Why did he appear to them all as taller and statelier? Why did his countenance exude so white and fearful a gleam? He almost seemed to tower above huge Mac. His Majesty, pain, thought the doctor, has entered the old Jew.

"Once," began Mendel, in the car, "Sam said to me that American medicine is the best in the world. Now it cannot help her. "God can help!" says the doctor. Tell me, Vega, have you ever seen God help a Mendel Singer? God can help!"

"You must live with us now," sobbed Vega.

"I shall not live with you, my child," answered Mendel. "You will marry another husband, you should not be without a husband, your child should not be fatherless. I am an old Jew. Soon I shall die. Listen, Vega! Mac was Shemariah's friend; he loved Miriam. I know he is no Jew, but you should marry him. Not Mr. Glueck! Do you hear, Vega? Are you surprised that I speak so, Vega? Don't be. I am not insane. I am old. I have seen a few worlds perish, and at last I am wise. All the years long, I was a silly teacher. Now I know what I say."

They came, helped Mendel out, led him to his room. Mac and Vega stood for a while, and did not know what to do.

Mendel sat down on a stool near the clothes closet and said to Vega, "Don't forget what I told you. Now, go, my children."

They left him. Mendel went to the window and watched them get into the car. It seemed to him that he must bless them, as though they were children who start out on a journey which may be very hard or may be very happy. I shall never see them again, he thought; then—I shall not give them my blessing, either. My blessing might be a curse, coming from me it could only harm them.

He felt light, lighter than ever in all his years. He had severed all relationships. It occurred to him that he had been alone for years. He had been alone since that moment when desire had ceased between his woman and himself. He was alone—alone. Wife and children had surrounded him and had hindered him from bearing his pain. Like useless poultices that do not aid healing, they had lain upon his wounds and had merely covered them. Now, at last, he indulged his misery in triumph! There was only one relationship still to be broken. He prepared to do it.

He went into the kitchen, ruffled newspapers together with kindling, and made a fire in the open stove. When the fire had reached a considerable height and breadth, Mendel walked with firm steps to the cupboard, and took from it the little red velvet sack which contained his phylacteries, his prayer shawl, and his prayerbooks.

He imagined to himself how these objects would burn. The flames would seize the yellowish shawl of pure sheep's wool, and destroy it with pointed, blue, greedy tongues. The glittering border of silver thread would slowly be reduced to embers, in tiny, glowing spirals. The fire would gently roll together the leaves of the books, change them into silvery ashes, and for a few seconds paint the black letters the color of blood.

The leather corners of the binding would curl up; like the strange ears with which books listen they would stand up to hear what Mendel called after them as they died. He called a terrible song after them:

"It is over, all over; it is the end of Mendel Singer!" he cried, and his feet stamped in time to the tune, so that the floorboards rumbled and the pots on the wall began to rattle.

"He has no son, he has no daughter, he has no wife, he has no country, he has no money! God said: I have punished Mendel Singer! For what has He punished him? Why has He not punished Lemmel, the butcher? Why not Skovronnek? Why not Menkes? He punishes only Mendel. Mendel has death, Mendel has madness, Mendel has hunger—all God's gifts are for Mendel! All, all over—it is the end of Mendel Singer!"

Thus stood Mendel before the fire, and bellowed, and stamped with his feet. He held the red velvet sack in his arms, but he did not cast it into the flames. A few times he lifted it high, but his arms let it sink again. His heart was angry against God, but in his sinews the fear of God still dwelt. Fifty years, day after day, these hands had spread the prayer shawl and folded it again, had unrolled the phylacteries, and bound them about his head and his left arm, had opened this book, paged in it, and closed it again. Now Mendel's hands refused to obey. Only his mouth did not refuse. Only his feet, which so often had danced to the glory of God, stamped in time to Mendel's paean of scorn.

Mendel's neighbors heard the crying and stamping and, when they caught sight of the blue-gray smoke through the cracks of his door, they knocked at Singer's door and cried that he should open for them. But he did not hear them. His eyes were filled with smoke from the fire, and in his ears sounded the noise of his great, painful exaltation. The neighbors were about to call the police, when one of them said: "Let us call his friends. They are at Skovronnek's. Perhaps they can bring the poor fellow to his senses."

When the friends came, Mendel actually did calm down. He pushed back the bolt and allowed them to come in, one after the other, as they were accustomed to enter Mendel's room: Menkes, Skovronnek, Rottenberg, and Groschel. They compelled Mendel to sit down on the bed, seated themselves beside him and before him, and Menkes said: "What is the matter, Mendel? Why do you make such a fire? Why do you want to set the house on fire?"

"I want to burn more than a house and more than a person. You will be astonished when I tell you what I really intended to burn. You will wonder and say: Mendel is crazy, too, like his daughter. But I assure you, I am not crazy. For more than sixty years I have been mad, but today I am not."

"Then tell us what you wanted to burn."

"I want to burn God."

At this, a cry burst simultaneously from all four listeners. They were not all pious and God-fearing, as Mendel had always been. All four had lived long enough in America, they worked on the Sabbath, their interest was in money, and the dust of the world already lay thick, high, and gray upon their ancient beliefs. Many ceremonials they had already forgotten; they had violated many laws, they had sinned with their heads and with their limbs. But God still dwelt in their hearts. And as Mendel blasphemed God, it seemed to them as though he had taken hold of their naked hearts with sharp fingers.

"Do not blaspheme, Mendel," said Skovronnek, after a long silence. "You know better than I, because you have studied more, that God's chastisements always have a hidden purpose. We do not know why we are punished."

"But I know, Skovronnek," answered Mendel. "God is cruel, and the more one obeys Him the more brutally He treats one. He is mightier than the most mighty; with the nail of one of His little fingers He can wipe them out, but He does not do it. Only the weak He gladly destroys. The weakness of a man tempts His strength, and obedience awakens His scorn. He is a great, brutal *ispravnik,* a real Russian official. Follow the laws, and He says you have but done it for your own advantage. Break but one of His commandments, and He persecutes you with a hundred chastisements. Seek to bribe Him, and He brings a judgment against you. Deal uprightly with Him, and He is impatient for bribes. In all of Russia there is no worse *ispravnik.*"

"Think, Mendel," began Rottenberg. "Think of Job. The same sort of things happened to him as to you. He sat upon the naked earth, ashes upon his head, and his wounds hurt him so much that he writhed upon the ground like an animal. He, too, blasphemed God. And yet, it was only a test, after all. What do we know, Mendel, of what goes on up there? Perhaps the Evil One came to God, as he did then, and said: We must tempt one of the righteous. And God said: Just try it with my servant Mendel!"

"And there you see," continued Groschel, "that your complaints are unjust. For Job was not weak, when God tested him, but strong. And you, too, were not weak, Mendel. Your son had a big store, he was getting richer from year to year. Your son Menuchim was almost well, and he was just about to come to America. You were well and strong, your wife was well, your daughter was beautiful, and soon you would have found a husband for her!"

"Why do you break my heart, Groschel?" answered Mendel. "Why do you tell me all that was, now, when I have nothing left. My wounds have not yet scarred, and you tear them open."

"He is right," said the other three, as though with one mouth.

And Rottenberg began: "Your heart is torn, Mendel, I know. But because we dare to speak about everything with you, and since you know that we share your grief as though we were your brothers, will you be angry with us, if I ask you to think of Menuchim? Perhaps, dear Mendel, you tried to disturb God's plans, when you left Menuchim behind? A sick son was allotted to you, and you acted as though he were a wicked son."

It was still. For a long time Mendel answered nothing at all. When he spoke again, it was as though he had not heard Rottenberg's words, for he turned to Groschel, and said:

"And why do you quote the example of Job? Have you really seen miracles with your own eyes? Miracles, such as were reported of Job, in the end? Shall my son Shemariah be resurrected out of the common grave in which he lies in France? Shall my son Jonas return alive from his long absence? Shall my daughter Miriam suddenly come home cured, from the insane asylum? And if she comes home, will she find a husband, and live peacefully on, as though she had never been insane? Shall my wife Deborah rise from her grave which is still fresh? Shall my son Menuchim, in the midst of the war in Russia, suddenly come here, even granted that he still lives? For it is not true"—and here he turned again to Rottenberg—"that I left Menuchim behind out of unkindness, to punish him. We had to leave for other reasons, because of my daughter, who had begun to run around with Cossacks—with Cossacks! And why was Menuchim sick? His sickness itself showed that God was wroth with me. It was the first blow, which I did not deserve."

"Although God can do all things," began Menkes, the most thoughtful of them all, "it is probable that He no longer performs the greatest miracles, because the world is no longer worthy of them. And even if God wanted to make an exception of you, the sins of the others would count against you. For the others are not worthy even to see a miracle happen to someone righteous. Thus

Lot had to leave his home, and Sodom and Gomorrah perished, and did not see the miracle of Lot.

"But today the world is everywhere populated—and even if you leave your home the newspapers can report what has happened to you. And so God can only perform moderate miracles today. But even those are great enough, praise His name! Your wife Deborah cannot live again, your son Shemariah cannot become alive. But Menuchim is probably alive, and after the war you will see him. Your son Jonas is probably in prison, and after the war you will see him again. Your daughter Miriam may be cured; the madness will be taken from her; she may be more beautiful than ever, and will get a husband, and bear you grandchildren. And you have one grandchild, Shemariah's son. Gather together all the love which you have had, up till now, for all the children and give it to this one grandchild! And you will be comforted."

"Between me and my grandchild," answered Mendel, "the tie is broken. For Shemariah is dead, my son and the father of my grandchild. My daughter-in-law, Vega, will marry someone else; my grandchild will have another father, who is not my son. My son's house is not my house. I have nothing to do there. My presence brings misfortune, and my love draws a curse upon it, as a lonely tree in a level field draws down the lightning.

"But as far as Miriam is concerned, the doctor himself told me that medicine could not heal her sickness. Jonas is probably dead, and Menuchim was ill even when he was better off. In Russia, in the midst of so dangerous a war, he has certainly perished. No, my friends. I am alone, and I will remain alone. During all these years I have loved God, and he has hated me. All the arrows from His quiver have already hit me. He can but kill me. But He is too cruel for that. I shall live, live, live."

"But His power," interrupted Groschel, "is in this world and in the next as well. Woe to you, Mendel, when you are dead!"

Then Mendel laughed outright, and said: "I am not afraid of hell; my skin is already burned, my limbs lamed, and the evil spirits are my friends. I have already suffered all the tortures of hell. The Devil is kinder than God. Since he is not so mighty, he cannot be so cruel. I am not afraid, my friends!"

Then the friends were silent. But they did not wish to leave Mendel alone, and so they remained seated, dumb. Groschel, the young-

est, went down to inform his own wife and the wives of the others
that their husbands would not come home that night. He brought
five more Jews to Mendel's dwelling, in order that they should be
ten and could say the evening prayer. They began to pray. But Mendel Singer did not participate in the prayer. He sat motionless upon
his bed. Even the prayer for the dead he did not say—and Menkes
said it for him.

The five strangers left the house. But the four friends remained
all night. One of the two blue lamps still burned. It was silent. This
man or that slept where he sat, snored, and awoke, disturbed by his
own noises, and nodded again.

Only Mendel did not sleep. With wide-open eyes he stared at the
window, behind which the deep blackness of the night finally began
to waver, was gray, then whitish. Six strokes sounded from inside
the clock. Then the friends awoke, one after another.

And without consultation with each other, they grasped Mendel
by the arms, and led him downstairs. They brought him into the
back room of Skovronnek's shop, and laid him upon a sofa.

Here he slept.

14

From now on Mendel Singer lived with the Skovronneks. His
friends bought his wretched furniture. They left him only his bedding and the red velvet sack with the prayer utensils, which Mendel
had almost burned. Mendel no longer touched the sack. Gray and
dusty, it hung on a huge nail in Skovronnek's back room. Mendel
Singer no longer prayed. Sometimes, to be sure, he participated
when a tenth man was needed in order to complete the stipulated
number of supplicants. Then he allowed them to count him as present. Sometimes, too, for a small consideration, he lent his phylacteries to this or that person.

People gossiped about him, saying that he went now and then
into the Italian section, in order to eat pork and irritate God. In his
fight against Heaven, the people with whom he lived took his part;
although they were believers, they thought he was right. Jehovah
had treated him too sorely.

War still raged in the world. Apart from Sam, Mendel's son, all members of this neighborhood who had enlisted still lived. Young Lemmel had become an officer, and had had the luck to lose his left hand. He came home on leave and was the hero of his quarter. He gave to all Jews the feeling that they had a right to count America as their real home. He was staying in the service only to assist in the training of raw troops. Great as was the difference between young Lemmel and old Mendel Singer, the Jews of the neighborhood linked them together in their minds. It was as though Mendel and Lemmel together had divided between them all the bad luck designed for all of them. And Mendel had lost more than just a left hand. If Lemmel was fighting the Germans, Mendel was fighting supernatural powers. Although they were convinced that the old man was no longer in full possession of his faculties, still the Jews could not help mixing a certain admiration with their sympathy, and feeling almost devout before such holy madness.

Undoubtedly Mendel Singer was a man marked by God. In the midst of those whose laborious days were undisturbed by terrors he lived as a pitiful witness of the cruel power of Jehovah. For many years he had lived his days like all the others, observed by few, by many not even noticed. Then one day he had been set apart, in a dreadful way. There were none, now, who did not know him. He spent the greater part of his days in the streets. It was as though it were part of his curse not only to suffer misfortune but to set an example, to wear the sign of his agony like a banner. And like a sentry over his own pain, he walked up and down in the middle of the street, greeted by all, presented with a small coin by some, questioned by many.

For the charitable gifts he returned no thanks, he hardly noticed the greetings, and questions he answered with yes or no. He rose early in the morning. In Skovronnek's back room no light entered; it had no window. He only felt the approach of morning, from a long way off. When the first noises began in the streets, Singer's day began. In an alcohol cooker the tea brewed. He ate with it some bread and a hard-boiled egg. He cast a shy but angry glance upon the sack with the holy objects, hanging on the wall. In the dark-blue shadows the sack looked like a still darker outgrowth of the shadow.

"I shall not pray," thought Mendel. Yet he suffered because he did not pray. His rage hurt him, and the impotence of his rage. Although Mendel was angry with God, God still ruled the world. Hate could move Him no more than piety.

Filled with such and kindred thoughts, Mendel began his day. Once, he remembered, his awakening used to be light; the happy anticipation of his prayers had awakened him, and the desire to renew the familiar close contact with God. From the snug warmth of sleep he had entered with confidence and trust into the even more comfortable glow of prayer, as into a splendid, yet homelike room, in which a strong but smiling father lived. "Good morning, Father," Mendel had said—and believed that he heard an answer.

He had been deceived. The room was splendid but cold; the Father was strong but harsh. No sound issued from His lips but thunder.

Mendel Singer rolled up the iron shutters, and laid the sheet music, the song texts, the phonograph records, in the little show-window. Then he took a mouthful of water, sprinkled the floor, seized the broom, and swept together the debris of the preceding day. On a little shovel he carried the scraps of paper to the stove, made a fire, and burned them. Then he went out, bought a few newspapers, and delivered them to some of the neighbors. He met the milkman and the early baker-boys, greeted them, and returned "to business."

Soon the Skovronneks arrived. They sent him on this errand or that. It was: "Mendel, run out and buy a herring," "Mendel, the raisins for wine haven't been put up yet," "Mendel, you have forgotten the laundry," "Mendel, the ladder is broken!" "A pane is out of the lantern!" "Where is the corkscrew?" And Mendel ran out and bought a herring, put up raisin wine, fetched the wash and fixed the ladder and carried the lantern to the glazier and found the corkscrew. Sometimes the neighbors called him to look after the little children, when the moving picture show changed its program or a new theater opened.

And Mendel sat with the children of strangers, and, as once with a light and tender finger he had set Menuchim's basket swinging, so now, with a light and tender tread of the foot, he rocked the cradles of children whose names he did not know. And as he rocked he sang an old, old song:

"Say after me, Menuchim: In the beginning God created the heaven and the earth. Say after me, Menuchim—"

It was in the month of Ellul, and the high holidays were beginning. All the Jews of the neighborhood wanted to fix a temporary house of prayer in Skovronnek's back room. (They did not like to go to the synagogue.)

"Mendel, we will pray in your room," said Skovronnek. "What do you say?"

"You can pray." said Mendel.

And he watched the Jews assemble and light the great yellow wax candles, with their overhanging tufts of wick. He himself helped every merchant to roll down his iron shutters and lock his door. He saw how they all drew on their white robes, so that they looked like corpses who had risen from the dead to praise God. They drew off their shoes and stood in their socks. They fell upon their knees and rose again. The great golden-yellow candles of wax, and the snow-white ones of paraffin, bent, and dropped hot tears upon the prayer shawls, and encrusted in no time. The white Jews themselves bent like the candles, and their tears, too, fell upon the floor, and dried.

But Mendel Singer stood, black and silent, in his everyday clothes, in the background, near the door, unmoving. His lips were closed, and his heart was a stone. The song of Kol-Nidre rose like a hot wind. Mendel Singer's lips remained closed, and his heart a stone. Black and silent, in his everyday clothes, he kept to the background, close to the door. No one noticed him. The Jews went out of their way not to see him. A stranger was among them. This one or that thought of him, and prayed for him. But Mendel Singer stood erect in the doorway and hated God. They are all praying because they are afraid, he thought. But I do not fear Him. I am not afraid!

After they had all gone, Mendel Singer lay down on his hard sofa. It was still warm from the bodies of the supplicants. Forty candles still burned in the room. He did not dare to extinguish them, and he could not sleep while they burned. So he lay awake, all night long. He thought out exceptional, unheard-of blasphemies. He imagined himself going out, now, into the Italian section, buying pork in a restaurant, and bringing it back to eat, here, in the presence of the burning candles. He even undid his handkerchief and counted his coins, but he did not leave the room, he did not eat. He lay undressed on the sofa, with great sleepless eyes, and murmured:

"It is over, all over; it is the end of Mendel Singer! He has no son, he has no daughter, he has no wife, he has no money, he has no house, he has no God! All, all over; it is the end of Mendel Singer!"

The yellow and blue flames of the candles trembled lightly. The hot waxen tears dropped with a hard sound upon the bases of the candlesticks, upon the yellow sand in the brazen mortars, on the dark-green glass of the bottles. The hot breath of the supplicants still lived in the room. The white prayer shawls still lay on the chairs that had been temporarily put in, awaiting the continuation of the service on the next day. The room smelled of wax and the glowing remnants of wicks.

Mendel left the room, opened the shop, walked into the open. It was a clear early autumn night. Nobody was in sight. Mendel walked up and down before the shop. The long, slow step of a policeman approached. Then Mendel went back into the shop. He still kept out of the way of men in uniform.

The holidays were over. Autumn came. Rain sang. Mendel bought herrings, swept the floor, fetched the wash, fixed the ladder, sought a corkscrew, put up raisin wine, and walked back and forth, in the middle of the street. For charitable gifts he returned no thanks, he hardly noticed greetings, and questions he answered with yes or no. In the afternoon, when people assembled to talk politics and read from the newspapers, Mendel lay on the sofa and slept. The talk of the others did not awaken him. The war did not concern him. The newest phonograph records sang to him in his sleep. He would awaken only when they had all gone, and it was still. Then he would talk for a while with old Skovronnek.

"Your daughter-in-law is going to marry again," said Skovronnek once.

"Good," answered Mendel.

"But she is going to marry Mac."

"I advised her to."

"Business is good."

"It is not my business."

"Mac has let us know he wants to help you, with money."

"I don't want money."

"Good night, Mendel."

"Good night, Skovronnek."

Exciting news was appearing in the newspapers which Mendel was accustomed to buy every morning. It flamed in their pages; against his will he was forced to notice its distant reflection—he wished to know nothing of it. In Russia there was no longer a Czar. Good, let the Czar go. In any case they could bring no news of Jonas and Menuchim, the newspapers. At Skovronnek's they were betting that the war would be over in a month. Good, let it be over. Shemariah would not come back. The administration of the asylum wrote that Miriam's condition had not improved. Vega sent the letter; Skovronnek read it aloud. "Good," said Mendel. "Miriam will never get well."

His old black caftan shimmered green on his shoulders, and, like a tiny drawing of the backbone, the seam was visible down the entire back. The skirts of his coat grew longer and longer. Now, when he walked, they did not touch the tops of his boots, but almost the ankles. His beard, which once had covered only his breast, reached to the lowest button of his caftan. The visor of his black, or rather greenish, red cap had become soft and pliable, and hung limply over Mendel Singer's eyes, not unlike an old rag.

In his pockets Mendel Singer carried many things: little packets that people had given him, newspapers, implements with which he repaired broken odds and ends at Skovronnek's, spools of colored string, brown paper, and bread. The weight of all these bowed Mendel's back even more, and, because the right pocket was usually heavier than the left, the old man's right shoulder was pulled awry. Thus he walked through the streets, oblique and bent, a wreck of a creature, with crooked knees and scuffling soles. The news of the world and the weekdays and feastdays of the others rolled past him, like carriages past an old house off the main road.

One day the war was really over. The neighborhood was empty. Everyone had gone to see the peace celebration and the homecoming of the regiments. Many had commissioned Mendel to watch over their houses. He went from one flat to another, tested the bolts and locks, and returned home, to the store. From an unconscionable distance he thought he heard the festive sound of a happy world, the detonation of fireworks, the laughter of tens of thousands of men. A tiny, silent peace crept over him. His fingers combed his beard, his lips drew themselves into a smile, yes, there was even a little burst of laughter from his throat.

"Mendel will celebrate, too," he whispered, and for the first time he approached one of the brown phonographs. He had seen how they wound the instrument. "A record, a record!" he said. That very morning a returned soldier had been there and had brought half a dozen new records, new songs from Europe.

Mendel unpacked the top one, laid it carefully upon the instrument, meditated for a while trying to recall exactly how the thing was run, and finally set the needle to the disc. The apparatus croaked. Then the song began. It was evening; Mendel stood in the dark near the machine and listened.

Every day he had heard records, gay ones and sad ones, slow and fast, dark and light. But never had he heard a song like this one. It ran like a little brook and murmured softly; it was vast as the ocean and roared. Now I am hearing the whole world, thought Mendel. How is it possible that the whole world can be engraved on such a little disc? Then a silver flute tone melted into the violin music; it sewed itself around the velvety fabric of the violin playing like an accurate little hem. Mendel began, for the first time in long, to weep. Then the song was over. He played it again, and then a third time. Finally, he accompanied it in a hoarse voice, beating time, with a timid finger, upon the phonograph stand.

Skovronnek, returning, found him thus. He stopped the phonograph and said, "Mendel, light the lamp! What are you playing here?"

"Look, Skovronnek, see what the song is called."

"Those are the new records," said Skovronnek. "I bought them today. The song is called—" and Skovronnek put on his glasses, held the disc under the lamp, and read: "The song is called *Menuchim's Song.*"

Mendel was suddenly faint. He had to sit down. He stared at the shining disc in Skovronnek's hands.

"I know what you are thinking," said Skovronnek.

"Yes," answered Mendel.

Skovronnek turned the crank again. "A beautiful song," said Skovronnek, his head on his left shoulder, listening.

Slowly the shop filled with late-returning neighbors. No one spoke. All listened to the song, and waved their heads in time. And they heard it sixteen times over, until they all knew it by heart.

Mendel was alone in the store. Carefully he locked the door on the inside, cleaned out the show-window, began to undress. At each step the song accompanied him. While he dropped off to sleep, it seemed to him that the blue and silver melody bound itself together with Menuchim's complaining whimper, with Menuchim's, his own Menuchim's only, long-unheard song.

15

The days lengthened. The mornings were so bright that they even penetrated through the closed iron shutters back into Mendel's windowless room. In April the street awakened a good hour earlier. Mendel lighted the spirit lamp, set on the tea, filled the little blue washbasin, ducked his face in it, dried himself with the corner of the towel which hung from the door latch, put up the store shutters, took a mouthful of water and carefully spat it over the floor, and regarded the tortuous patterns which the bright stream from his pursed lips drew in the dust. The clock had not yet struck six when the water on the spirit lamp began to purr. Mendel stepped outside. The windows in the street were opening as of their own accord. It was spring.

It was spring. People were preparing for Easter, and in all the houses Mendel helped. He ran the plane over the wooden tabletops to rid them of the profane remains of food accumulated during the year. He placed in the white partitions of the show-windows the cylindrical packages in which the layers of Passover bread were wrapped in bright red paper. He freed the Palestine wines of the cobwebs under which they had been resting in the cool cellars. He took apart the neighbors' beds, and carried them, piece by piece, into the courtyards, where the gentle April sun lured the vermin into the open and made possible their destruction with benzine, turpentine, and kerosene.

Out of pink and sky-blue tissue paper he cut with his shears fringes and round and angular designs, and fastened them with thumbtacks to the kitchen shelves, as an artistic setting for the china.

He filled tubs and barrels with hot water, and held great iron balls at the end of wooden rods in the fire of the stove, until they glowed red-hot. Then he immersed the balls in the barrels and tubs; the water hissed, and the vessels were clean, as was commanded by the precepts. In enormous mortars he pounded the Easter bread into flour, poured it into clean sacks, and bound them with blue ribbons.

All this he had once performed in his own house. Spring had come more slowly there than in America. Mendel remembered the aging gray snow that edged the wooden pavement of the sidewalks at this time of year in Zuchnow. He remembered the crystal icicles which hung from the faucets; the sudden, soft rains which sang in the gutters of the eaves the whole night long. He remembered the distant thunder rolling far away behind the fir forest, the white rime which tenderly decked each bright blue morning. He remembered Menuchim, whom Miriam had stuck into a roomy vat in order to get him out of the way, and he remembered the hope that at last, at last, in this year the Messiah would come.

He had not come. He did not come, thought Mendel; he will not come. Let others await him. Mendel did not.

And yet to Mendel's friends and neighbors he seemed this spring, to be changed. They observed that he sometimes hummed a little song, and they caught a gentle smile under his white beard.

"He is becoming childish; he is already old," said Groschel.

"He has forgotten everything," said Rottenberg.

"He is happy that he will soon die," said Menkes.

Skovronnek, who knew him best of all, was silent. But once, in the evening, before he went to sleep, he said to his wife:

"Since the new records arrived our Mendel is another man. I have caught him now and then winding up a phonograph himself. What do you think of that?"

"I think," answered Mrs. Skovronnek impatiently, "that Mendel is getting old and childish and soon will be no use to us."

For some time she had been dissatisfied with Mendel. The older he became the less pity she felt for him. Gradually she was forgetting that Mendel had once been a well-to-do man, and her sympathy, which had been nourished by her respect (for she had little heart), died at the same time. She no longer called him, as at the beginning, Mister Singer, but simply Mendel, as indeed the whole world did. And whereas she had formerly given him orders with a certain reserve which showed that his obedience both honored and shamed her, she now ordered him about so impatiently that her dissatisfaction with him was visible even before he acted. Although Mendel was not deaf, Mrs. Skovronnek raised her voice whenever she spoke with him, as though she feared that she would be misunderstood, and as though she sought to imply by her screaming that Mendel had carried out her orders badly when she had spoken to him in an ordinary tone of voice.

Her precautionary screams were the only thing that offended Mendel.

For he, so humiliated by Heaven, cared little for the careless and good natured mockery of mankind, and was only insulted when people doubted his ability to understand.

"Hurry up, Mendel," was the way Mrs. Skovronnek prefaced every order. He made her impatient; he seemed so slow.

"Don't yell so," Mendel would occasionally answer. "I hear you."

"But you don't hurry; you take your time so."

"I have less time than you, Mrs. Skovronnek, because I am older."

Mrs. Skovronnek, who did not immediately grasp the double meaning of his answer, nor the reprimand in it, but felt that she was being mocked, immediately turned to the nearest persons in the shop.

"Now what do you say to that? He is getting old! Our Mendel is certainly getting old!"

She would have liked to accuse him of entirely other peculiarities, but she contented herself with calling attention to his age, which she held to be in itself a vice. When Skovronnek heard this sort of talk, he said to his wife:

"We will all be old some day. I'm just as old as Mendel, and you won't grow any younger yourself."

"You can marry a young one if you like," said Mrs. Skovronnek.

She was happy at last to have a ready-made reason for a marital quarrel. And Mendel, who knew very well the development of such disputes, and foresaw from the beginning that Mrs. Skovronnek's rage would finally vent itself against her husband and his friend, trembled for their friendship.

Today Mrs. Skovronnek was angry with Mendel for special reasons.

"Imagine," she said to her husband. "For several days now I have missed my meat chopper. I could swear that Mendel has taken it! But ask him, and he pretends to know nothing about it. He's getting older and older; he's like a child."

As a matter of fact Mendel had taken Mrs. Skovronnek's meat chopper and hidden it. In secret he had long been working on a great plan, the last of his life.

One evening he thought he could carry it out. He pretended to nod, lying on the sofa, while the neighbors amused themselves at Skovronnek's. In reality Mendel did not doze at all. He lay in ambush and listened with closed eyelids until the last guest had departed. Then he drew the meat chopper from under the pillow of the sofa, hid it under his caftan, and glided swiftly into the darkening street. The street lamps were not yet lit; although from many windows yellow lamplight already shone.

Opposite the house in which he had lived with Deborah, Mendel Singer took his stand and spied at the windows of his former dwelling. A young married couple named Frisch lived there now; underneath they had opened a modern ice-cream parlor. Now the young people came out of the house. They locked the ice-cream parlor. They were going to a concert. They were saving, even stingy, industrious, and music-loving. The father of young Frisch had once been conductor in an orchestra in Kovno, which played at weddings. Today a philharmonic orchestra, just come from Europe, was playing. Frisch had not spoken about it for days. Now they went out. They did not see Mendel.

He crept across the street and into the house, felt his way up along the familiar banister, and drew all the keys out of his pocket. He got them from the neighbors who made him watchman over their dwellings when they went to the moving pictures.

He opened the door without difficulty. He shoved the bolt to, laid himself flat on the floor, and began to knock on the floorboards, one after another. It lasted a long time. He was tired, allowed himself a small pause, and then went on with his knocking. Finally, he heard a hollow sound, just at the place where Deborah's bed had once stood. Mendel cleaned the dirt out of the joint, loosened the board at all four edges with the meat chopper, and forced it up. He was not disappointed; he found what he was looking for. He grasped the strong, knotted handkerchief, hid it in his caftan, laid the floorboard back in place, and quietly let himself out. No one was on the stairs; no one had seen him.

Earlier than usual he closed the shop, rolling down the iron shutters. He lighted the great hanging lamp, and sat down in the circle of its light. He unknotted the handkerchief and counted its contents. Deborah had saved sixty-seven dollars, in bills and coins. It was much, but not enough for Mendel. If he added his own savings, the gifts and little fees for his work in the neighbors' houses, it made exactly ninety-six dollars. It was still not enough. "A few months more!" whispered Mendel. "I have time."

Yes, he had time. He must live for quite a long time still. Before him lay the vast ocean. Once again he must cross it. The whole great sea waited for Mendel. All of Zuchnow and its surroundings waited for him: the barracks, the fir forest, the frogs in the swamp, and the crickets in the fields. If Menuchim were dead, he lay in the little cemetery and waited. And Mendel would lay himself down there, too. Before that he would enter Sameshkin's yard; he would no longer be afraid of the dogs—give him a wolf from Zuchnow, and he would not fear. Careless of beetles and snakes, of toads and grasshoppers, he would be prepared to lie down upon the naked earth. The church bells would sound for him, and remind him of the listening light in Menuchim's foolish eyes.

Mendel would say: "I have come home, dear Sameshkin. Let others wander through the world. My worlds are dead, I have come back in order to sleep for ever here."

The blue night is stretched over the land, the stars glitter, the frogs croak, the crickets chirp, and over there, in the dark forest, someone sings Menuchim's song.

So Mendel went to sleep, the knotted handkerchief in one hand.

The next morning he went into the Skovronneks' flat, laid the meat chopper on the cold kitchen stove, and said: "Here, Mrs. Skovronnek, is the chopper; it is found."

He tried to hurry away, but Mrs. Skovronnek began: "Found, is it? That wasn't hard! You hid it yourself! Besides, you certainly slept soundly last evening. We stopped again at the shop and knocked. Did you hear? Frisch, from the ice-cream parlor, has something very important to say to you. You should go over to him right off."

Mendel was scared. So, someone had seen him yesterday; perhaps someone else had robbed the flat, and they suspected Mendel! Perhaps, too, it wasn't Deborah's savings, but Mrs. Frisch's that he had taken, and he had robbed her! His knees trembled.

"Let me sit down," he said to Mrs, Skovronnek.

"You can sit just two minutes," she said. "Then I must start cooking."

"What sort of important thing is it?" he inquired. But he knew that the woman would tell him nothing. She gloated over his curiosity, and was silent. Then, when Mendel's two minutes were up, she said:

"I don't concern myself with other people's business. Just go to Frisch."

Mendel went out, resolved not to go to Frisch's. It could only be something bad. Frisch would come soon enough himself. He waited.

But in the afternoon Skovronnek's grandson came visiting. Mrs. Skovronnek sent Mendel for three portions of strawberry ice cream. Mendel entered the shop faint-heartedly. Luckily Mr. Frisch was not there. His wife said:

"My husband has something very important to tell you. You must surely come this afternoon."

Mendel acted as though he had not heard. His heart was beating stormily, as though it would spring from his breast. He held it with both hands. In any case something evil was threatening him. He would tell the truth; Frisch would believe him. If he didn't believe him he would go to jail. Well, and what of it? In prison, he would die. Not in Zuchnow.

He could not leave the vicinity of the ice-cream parlor. He walked up and down before the shop. He saw Frisch return home. He wanted to wait longer, but his feet hurried, by themselves, into the shop. He opened the door, setting a shrill bell ringing, and found no strength to close it, so that the alarm went on and Mendel stood deafened by its violent noise, incapable of moving.

Mr. Frisch himself closed the door. And in the quiet which followed, Mendel heard Mr. Frisch say to his wife:

"Quick, a raspberry soda for Mr. Singer."

How long had it been since anyone had said "Mister Singer" to Mendel? In this moment he realized for the first time that people had been calling him Mendel in order to humiliate him. It's a mean joke of Frisch's, he thought. The whole neighborhood knows that this young man is stingy; he knows that I won't pay for the raspberry soda. I won't drink it.

"Thanks, thanks," said Mendel. "I don't care for anything."

"You mustn't turn us down," said the woman, smiling.

"He won't refuse me," said young Frisch.

He drew Mendel to one of the thin-legged iron tables and pressed him into a wicker chair. He himself sat down on an ordinary wooden chair, pulled himself close to Mendel, and began:

"Yesterday, Mr. Singer, I was at the concert, as you know."

Mendel's heart palpitations started again. He leaned back and took a swallow, in order to sustain life.

"Now," Frisch went on, "I have heard a lot of music, but this was like nothing in the world. Thirty-two musicians, understand, and almost all of them from around our part of the world. And they played Jewish melodies, understand? It warmed the heart; I cried. Almost the whole audience cried. And at the close they played *Menuchim's Song,* Mr. Singer. You know it from the phonograph record. A beautiful song, isn't it?"

"What does he want," thought Mendel. "Yes, yes, a lovely song."

"During the intermission, I went back to the musicians' room. It was crowded. Everybody wanted to meet the musicians. This one and that discovered a friend, and I, too, Mr. Singer—I, too!"

Frisch paused. People entered the shop. The bell rang shrilly.

"I found—but have a drink, Mr. Singer—I found my own cousin, Berkovitch, from Kovno. The son of my uncle. And we kissed. And we talked. And suddenly Berkovitch said, 'Do you known an old man—named Mendel Singer?'"

Frisch waited again. And Mendel Singer did not move. He accepted the fact that a certain Berkovitch had asked after an old man, Mendel Singer.

"Yes," said Frisch, "I answered that I knew a Mendel Singer from Zuchnow. 'That's he,' said Berkovitch. 'Our conductor is a great composer, still young, and a genius; he wrote most of the pieces that we play. His name is Alexis Kossak, and he is also from Zuchnow.'"

"Kossak?" answered Mendel. "My wife was born a Kossak. He must be a relative."

"Yes," said Frisch, "and it seems that this Kossak is looking for you. Probably he has news for you. And I should ask you if you would like to hear it. You can either go to his hotel, or I will write Berkovitch your address."

Mendel felt at the same moment relieved and depressed. He drank the raspberry soda, leaned back, and said:

"Thank you, Mr. Frisch. But it is not so important. This man Kossak will tell me all sorts of sad things that I already know. And apart from that, I will tell you the truth: I had wanted for some time to get your advice. Your brother has a steamship agency, hasn't he? I want to go home, to Zuchnow. It is no longer Russia; the world has changed. What does a ticket cost today? And what documents would I have to have? Talk with your brother, but don't tell anyone else."

"I will inquire," answered Frisch. "But you certainly haven't enough money. And at your age! Perhaps this Kossak will tell you something. Perhaps he will take you with him! He is only staying for a short time in New York. Shan't I give Berkovitch your address? Because, if I know you, you won't go to the hotel."

"No," said Mendel. "I won't go. Write him if you like."

He got up to depart. Frisch pressed him into his chair again.

"Just a moment, Mr. Singer," he said. "I brought the program with me. This Kossak's picture is on it."

From his waistcoat pocket he drew a large program, unfolded it, and held it for Mendel to see.

"A good looking young man," said Mendel. He looked at the photograph. Although the picture was worn, the paper dirty, and the portrait seemed about to dissolve into a hundred thousand tiny molecules, it looked up from the program with vitality. He wanted to return it immediately, but he held it and stared. Under the black hair the forehead was broad and white as a smooth, sunny stone. The eyes were large and clear. They looked directly at Mendel Singer. He could not free himself from them. They made him happy and light-hearted, Mendel believed. He saw the light of their intelligence. They were old, and at the same time young. They knew everything; the whole world reflected itself in them. It seemed to Mendel Singer, looking at these eyes, that he himself was younger;

he was a youth who knew nothing. He must learn everything from these eyes.

Years ago, when he had begun the study of the Bible, these had been the eyes of the prophets. Men to whom God Himself had spoken had such eyes. They knew all, they betrayed nothing; they were full of light.

Mendel looked at the picture for a long time. Then he said, "I will take it home with me, if you permit, Mr. Frisch." And he folded up the paper and went.

He went around the corner, unfolded the program, looked at it again, and stuck it in his pocket. A long time seemed to have elapsed since he entered the ice-cream parlor. The few thousand years which shone in Kossak's eyes lay between, and the years when Mendel was still so young that he could imagine the countenances of the prophets. He wanted to turn around, to ask where the concert hall was, where the orchestra was playing, and to go in. But he was ashamed. He went to Skovronnek's shop and told them that a relative of his wife was in America and looking for him. He had given Frisch permission to tell his address.

"Tomorrow evening you will eat with us, as you do every year," said Skovronnek. It was the first Passover evening. Mendel nodded. He would rather remain in his back room; he knew the oblique glance of Mrs. Skovronnek, and the calculating hands with which she apportioned to Mendel his soup and fish. It is the last time, he thought. In another year I shall be in Zuchnow, living or dead; rather dead.

He was the first guest to arrive the next night, but the last to sit down to table. He came early, in order not to offend Mrs. Skovronnek; he took his place last in order to show that he considered himself the least of those present. Already they sat about the table—the hostess, both of Skovronnek's daughters with their husbands and children, a strange music salesman, and Mendel. He sat at the end of the table, upon which a planed board had been laid to make it longer. Mendel's concern was not only to maintain the peace, but to keep the precarious extension balanced on the tabletop.

When a plate or tureen had to be set on the end of the board, Mendel held it fast. Six thick snow-white candles burned in the silver candlesticks upon the snow-white tablecloth, from the starched surface of which were reflected the six lights. Like white and silver

watchmen, all of the same height, the candles stood before Skovronnek, the host, who sat in a white robe upon a white cushion,
leaning against another cushion, a purified king upon a purified
throne. How long had it been since Mendel in the same costume
had ruled the feast in the same fashion? Today he sat, bent and broken, in his greenish coat, at the far end of the table, the least among
the guests, concerned with appearing to be modest, a miserable support for the festivities.

The unleavened bread lay covered with a white napkin, a snowy
mound beside the juicy green of the kale, the dark red of beets, and
the acid yellow of the horseradish root. The books with the account
of the exodus of the Jews from Egypt lay open before each guest.
Skovronnek began to chant the legend, and all repeated his words,
caught up with him, and sang in unity the comforting, smiling melody, a chorused account of the various miracles, numbered over
and over again, and always manifesting the same virtues of God:
His greatness, His goodness, His compassion, His mercy toward Israel, His anger with Pharaoh.

Even the music salesman, who could not read the Holy Writ and
did not understand the customs, could not resist the melody, which
wooed him with every verse, caressed him, drew him into its net, so
that he began to hum it unwittingly. And even Mendel became
milder toward Heaven, which four thousand years ago had generously lavished such marvelous miracles, and it was as though, because of God's love for his whole people, Mendel could almost be
reconciled to his own fate. He still did not participate in the song,
but his body swung backward and forward, cradled in the song of
the others. He heard Skovronnek's grandchildren singing in their
clear voices, and recalled the voices of his own children. He still saw
the helpless Menuchim raised on his unaccustomed chair at the festive table. Only the father had, from time to time during the singing, cast a hasty glance upon his youngest and least gifted son, had
seen the listening light in his foolish eyes, and had felt how the little
one tried in vain to express what sounded in him, and to sing what
he heard.

It was the only evening in the year when Menuchim wore a new
suit, like his brothers, the white collar of his shirt with its bright red
edging about his flabby double chin. When Mendel reached him the
wine, he drank half the glass, with one greedy draught, then

sneezed, and distorted his face in an ineffectual attempt to laugh or to cry; who knew which?

Mendel thought of these things as he swayed to the song of the others. He saw that they were already far ahead of him. He turned over a few pages, and prepared to stand up and to free the corner of the plates so that there would be no catastrophe when he let go of it. For the moment was approaching when the red beaker of wine would be filled, and the door opened in order to admit the prophet Elijah. The dark-red glass was waiting, the six candles glittered in its curved surface. Mrs. Skovronnek lifted her head and looked at Mendel. He stood up, glided to the door, and opened it. Now Skovronnek sang the invitation to the prophet. Mendel waited until he was finished, for he did not want to go to the door twice. Then he closed the door, braced a supporting fist under the table-leaf, and the singing went on.

Hardly a minute had passed after Mendel had seated himself, when a knock sounded. Everyone heard the knock, but everyone thought he was mistaken. On this evening all their friends were at home, the streets of the quarter were empty. At this hour no visitor was possible. It was certainly the wind which knocked.

"Mendel," said Mrs. Skovronnek, "you haven't closed the door properly."

Then the knock sounded again, longer and more clearly. All waited. The smell of the candles, the flush of the wine, the unusual yellow light, and the old melody had brought grown-ups and children to the point where they almost awaited a miracle, so that they held their breaths for a moment, and stared at each other, perplexed and pale, as though they asked themselves whether the prophet were indeed at the door. And so there was silence, and no one trusted himself to move. Finally Mendel stirred. Again he pushed the plates toward the center of the table. Again he glided to the door and opened it . . . There in the half-dark passage stood a tall stranger who wished him good evening, and asked whether he might enter. Skovronnek got up from his cushions with some difficulty. He went to the door, looked at the stranger, and said: "If you please," as he had learned one should do, in America.

The stranger entered. He wore a dark overcoat. His collar was turned up, he kept his hat on his head, obviously out of reverence for the ceremony into the midst of which he had stepped, and because all the men present sat with their heads covered.

"He is a sensitive person," thought Skovronnek. And without saying a word, he unbuttoned the stranger's coat. The man bowed and said:

"My name is Alexis Kossak. I beg your pardon. I sincerely beg your pardon. I had been told that I would find here a certain Mendel Singer from Zuchnow. I should like to speak with him."

"I am he," said Mendel, approached the guest, and lifted his head. His forehead but reached to the shoulder of the stranger. "Mr. Kossak," he continued, "I have heard of you already. We are relatives."

"Lay off your things, and sit down with us at the table," said Skovronnek.

Mrs. Skovronnek rose. They all pushed together. They made a place for the stranger. Skovronnek's son-in-law set another chair at the table. The stranger hung his coat on a nail, and sat down opposite Mendel. They placed a glass of wine before the guest.

"Do not let me interrupt you," bade the stranger. "Please go on with your prayers."

They continued. Silent and slender, the guest sat in his place. Mendel gazed at him without stopping. Alexis Kossak's gaze at Mendel Singer was unbroken. Thus they sat opposite each other, fanned by the singing of the others, but separated from them.

They both felt grateful that the presence of the others kept them from talking to each other. Mendel sought the stranger's eyes. If Kossak cast them down, it seemed to the old man that he must beg him to open them again. In this countenance, everything was strange to Mendel Singer except the eyes behind the rimless glasses, which were familiar. His gaze always strayed back to them, like a homecoming to well known lights behind windows, in the unfamiliar landscape of the narrow, pale, and youthful face.

His lips were thin, tight, and smooth.

"Were I his father," thought Mendel, "I should say, 'Smile, Alexis.'"

He drew the program quietly from his pocket, unfolded it under the table in order not to disturb the others, and handed it to the stranger. He took it and smiled, thinly, tenderly, and for but a moment.

The singing ended, and the feast began. Mrs. Skovronnek pushed a plate of soup before the guest, and Mr. Skovronnek bade him eat with them. The music salesman began a conversation in English with Kossak, of which Mendel understood nothing. Then the salesman declared to them all that Kossak was a young genius, that he was staying only a week in New York, and that he would be happy to present all of them with free tickets to his concert.

Other conversations failed to start. They ate in unfestive haste, approaching the close of the celebration, and every second bite was accompanied by a polite word from the host or from the guest. Mendel did not speak. To please Mrs. Skovronnek he ate even faster than the others, not to contribute to any delay.

All of them greeted the end of the feast, and eagerly began the recitation of the miracles. Skovronnek struck an even quicker rhythm; the women could hardly follow him. But when he came to the Psalms, his voice changed, as did the tempo and the melody, and the words which he sang sounded so enchanting that even Mendel, at the end of each strophe, joined in the Hallelujah! Hallelujah! He shook his head so that his long beard swept over the open leaves of the book, and a gentle rustling was audible, as though the beard of Mendel participated in the prayer which the mouth of Mendel so reluctantly celebrated.

Soon they were finished. The candles had burned to half their size, the table was no longer smooth and festive, spots and crumbs of food were visible on the white cloth and Skovronnek's grandsons were already yawning. At the close the book was lifted. In a loud voice Skovronnek repeated the traditional wish: "Next year in Jerusalem!" They all repeated it, closed the books, and turned to the guest.

Now it was Mendel's turn to question the guest. The old man cleared his throat, smiled, and said, "Now, Mr. Alexis, what have you to tell me?"

In a low voice the stranger began. "You should have heard from me long ago, Mr. Mendel Singer, had I had your address. But after the war no one knew it. Billes's son-in-law, the musician, died of typhus; your house in Zuchnow stood empty, for Billes's daughter went to her parents who already lived in Dubno; and in Zuchnow, in your house, Austrian soldiers were quartered. Now, after the war, I wrote to my manager here, but the man was not clever enough to find you."

"Too bad about Billes's son-in-law," said Mendel, and thought of Menuchim.

"And now," continued Kossak, "I have some pleasant news."

Mendel lifted his head. "I bought your house from old Billes before witnesses, and on the basis of an official estimate of its worth. And I will pay you the money."

"How much is it?" asked Mendel.

"Three hundred dollars!" said Kossak.

Mendel gripped his beard and combed it tremblingly with spread fingers.

"Thank you," he said.

"As far as your son Jonas is concerned," said Kossak, "he disappeared in the year 1915. No one had news of him, either in Petersburg, Berlin, Vienna, or in the Swiss Red Cross. I asked or had inquiries made everywhere. But two months ago I met a young man in Moscow. He had just escaped over the Polish border, for, as you know, Zuchnow now belongs to Poland. And this young man had been in Jonas's regiment. He told me that he had once heard, by accident, that Jonas was alive and fighting in a White Guard regiment. In that case it would of course have been difficult to get any news from him. But you need not yet give up hope."

Mendel wanted to open his lips to ask after Menuchim. But his friend, Skovronnek, who anticipated Mendel's question and was certain of a sad reply, was anxious to avoid unhappy talk on this particular evening, or to postpone it, at least, as long as possible, so he interrupted the old man, and said:

"Now, Mr. Kossak, that we have the pleasure of having so distinguished a guest as you, won't you tell us something, perhaps, of your own life? How does it happen that you escaped the war, the revolution, and all dangers?"

The stranger had obviously not expected this question, for he did not answer immediately. He cast down his eyes, as one who was ashamed or had to think, and answered only after a long pause.

"I have not gone through anything special. As a child I was sick for a long time. My father was a poor teacher, like Mendel Singer, to whose wife I am related. It is not the time, just now, to explain the relationship more exactly. To be brief, because of my illness, and because we were poor, I was sent to a great city, to a public medical institute. And there I was well treated, a physician took a special interest in me, I was cured, and the doctor took me into his own house.

"There"—and here Kossak's head sank, and it was as though he spoke to the table, and everyone held his breath in order to hear his exact words—"there I sat down at the piano one day and played out of my head my own songs. And the doctor's wife wrote notes to these songs. The war was my good fortune. For through it I came to perform military music, and became the leader of a band, stayed the whole time in Petersburg, and even played a few times before the Czar. After the revolution my band went abroad with me. A few left us, new ones came; in London we made a contract with a concert agency, and thus my orchestra came into being."

They all continued to listen, although the guest spoke no more. But his words still lingered in the room, and now struck first this one and then that. Kossak spoke the Yiddish jargon badly, he interspersed half Russian sequences in his account, and Mendel and the Skovronneks missed many details but grasped the sense of it all. Skovronnek's sons-in-law, who had come as small children to America, understood less than half of what was said, and had their wives translate the stranger's words into English. The music salesman then went over Kossak's biography again, in order to impress it upon them.

The candles had burned down in the candlesticks to short stumps; it was dark in the room; the grandchildren slept in their chairs with their heads on the side, but no one made a move to go. Yes, Mrs. Skovronnek even fetched two candles, stuck them upon the old stumps, and thus reopened the evening. Her ancient respect for Mendel Singer reawakened. This guest, who was a great man, had played before the Czar, wore a remarkable ring on his little finger and a pearl in his cravat, and was dressed in a suit of good European stuff—she knew what was what, because her father had been a draper—this guest could hardly go with Mendel into the back room. Yes, to the astonishment of her husband, she said:

"Mr. Singer! It is a good thing that you came to us this evening. Usually"—and she turned to Kossak—"he is so modest and sensitive that he refuses my invitations. And yet he is like the oldest child in our house."

Skovronnek broke in. "Make us some more tea!" And as she stood up, he said to Kossak: "We all have known your songs for some time. *Menuchim's Song* is yours, isn't it?"

"Yes," said Kossak. "It is by me."

It seemed as though this question was unwelcome to him. He looked quickly at Mendel and said: "Your wife is dead?"

Mendel nodded.

"And as far as I know, you have a daughter?"

In Mendel's place Skovronnek answered: "Unfortunately, her mother's death, and that of her brother Sam made her insane, and she is in the asylum."

The stranger bowed his head. Mendel rose and went out.

He wanted to ask after Menuchim, but he had not the courage. He knew the answer in advance. He put himself in the place of the guest and answered himself: "Menuchim is long since dead. He perished miserably." He practiced this sentence, tasted in advance its whole bitterness, in order, when he really heard it, to be able to sit quietly. And because he still had a shy hope in his heart, he sought to kill it. If Menuchim were alive—he said to himself—the stranger would have told me right away. No! Menuchim is long since dead. And now I will ask him, so that this stupid hope will come to an end at last!

But still he did not ask. He sat silent for a while, and the noisy activity of Mrs. Skovronnek, who was busy in the kitchen with the tea kettle, gave him an excuse to leave the room, in order to help the hostess.

But she sent him back. He had three hundred dollars and a distinguished relative.

"It isn't right for you, Mister Mendel," she said. "Don't leave your guest alone."

Anyhow, she was already finished. With full tea glasses on a broad tray, she entered the room followed by Mendel. The tea was steaming. Mendel had finally made up his mind to inquire after Menuchim. Skovronnek, also, felt that the question could no longer be postponed. He would rather ask himself; Mendel, his friend, should not add to the pain which the answer would cause, the misery of asking it.

"My friend, Mendel, had another poor, sick son, named Menuchim. What has happened to him?"

Again the stranger did not answer. He poked around in the bottom of his glass with his spoon, crushed the sugar, and gazed at the pale brown glass as though he would read the answer in it. And with the spoon still held between his thumb and forefinger, his narrow brown hand gently waving to and fro, he said finally, in an unexpectedly loud voice, as though by sudden decision:

"Menuchim is alive!"

It did not sound like an answer; it sounded like a cry. At once a laugh burst from Mendel Singer's breast. Everyone started, and stared at the old man. Mendel sat, leaning back in his chair, and shook, and laughed.

He is so bent that he no longer can touch the whole of the chair back. Between the back of the chair and Mendel's old neck (white hairs curl over the shabby collar of his coat) there is a wide space. Mendel's long beard moves violently; it almost flutters, like a white flag. And it, too, seems to laugh. From Mendel's breast comes now a rumbling, now a tittering. Everyone is scared. Skovronnek rises with some difficulty from his swollen cushions, hampered by his long white robe, and, going to Mendel, bends over him, taking both his hands in his. Now Mendel's laughter turns to weeping. He sobs, and the tears flow over his old, half-veiled eyes, into the wild beard, losing themselves in the tangled brush; others remain for a while, hanging in the hair of his beard, round and full as drops of glass.

Finally Mendel becomes quiet. He looks straight at Kossak, and repeats:

"Menuchim is alive?"

The stranger looks at Mendel calmly and says:

"Menuchim lives. He is alive, he is well, he is even prosperous."

Mendel folded his hands, lifting them as high as he could toward the ceiling. He tried to stand up. He had the feeling that now he must stand up, stand straight, grow, become taller and taller, higher than the house, and with his hands touch the skies. He can no longer unclasp his folded hands. He looks at Skovronnek, and the old friend knows what he has to ask, in Mendel's stead.

"Where is Menuchim now?" asks Skovronnek.

And slowly Alexis Kossak answers:

"I am Menuchim."

All arise suddenly from their places. The children, who were already asleep, awake and burst into tears. Mendel stands up so violently that behind him the chair falls down with a loud crash. He walks, he runs, he hastens, he skips to Kossak, who alone has remained seated. There is a great commotion in the room. The candles begin to flicker as though they are moved by a sudden wind. On the wall flutter the shadows of the standing people. Mendel sinks down before Menuchim; he searches with impatient mouth and waving beard for the hands of his son; his lips kiss whatever they touch, the knees, the legs, the waistcoat of Menuchim.

Mendel stood up at last. He lifted his hands, and as though he were blind, began to touch his son's face, with eager fingers. The blunt old fingers glided over Menuchim's hair, over his smooth, broad brow, over the cold glass in his spectacles, over the thin closed lips. Menuchim sat quietly, and did not move. All present surrounded Menuchim and Mendel. The children cried, the candles flickered, the shadows on the wall merged into a dark cloud. No one spoke.

Finally, Menuchim's voice sounded.

"Stand up, Father," he said, and grasped Mendel under the arms, lifted him high, and seated him upon his knees, like a child. The others drew away. Now Mendel sat upon the lap of his son, and smiled into the face of each person in the circle. He whispered:

"Pain will make him wise, ugliness good, bitterness mild, and sickness strong!"

Deborah had said it. He heard her voice still.

Skovronnek left the table, laid his robe aside, drew on his coat and said: "I shall be back immediately."

Where was Skovronnek going? It was not yet late; the friends were still at their tables. He went from house to house, to Groschel, Menkes, Rottenberg. He would find them all, still at their tables.

"A miracle has happened! Come with me and witness it!"

He led all three to Mendel. On the way they met Lemmel's daughter, who had been accompanying her guests. They told her about Mendel and Menuchim. Young Frisch, who had gone out for a little walk with his wife, also heard the news. And thus a few learned what had happened. Below, before Skovronnek's house, stood, as proof, the automobile in which Menuchim had come. A few people opened their windows and looked at it. Menkes, Groschel, Skovronnek, and Rottenberg entered the house. Mendel went toward them all and silently pressed their hands.

Menkes, the most thoughtful of them all, was spokesman.

"Mendel," he said, "we have come to visit you in your good luck as we visited you in your misfortune. Do you remember how crushed you were? We tried to comfort you, but we knew it was in vain. Now you in the flesh experience a miracle! As we mourned with you then, so we rejoice with you now. Great are the wonders of the Eternal, today, as they were a thousand years ago! Praise His name!"

All stood. Skovronnek's daughters, the children, the sons-in-law, and the music salesman had already put on their coats, and were departing. Mendel's friends did not sit down because they had only come to offer congratulations. Smaller than any of them, with his bent back, in his greenish coat, Mendel stood in their midst like a disguised king. He had to stretch himself up to look into their faces.

"I thank you," he said. "Without your help I should never have seen this hour. Look at my son!"

He pointed toward him with his hand, as though one of the friends might perhaps have failed to regard Menuchim closely enough. Their eyes felt of the stuff of his suit, of his silk cravat, the pearl, the slender hands, and the ring. Then they said:

"A noble young man! One sees that he is someone special."

"I have no house," said Mendel to his son. "You come to your father and I have no bed to offer you."

"I want to take you with me, Father," answered the son. "But I do not know whether you will go, because today is a feast day."

"He can go," they all answered, as though with one mouth.

"I think that I may go with you," said Mendel. "I have committed grave sins; God has closed His eyes. I called Him an *ispravnik*. He held His ears. He is so great that our badnesses seem to Him very small. I can go with you."

They all accompanied Mendel to the car. At this window and that neighbors stood and looked down. Mendel fetched his key, unlocked the shop once more, went into the back room, and took down the red velvet sack from its nail. He blew upon it to disperse the dust, rolled down the iron shutters, locked up, and gave Skovronnek the key. With the sack in his arms he climbed into the automobile. The motor whirred. The headlights shone. From this window and that voices called: "Auf wiedersehen, Mendel!"

Mendel Singer grasped Menkes by the arm and said:

"Tomorrow, at prayers, you will announce that I am giving three hundred dollars to the poor. Good bye!"

And at the side of his son he rode to the Astor Hotel.

16

A bent, pitiable figure in a greenish coat, with the red velvet sack under his arm, Mendel Singer entered the lobby, observed the electric light, the blond doorman, the white bust to an unknown God at the entrance of the stairs, and the black Negro who tried to take the sack from him. He entered the lift, and saw himself in its mirror beside his son. He closed his eyes, for he felt dizzy. He was, perhaps, already dead, he thought; he floated in heaven; it would go on like this for ever.

His son took his hand; Mendel walked on the silent carpet, through the long corridor. He only opened his eyes when he finally stood in the room. As was his custom, he immediately stepped to the window. There he saw for the first time America's night close at hand. He saw the reddened heavens, the flaming, sparkling, dropping, glowing, red, blue, green, silver, golden letters, pictures, and signs. He heard the noisy song of America, the whistle, the rumble, the ringing, the screaming, the rattling, the piping, the howling. Across from the window on which Mendel leaned appeared every fifth second the broad laughing face of a girl, put together out of sparkling points of light, between her parted lips a blinding set of teeth made, seemingly, of a single piece of molten silver. A foaming ruby-red goblet swam toward this face, tipped of itself, spilled its contents into the open mouth, and disappeared, only to return refilled and foaming over with white froth.

It was an advertisement for a new soft drink. Mendel admired it as the perfected representation of nightly joys and golden health. He smiled, watched the picture several times as it came and went, and then turned again toward the room. There stood a white bed, already made. Menuchim rested in a deep chair.

"I shall not sleep tonight," said Mendel. "You go to bed. I will sit beside you. In Zuchnow you slept in the corner, next to the oven."

"I remember perfectly the day—began Menuchim, and laid aside his glasses, and Mendel saw the naked eyes of his son, and they seemed to him weary and sad—"I remember perfectly a certain morning. The sun is very bright and the room is empty. Then you come in. You lift me up. I sit on a table, and you strike upon a glass with a spoon. There was a lovely ringing. I wish that I could reproduce that sound and play it today. Then you sang. And then the bells began to ring, the old, old bells. They were like enormous spoons striking upon enormous glasses."

"Go on, go on!" cried Mendel. He, too, remembered the exact day. It was the day Deborah went out of the house to prepare for the journey to Kapturak.

"From the early days that is all I can recall," said Menuchim. "Then the time came when Billes's son-in-law played the violin. I believe that he played every day. When he stopped playing I still heard him. The music went on in my years, day and night."

"Go on, go on!" cried Mendel, in the tone in which he had urged his pupils to more zealous effort.

"Then for a long time, nothing. Then one day I saw a great red and blue fire. I lay down on the floor. I crept to the door. Suddenly someone seemed to lift me up and push me. I ran. I was outside. People were standing on the other side of the street. 'Fire!' I cried."

"Go on, go on!" said Mendel.

"I cannot remember the rest. Later people told me that I was sick and unconscious for a long time. After that I remember only the time in Petersburg, a white room, white beds, many children in the beds, an accordion or an organ playing, and I singing with a loud voice in accompaniment. Then the doctor takes me home in his car. A tall blonde woman in a pale blue dress plays the piano. She stands up. I go to the keys. When I touch them, they sound. Suddenly I see that I can play the songs of the organ and everything that I can sing."

"Go on, go on!" said Mendel.

"I remember nothing more from the early times except these few days. I remember my mother. It was warm and soft with her, she had a very deep voice, and her face was big and round, like a whole world."

"Go on, go on," said Mendel.

"I cannot remember Miriam, Jonas, or Shemariah at all. I heard about them much later, from Billes's daughter."

Mendel sighed. "Miriam," he repeated. She stood before him, in a golden yellow shawl, with her blue-black hair, quick and light-footed, a young gazelle. She had his eyes.

"I was a bad father," said Mendel. "I treated you badly, and her, too. Now she is lost. No medicine can help her."

"We will go to her," said Menuchim. "Wasn't I healed, Father?"

Yes, Menuchim was right. Man is never content, thought Mendel to himself. Just now he had experienced a miracle, and already he wanted another! Wait, wait, Mendel Singer! Only see what has become of Menuchim, a cripple! Slender are his hands, wise are his eyes, soft are his cheeks.

"Go to sleep, Father," said the son.

He sat upon the floor and drew off Mendel Singer's old boots. He looked at the soles, which were torn, with broken edges. He looked at the yellow patched tops, the roughened shafts, the holes in the socks, the ragged trousers. He undressed the old man and laid him in bed.

Then he left the room, took a book from a trunk, and returned to his father, sat down in the easy chair beside the bed, lighted the little green lamp, and began to read. Mendel pretended to sleep. He peeped through a narrow little crack between his lids. His son laid the book aside, and said:

"You are thinking of Miriam, Father! We will visit her. I shall get another doctor. They will heal her. She is still young. Go to sleep."

Mendel closed his eyes, but he did not sleep. He thought of Miriam, heard the strange noises of the world, felt through his closed eyelids the brightness of the night skies. He did not sleep, but he felt well. He rested. With his head awake he lay bedded in sleep and awaited the morning.

His son prepared a bath for him, dressed him, set him in an automobile. They rode for a long time, through noisy streets. They left the city. They came to a long, wide road, on the edges of which stood budding trees. The motor hummed brightly. Mendel's beard waved in the wind. He was silent.

"Do you want to know where we are going, Father?" asked the son.

"No," answered Mendel. "I do not want to know. Wherever you go is well."

And they reached a world where the sands were yellow, the wide ocean blue, and all the houses white. Mendel Singer sat upon the terrace of one of these houses, before a small white table. He drank a golden brown tea. Upon his bent back shone the first warm sun of the year. Robins hopped around them, and their sisters piped before the terrace. The waves of the sea splashed upon the strand with a soft, regular beat. A few white clouds stood in the pale blue sky. Under this sky it was possible for Mendel to think that Jonas might be found again, and Miriam come home, "in all the land no woman so fair," he quoted, silently, to himself. He himself, Mendel Singer, would have a good death, after many years, surrounded by grandchildren, "old and full of days," as was written of Job. He felt a curious and forbidden desire to lay aside his old cap of silk rep, and feel the sun upon his old skull. And for the first time in his life, Mendel Singer voluntarily uncovered his head, as he had only done in public offices, and in his bath. The few kinky hairs upon his bald head were moved by a gentle spring wind as though they had been rare and tender plants.

Thus Mendel Singer greeted the world.

And a gull, like a silver shot from heaven, flew under the awning of the terrace. Mendel watched its headlong flight, and its shadowy white wake in the blue air.

Then the son said: "Next week we go to San Francisco. On the way back we play for ten days in Chicago. I think, Father, that in four weeks we can return to Europe."

"Miriam?"

"I shall see her today, and talk with the doctors. Everything will be all right, Father. Perhaps we can take her with us. Perhaps she will get well in Europe."

They went back to the hotel. Mendel went into his son's room. He was tired.

"Lie down on the sofa; sleep a little," said the son. "I shall be back in two hours."

Mendel lay down obediently. He knew where his son was going. He was going to his sister. He was a wonderful man, his son. Blessing rested upon him. He would make Miriam well.

Mendel caught sight of a big photograph in a brown frame, upon the little dressing table.

"Give me that picture!" he begged.

He looked at it a long time. He saw a blonde young woman in a light colored dress, light as the day, and she sat in a garden through which the wind walked, moving the sprays at the edges of flower beds. Two children, a girl and a boy, stood beside a little carriage with a donkey hitched to it."

"God bless her," said Mendel.

The son went out. The father rested on the sofa, laying the photograph gently down beside him. His tired eyes wandered through the room, to the window.

From the depths of his couch he could see a broken bit of cloudless sky. He took the picture up again. That was his daughter-in-law, Menuchim's wife; those were his grandchildren, Menuchim's children. When he looked at the girl closely, he thought he saw a childhood picture of Deborah. Deborah was dead. Perhaps with strange otherworldly eyes she saw the miracle from the other side. With gratitude, Mendel remembered the young warmth which he had once delighted in, her red cheeks, her half-open eyes, which had shone in the darkness of their love nights like narrow, luring lights. Dead Deborah!

He stood up, pushed a chair to the sofa, set the picture on the chair, and lay down again. As his eyes slowly closed, they took with them into sleep the whole gay blueness of the sky and the faces of the new children. Beside them arose out of the brown background the portraits of Miriam and Jonas. Mendel fell asleep. And he rested from the burden of his happiness, and the greatness of the miracle.

Translated by Dorothy Thompson

Concerning the passages excised from Joseph Roth's *Job*:

1. A passage of less than one page in which is told of Deborah's neglect of the household as she waits for Menuchim's return to health.
2. This is followed by two pages that describe the journey to Kluczysk and the night before the visit to the Rabbi.
3. The second chapter begins with a one-and-a-half page report of Deborah's return to Zucknow: Mendel teaches, and the basket containing Menuchim is again hung from the ceiling. The next three pages tell of his siblings' unsuccessful attempt to drown the sick brother, and of how the love between Mendel and Deborah dies.
4. In a passage of a short page, Deborah's pervasive fear of her two sons' imminent military duty is made clear.
5. Four pages tell of the two brothers' return journey. Jonas is eager to leave the strict Jewish way of life. He drinks schnapps with the Russian farmers, and is willing to become a soldier.
6. The third chapter closes with a passage of not quite one page. It deals with Deborah's headlong flight to the cemetery, to lament her sufferings with the dead.
7. The next two pages tell of Deborah's preparation for the journey. In the meantime, Mendel takes care of Menuchim. He arouses in the boy an unusual degree of attention by tapping a spoon against a glass and singing a little song. At the end of the novel, it becomes clear that this counts as one of Menuchim's earliest clear memories.
8. The following one-and-a-half pages describe Schemarjah's taking leave of his family.

9. On one page, Mendel, now alone, reflects upon events.
10. A report, over two pages, of how Deborah bargains with the ferryman, Sameschkin, and persuades him to take her to Dubno.
11. A three segment description, over about one-and-a-half pages, of Mirjam—how she feels herself to be restricted, of her spending the following Sunday with Stepan, and of her sleeping with him in the woods.
12. On one full page, the journey home is recounted. It tells of the surprising development of a common bond between Sameschkin and Mendel.
13. On about a page, information about the Billes family is given.
14. About a page covers Mendel's farewells to the neighbors, and Deborah's final night with Menuchim.
15. The following three-quarters of a page make clear that Deborah is unhappy, although her circumstances appear satisfactory.
16. On a half-page, is told of how Mendel, on his way home, sees a small boy crying. For a moment, he believes he sees Menuchim before him.
17. On the last page of the eleventh chapter, Mendel cares for his two sons, who had been left behind. He reproaches himself for not having gone back to Zucknow, and for having returned to America with Menuchim. He is still pious, and has faith in the Psalms he sings.
18. There follows a passage of just over one page. In the waiting room, Mendel's thoughts slip back to Zucknow. He wonders, impiously (for which he immediately chastises himself), if it wouldn't have been better to stay? To accede to Miriam's wishes and to surrender to Jewish conformity?

Titles Available in The German Library

All titles available at your bookstore or
from Continuum International
15 East 26 Street, New York, NY 10010
www.continuumbooks.com

Titles Available in The German Library

Titles Available in The German Library

Titles Available in The German Library

Titles Available in The German Library

Titles Available in The German Library

Titles Available in The German Library